Quality of Life and Human Difference

This innovative volume brings together two important literatures for the first time. One concerns the role of quality-of-life assessments in social policy, and especially in health policy. The second concerns ethical and social issues raised by prenatal testing for disability; a theme of this literature has been the role played by controversial assumptions about the quality of life of people with disabilities.

Hitherto, these two literatures have had little contact with each other. Few scholars have written about both or have compared the two domains in a systematic way, and people with disabilities and disability scholars are underrepresented in recent discussions about health policy and quality-of-life assessment. This book brings to bear the perspectives of disability scholars on issues that have largely been the province of health methodology, policy, and philosophy, while focusing philosophical policy analysis on problems that have largely been the province of disability scholarship.

This volume will be sought after by bioethicists, philosophers, and specialists in disability studies and health care economics.

David Wasserman is Research Scholar at the Institute for Philosophy and Public Policy, University of Maryland.

Jerome Bickenbach is Professor in the Department of Philosophy and Faculties of Law and Medicine, Queen's University, Ontario.

Robert Wachbroit is Research Scholar at the Institute for Philosophy and Public Policy, University of Maryland.

Cambridge Studies in Philosophy and Public Policy

General editor: Douglas MacLean, University of North Carolina,
Chapel Hill

Quality of Life and Human Difference

Genetic Testing, Health Care, and Disability

Edited by

DAVID WASSERMAN
University of Maryland

JEROME BICKENBACH
Queen's University

ROBERT WACHBROIT
University of Maryland

CAMBRIDGE
UNIVERSITY PRESS

CAMBRIDGE UNIVERSITY PRESS
New York, Melbourne, Madrid, Cape Town, Singapore, São Paulo

Cambridge University Press
40 West 20th Street, New York, NY 10011-4211, USA

http://www.cambridge.org
Information on this title: www.cambridge.org/9780521832014

First published 2005

Printed in the United States of America

A catalog record for this publication is available from the British Library.

Library of Congress Cataloging in Publication data

Quality of life and human difference : genetic testing, health care, and
disability/edited by
David Wasserman, Jerome Bickenbach, Robert Wachbroit
p.   cm. – (Cambridge studies in philosophy and public policy)
Includes bibliographical references and index.
ISBN 0-521-83201-2 – ISBN 0-521-53971-4 (pbk.)
1. Prenatal diagnosis – Moral and ethical aspects. 2. Prenatal diagnosis – Social
aspects. 3. Fetus – Abnormalities – Diagnosis. 4. Genetic screening – Moral and
ethical aspects. 5. Genetic screening – Social aspects. 6. Medical ethics. 7. Quality of
life.   I. Wasserman, David T.   II. Bickenbach, Jerome Edmund.   III. Wachbroit,
Robert Samuel.   IV. Series.
RG628.Q35   2005
618.3'2042–dc22   2004062839

ISBN-13   978-0-521-83201-4 hardback
ISBN-10   0-521-83201-2 hardback

ISBN-13   978-0-521-53971-5 paperback
ISBN-10   0-521-53971-4 paperback

Contents

Contents

Contributors

Ron Amundson, University of Hawaii
Adrienne Asch, Wellesley College
Jerome Bickenbach, Queen's University, Ontario
Dan W. Brock, Harvard Medical School
Jeff McMahan, Rutgers University
Erik Nord, National Institute of Public Health, Oslo, Norway
Tom Shakespeare, Ethics and Life Sciences Research Institute,
    Newcastle, UK
Anita Silvers, San Francisco State University
Robert Wachbroit, University of Maryland
David Wasserman, University of Maryland

Acknowledgments

The present volume explores the relationship of variations in physical and mental functioning to the quality of human lives, and the relevance of the expected or assessed quality of a human life to decisions about whether to create or extend it. It arises from a working group the editors convened in January 2001 (with support from NIH Grant HG011979-02) to address issues about disability, well-being, and the valuation of lives raised by recent developments in health technology and methodology. Most of the chapters in this volume were initially prepared for the working group and were revised in light of its deliberations.

Introduction

DAVID WASSERMAN, JEROME BICKENBACH,
AND ROBERT WACHBROIT

I

Genetic technology has enabled us to test fetuses for an increasing number of diseases and impairments. On the basis of this genetic information, prospective parents can predict – and prevent – the birth of children
likely to have those conditions. In developed countries, prenatal genetic
testing has now become a routine part of medical care during pregnancy.
Underlying and driving the spread of this testing are controversial assumptions about health, impairment, and quality of life. While the early
development of prenatal testing and selective abortion may have been
informed by the questionable view that they were just another form
of disease and disability prevention, these practices are now justified
largely in other terms: prospective parents should be permitted to make
reproductive decisions based on concern for the expected quality of their
children's lives. These practices, and their prevailing rationale, reinforce
a trend in biomedical ethics that began in the 1970s, one giving a central
role to quality of life in health care decision making.

In this Introduction, we will briefly review how quality of life came
to assume such importance in health care and reproductive practice
and policy. We will then discuss some of the conceptual and ethical issues raised by attempts to measure health-related quality of life and
to use such measures in the evaluation of health care interventions.
Next, we will examine the bearing of these issues on the current rethinking of disability, a category that has been widely associated with
poor quality of life. We will describe the tension that has arisen between the emerging understanding of disability as an interaction between health and nonhealth conditions and environmental factors, and
the effort to systematically measure health-related quality of life. Finally,

1

we will preview the discussions of these issues by the contributors to this volume.

Concerns about quality of life first surfaced in the public debate as a basis for limiting medical interventions. As physicians became capable of indefinitely sustaining the mere biological functioning of individuals who had lost (or appeared to have lost) all capacity for consciousness, a sharp controversy emerged in the 1970s over whether continued health intervention was an appropriate use of health care resources, especially when it went against the previously expressed wishes of the patient or the current wishes of the family. An emerging consensus that the patient herself should make that decision whenever possible was reflected in the development of standardized living wills, medical powers of attorney, and do-not-resuscitate orders. This consensus has not reached two controversial areas: physician assistance in bringing about death sought by competent individuals hoping to avoid a continued existence with chronic impairment or pain, and the withdrawal of life support sought "on behalf" of cognitively incapacitated patients who have left no written instructions (for a summary of, and comprehensive references on, these debates, sce Battin, 2003).

The controversy over end-of-life treatment thus continues, now focused on the morality and legality of physician-assisted suicide and of decision making for those who appear unable to decide for themselves. In the former case, the salient issue is typically the right of competent individuals to enlist physicians' assistance in committing suicide; in the latter, the difficulties of ascertaining the prior or hypothetical wishes of the patient and their relevance to the present decision. In both areas, the notion of quality of life is firmly entrenched as an important, if often suspect, consideration. On the one hand, interventions that are technically feasible, but produce no discernible improvement in quality of life, are often opposed as pointless and undignified. On the other hand, the opposition to withdrawing life support from individuals who retain some cognitive functioning, or the possibility of recovering it, often emphasizes the quality of life still possible for those individuals.

Patients are not the only group to have become more concerned about the quality of life that results from medical interventions. The interest of health researchers, policy makers, and administrators predates the public's by at least a decade. Beginning in the 1960s, a variety of medications were developed to increase patients' functioning or to lessen their pain, discomfort, depression, or anxiety without curing their diseases or increasing their prospects for survival. In order to assess the benefits of these new medications, the pharmaceutical industry financed the design and use of some of the earliest quantitative measures of quality of life. That industry continues to play a major role in developing and utilizing increasingly sophisticated quality-of-life measures (Walker, 1993; Spilker, 1996). In the past thirty years, quality-of-life measurement has been eagerly taken up by researchers, epidemiologists, public and private health administrators, health economists, and health policy makers.[1] Together with estimates of survival and tests of physiological function, these measures have now become a standard part of the calculus employed to compare the "cost-effectiveness" of treatments for the same and different health conditions, a calculus that is used to justify trade-offs among limited medical resources.

The roughly concurrent emergence of drugs that improve the quality of living without extending life, and of medical interventions that extend life without improving or restoring its quality, raised issues about the very meaning of quality of life, and about its importance as a goal of health care practice and policy. While the growing use of treatments that appear to improve life quality without increasing longevity suggests a greater concern for patient welfare, the increasing scrutiny of life-preserving and other expensive medical technologies suggests a greater concern for resource allocation. The expense of many of these technologies has been a major stimulus for cost containment, as well as for a precise, objective assessment of the actual improvements that these technologies produce. The result has been the imposition of cost-effectiveness analysis in professions where rationing had rarely been explicit. Interventions sought by desperate patients and families, as well as interventions opposed by patients or their families as undignified or pointless, are routinely challenged by health economists, administrators, and policy makers because they are not "cost-effective."

A concern about quality of life also came to play a central role in reproductive decision making during the same period. In 1973, the U.S. Supreme Court recognized early and midterm abortion as a constitutional right. After *Roe v. Wade*, a woman could have a legal abortion through the second trimester anywhere in the United States, for any reason. Genetic and other reproductive technologies were soon providing a stock of reasons for aborting that women had never previously had, through the use of tests that could reveal a variety of diseases, susceptibilities, and impairments. Because public acceptance of such tests depended on their being seen as noncoercive, they could not be presented as public health measures intended to eliminate or reduce genetic diseases and defects. Rather, prenatal tests were justified as tools for expanding individual reproductive choice. Whether this represented eugenics "though the back door," as some critics claimed (e.g., Duster, 1990), or the distinct, if still unwelcome, intrusion of a consumer mentality into reproductive decision making (Lippman, 1991), the use of prenatal tests soon became a standard part of medical care for pregnant women deemed to be "at risk" of bearing diseased or disabled children.

The notion of quality of life, given currency by other developments in health care, offered a convenient "child-centered" rationale for prenatal testing and selective abortion: couples should be concerned not only about whether to have children, or indeed about whether it is moral to do so (e.g., Brock, 1995; Purdy, 1996), but also about the quality of life that a particular child could be expected to have. If the chromosomal or genetic constitution of a fetus appeared to preclude a life of reasonable quality, it was appropriate to abort. Until recently, selective abortion escaped the controversy that has accompanied efforts to limit the medical care given to severely impaired neonates (e.g., Kuhse and Singer, 1985) – a limitation also justified by low expected quality of life – in part because newborns are generally accorded higher legal and moral status than fetuses. Despite the continuing controversy over abortion in general, abortion for disease and impairment was seen, even by many who were troubled or ambivalent about abortion in general, as a responsible exercise of reproductive choice (see Asch, 1999).

Although prenatal testing has rarely been publicly justified in terms of its cost-effectiveness, public health administrators and policy makers concerned about the costs of "heroic" lifesaving interventions for neonates could hardly be oblivious to the actual and potential savings implicit in selective abortion. Many of the most expensive health conditions are not, and never will be, detectable by prenatal genetic testing, because they arise from accidents of various sorts or have complex etiologies in which genetic variations play only a slight or probabilistic role. Nevertheless, there is evidence that the incidence of several diseases and impairments thought, correctly or not, to impose significant health care costs has fallen – or has failed to increase as expected because of other factors, such as increased maternal age – as the vast majority of women who employ prenatal testing chose to abort fetuses found to have the conditions tested for (Huether, 1983; Huether, 1990; Kuppermann, Gates, and Washington, 1996; NDAD, 1996). Meanwhile, the costs and risks of prenatal testing have continued to decrease (Roan, 2004), creating a situation in which health care administrators and policy

4

makers have strong incentives to encourage prospective parents to make quality of life a critical factor in their reproductive decisions.

From Quality of Life to Health-Related Quality of Life

Despite its obvious appeal and growing currency in discussions of health policy and health care, the notion of quality of life raises a difficult conceptual issue for health professionals and policy makers: what outcomes (or types of outcomes) are connected closely enough with health to be taken account of in assessing the impact of health interventions on quality of life? Health care cannot be concerned with all aspects of life or well-being without giving it an impossibly broad mandate. That is just what the World Health Organization (WHO) appeared to have done in 1947, adopting a definition of "health" that made it virtually coextensive with quality of life: health was "not merely the absence of disease, but a state of complete physical, mental, and social well-being."[2] That definition, which set no limits on the scope of health policy or health care, was widely criticized and, though it remains a piece of interagency political rhetoric, plays no scientific role today even at the WHO.

But its rejection leaves a difficult question: if health is something less that complete physical, mental, and social well-being, how is its scope to be limited? Health professionals, researchers, and policy makers have acknowledged the need for such limits, and have introduced the notion of health-related quality of life (HRQL) as a way to set them. HRQL assessment tools evolved from older mortality and morbidity indicators, augmented by measures of functional status, subjective health experience, and perceived components of "social health." These instruments were designed to assess the patient's performance in, or satisfaction with, areas of activity affected by her physical and mental functioning. Since virtually all areas of activity are affected by health, however, these measures had to limit themselves to the areas most directly or substantially affected by health. Yet without an understanding of what counts as "health-related" in this sense, that term does more to label than to resolve the issue. The proliferation of HRQL instruments has not been informed by a careful analysis of, or an explicit agreement on, that issue.[3]

The lack of agreement about what falls within the bounds of health poses a serious practical problem, because narrower measures of health cannot serve as adequate proxies for broader ones. The notion of HRQL depends, both historically and conceptually, on the common observation that there is an uncertain relationship between diagnostic categories – the signs and symptoms that doctors use to identify disease, injury, and other conditions of ill health – and the full range of outcomes that, arguably, should be taken into account in assessing the success of a health intervention. Most health professionals recognize that diagnostic measures, such as ejection fractions and viral loads, correlate poorly with how well the patients functions at a "macro" level, from walking and stretching to getting and holding a job, let alone with how satisfied the patient is with his health or his life.[4]

Uncertainty about what aspects of quality of life count as health-related arises in part because a wide variety of economic, social, and psychological factors mediate the impact of health conditions on the activities and states of mind that people value, and because those activities and states of mind vary in how closely they appear to be related to health. Thus, for example, an instrument assessing the quality of life associated with pulmonary diseases or interventions would surely take too narrow a view of what counted as health-related if it took no account of patients' chronic pain, pervasive anxiety about breathing, or perceived incapacity to engage in routine activities because of shortness of breath. But what about the difficulties the patients had in getting jobs that required strong lung capacity? What about their difficulty in getting jobs because of a true or false belief that their conditions were contagious? What about the high blood pressure, anxiety, or marital conflict associated with their unemployment? Should any or all of these employment difficulties be considered health-related and thereby be included in what the pulmonary specialist should be assessing as HRQL?

If the health professions lack an account of what aspects of living or features of the environment are health-related (i.e., directly or substantially related to health conditions), they also, and perhaps more basically, lack a theory of quality of life itself. What qualities should a life have; what does it mean to live well? Has a person's quality of life improved or declined if his expectations increase faster than his lung capacity, leaving him more frustrated than he was before treatment? What if his decline in lung capacity is offset by his embrace of a more leisurely and personally rewarding lifestyle? Is his quality of life enhanced by a breathing apparatus that dramatically improves his respiration if he is ashamed to appear with it in public?

Health researchers and methodologists implicitly answer such questions when they select items and assign weights for their HRQL assessment instruments. Yet the answers they give are rarely the product of sustained reflection. Rather than responding to philosophical questions about what it means to live well, their instruments tend to be modified and refined in response to psychometric and statistical considerations. Nevertheless, this lack of reflection on the meaning of fundamental concepts has not precluded a rough consensus. Surveying some 300 instruments currently in use, Ann Bowling notes that despite the differences in the specific components of quality of life included in those instruments, there is broad agreement about the general categories of items that need to be represented and measured (Bowling, 1997; see also McDowell and Newell, 1991).[5] But this agreement appears to reflect conformity to precedent, or a methodological preference for comparability, rather than any clear, widely accepted conception of HRQL. Bowling and other HRQL scholars readily admit that despite substantial progress in developing quantitative tools to operationalize and measure specific components of HRQL, attempts to bring these tools together into a single, integrated assessment instrument have been utter failures, because of the lack of consensus on the definition of the terms "health," "health-relatedness," and "quality of life."

Objective and Subjective Components of HRQL

One of the most basic, and recalcitrant, issues in assessing quality of life is whether it should be regarded as subjective, based on the patient's own judgments and feelings, on objective measures of functioning and participation, or on some combination of the two. Is it enough to look at subjective measures, the individual's satisfaction with his health status or condition, or should we also include measures of physiological functioning, bodily performance, role fulfillment, and social participation in our assessment? Most HRQL instruments in fact include both types of measure, to varying extents, but this inclusiveness itself needs justification. Otherwise, it obscures sharp disagreements about the extent to which quality of life or HRQL is an objective matter; it risks treating conflicting accounts of quality of life as if they were just different aspects of a complex phenomenon.

The objective measures incorporated in HQRL instruments typically concern "functional status," which refers to the full range of human functions: (1) physiological functions, such as blood pressure, digestion, and respiration rate; (2) the capacity to perform basic physical and cognitive activities, such as walking, reaching, focusing attention, and communicating, or the various combinations of these needed to perform routine activities of daily living, such as eating, bathing, dressing, transferring, and toileting; and (3) socially shaped tasks or life roles, such as those needed by children for school and play and those needed by adults for work, household maintenance, and participation in social activities. Given its breadth, functional status is a composite measure more often used by rehabilitation therapists than by physicians. Rehabilitation professionals have developed clinical tools to assess many of these functional capacities, at least those at the more basic levels. For this reason, there is a vast rehabilitation research literature describing clinical questionnaires and other tools to assess physiological functioning and capacities for the "activities of daily living." Assessment tools for the more complex social tasks and life roles are arguably needed, but they are less frequently attempted. It should be clear that functional status categories go beyond standard medical diagnostic categories, in that people with the same diagnosis can nevertheless have different levels of functioning.

The subjective measures incorporated in HQRL instruments typically concern the patient's satisfaction with his health state and functional status. Clinical questionnaires assessing these matters have a long history, going back to the late 1940s if not earlier (Bowling, 1997), and their availability and familiarity may have influenced the early stages of the development of HRQL instruments. Even more than ratings of functional status, judgments of satisfaction vary widely for the same or similar health conditions.

The discussion of subjective quality of life in the health literature has been confused by the failure to make two basic distinctions, clear in theory even if vague or uncertain in application. The first is that between satisfaction as a mental state – a feeling, mood, or affect – and as a judgment or belief. (This distinction is especially important, and elusive, in mental health, where one main concern is how a patient feels. It may be hard to distinguish how the patient feels from what he believes about how he feels.) Feeling satisfied, in the sense of feeling pleasure or euphoria, is very different from believing that one's needs, desires, or preferences are being satisfied. The former is a psychological state, which can be inapt but not mistaken, while the latter is a judgment, which can be mistaken.

The second distinction sometimes overlooked in the quality of life literature is that between the patient's preferences and his choices. A generation of health professionals who have, at least officially, rejected paternalism have good reason to be concerned about the latter – the patient should be free to decline treatment that the physician finds medically valuable or necessary, even for reasons that the physician thinks are bad. But if it is imperative to honor the patients' choices about health intervention – to do as he decides – it hardly follows that it is necessary to adopt the patient's preferences in assessing the outcome of an intervention that he consents to. Why should the physician or researcher be obliged to evaluate its success by the same criteria as the patient?

Over the past few decades, hundreds of HRQL instruments have been developed, some designed for specific diseases, others more generic (see the standard texts, McDowell and Newell, 1991; Bowling, 1997). Almost all of them attempt to mix objective components (functional status) and subjective ones (self-reported health perceptions or levels of satisfaction). Given the obvious conceptual difficulties involved in combining these distinct and possibly incommensurable measures of well-being, a surprisingly large number of survey articles on HRQL blithely assert that the only viable candidates for HRQL instruments are "holistic" ones that merge subjective and objective measures (Day and Jankey, 1996). Some leaders in the field have argued forcefully, as does one of our contributors, that "quality of life" is inherently a measure of subjective reaction to one's health and functional status (Patrick and Erickson, 1993; Gill and Feinstein, 1994; Nord et al., 2001). They acknowledge that there are potential regularities between health or functional status and (subjective) quality of life, but insist that these must be empirically established, not conflated into a single notion. Reducing quality of life to functional status, or conflating the two in a single HRQL score, ignores or obscures the individual's own perceptions of how well life is going for her or replaces them with professional judgments in the guise of functional assessment. Yet hybrid measures continue to predominate, without clear justification.

This dispute among methodologists reflects broader disagreement, of far older vintage, about what it means to live well. The idea of well-being has played an important role in Western philosophical and moral inquiry for millennia, in perennial debates about what makes human lives go better or worse, what makes a life worth living at all, what we should promote in our own and others' lives, and whether the standards for living well are culturally variant or universal (see., e.g., Griffin, 1986; Nussbaum, 1990; Nussbaum, 1992; Brock, 1993; Griffin, 1993; Sen, 1993; Sumner, 1996; Nussbaum, 1998). These debates raise questions that are clearly relevant to those seeking to measure HRQL. Is quality of life or well-being to be understood mainly or exclusively in terms of pleasure and pain; in terms of happiness in some broader but still subjective sense; in terms of the satisfaction of actual desires, or of adequately informed desires; in terms of inherently valuable activities and achievements; or in terms of all, or some combination of, these diverse elements? If the last, then how, if at all, should those elements be combined in an overall assessment?

We can hardly expect health methodologists to resolve issues that have vexed generations of philosophers, but it is not unreasonable to expect them to acknowledge the conflict, and to recognize that it cannot be resolved by methodological refinement alone. The uncertainty about what counts as health-related, and what constitutes quality of life, suggests the need for a broader inquiry into what health professionals and policy makers should be measuring, and for what purposes. While the health context is often thought to present special considerations and constraints, it is important to bring the philosophical analysis of well-being to bear on the problematic notion of HRQL.

Health-Related Quality of Life and People with Disabilities

It might appear that people with disabilities would welcome the growing interest of health professionals and policy makers in quality of life. Many of the challenges facing individuals with impairments arise not only from their biomedical conditions, but also from a physical and social environment that renders those conditions disabling. Having an instrument that took account, not only of their physical or mental condition, but also of the effects of features of the world in which they live, would give a better picture of the quality of their lives. And yet the increased attention of health professionals to a broader range of causal factors and outcomes may also have some troubling implications for people with disabilities.

This is so for several reasons. First, as health professionals and policy makers have broadened the range of outcomes they regard as health-related, they have taken a correspondingly broader view of what counts as a health problem. In the case of mobility impairments, for example, difficulties in caring for oneself, in performing the activities of daily living, and in getting from place to place are typically seen, no less than difficulties in moving one's arms or legs, as the "consequences of a health condition" and thus, in an important sense, as health problems. This expansive view of health problems appears to contradict, and to undermine, the effort of two generations of disability activists to present such difficulties as problems of environmental fit and social justice. Their classification as health-related, and as health problems, may obscure the critical role of the physical and social environment in mediating the impact of limited arm or leg movement on the ability to care for oneself, to perform the activities of daily living, and to get from place to place – a role that disability advocates have done so much to expose.

Second, those who assess HRQL tend to treat one of the core phenomena of disability – adaptation – as an artifact and a distortion (e.g., Murray, 1996). People who lose functioning as a result of disease or accident typically report, despite initial disruption and feelings of loss, increasing satisfaction and proficiency with the passage of time, whether or not they receive a particular health intervention (e.g., Albrecht and Devlieger, 1999). For those trying to gauge the broader success of an intervention, this background improvement presents a complication and possibly a confounding factor. And for those who attempt to develop accounts of quality of life or well-being based on objective functioning, such changes are often taken to reveal the inadequacy of more subjective measures, such as personal satisfaction, as an index of life quality or well-being (see Wasserman, 2001). Tiny Tim's euphoria, to use the classic example, is not taken as evidence of his doing well despite his impaired mobility, but as proof that his feelings have but a tenuous relationship to his quality of life. While disability advocates recognize the possibilities for self-deception and false consciousness, they would argue that Tiny Tim's euphoria, should, at least at the outset, be taken at face value – that it should be regarded either as partially constitutive of a high quality of life, on a subjective account quality of life, or as evidence of a high quality of life, on a suitably refined objective account.

The two conceptual issues just raised – delineating the scope of health problems and assessing the significance of adaptation –give rise to both expressive and practical concerns. The main expressive concern is that the treatment of the personal and social challenges of people with disabilities as health problems, and of their satisfaction in the face of those problems as suspect, supports a false, demeaning impression of the impact of impairment (e.g., Asch, 2003). The lives of people with disabilities are assumed to be of low quality, whatever environmental factors mediate the impact of their impairments, and their own testimony to the contrary is seen as inherently unreliable. Their adaptations to their impairments appear not as instances of the universal processes of adjustment to changed circumstances, but as disability-specific strategies for recovering the ground that has been lost, or for covering up its loss through benign self-deception.

Significant practical concerns arise because this misleading impression threatens to jeopardize the hard-won gains of disability advocates in framing the challenges of impairments as problems of environmental design and social justice rather than, or as well as, problems of health. Professionals and policy makers who regard a wide range of environmentally mediated outcomes as health problems may be inclined to "prescribe" health interventions rather than environmental modification or social reform, and to see modifications and reforms that increase the functioning and participation of people with disabilities not as requirements of equality, but as a special provision for badly off individuals, an issue with less moral and political urgency or priority.

Admittedly, an expansive notion of health problems need not limit the range of interventions for people with disabilities. For some professionals and policy makers, a broad view of what counts as a health problem has underwritten a broad view of what counts as an appropriate intervention. Some rehabilitation specialists, for example, see environmental barriers to access and participation as health problems and "prescribe" their removal or modification. But they are not the dominant players in the health care and health policy fields, where treating disability as a health problem more often leads to its medicalization.

The belief that people with disabilities must lead lives of poor, or at least substantially lower, quality because of their impairments lends support to two policies seen by disability advocates as particularly threatening: the assignment of lower priority to the preservation of disabled lives in allocating scarce resources, and the development of health practices designed to reduce or eliminate the creation of people with such impairments. Neither of these policies is strictly implied by the view of impairment and quality of life that we have been describing; indeed, the second policy does not entail the first, and many who support the second, including one of our contributors, strongly oppose the first. But there is undeniably some association between that view and those policies, especially in light of the historical role of quality-of-life considerations as a basis for ending, or not extending, severely impaired lives.

Not surprisingly, people with disabilities were among the earliest, most vocal, and most trenchant critics of the actual and proposed uses of HQRL measures to assess health and allocate health care resources. They have argued that those measures are typically informed by simplistic assumptions about the causes and nature of disability, assumptions that have been rejected in other policy domains. The same three decades that saw the embrace of quality of life as a health concern and the proliferation of HRQL instruments to measure health outcomes saw the emergence of a public recognition of disability as a civil rights issue, as much as, if not more than, a health problem. The tension between these two developments is crystallized in the reconceptualization of disability as an interaction rather than a condition or property of an individual, perhaps the leading theoretical achievement of the disability rights movement.

Relying on a substantial body of work by sociologists and psychologists, many disability advocates have embraced an interactive model of disability (Safilos-Rothschild, 1970; Sagarin, 1971; Wright, 1983; Bury, 1987). On this model, disability is a product of, or an interaction between, the biological dysfunctions of the individual's body or mind (usually called impairments) and the social and physical context or environment in which the person lives (Amundson, 1992; Imrie, 1997). To be disabled is, roughly, to have limitations on the activities and roles one can perform that result in part, but only in part, from biological dysfunction. Those limitations also depend on the environment, on physical or social obstacles that limit, prevent, or fail to promote performance. Disability, therefore, is not a feature of an individual's body or mind, but a complex interaction of biological features of the individual and features of the physical and social environment.

A more radical model was suggested in 1976 by a group of disabled activists in the UK, the Union of the Physically Impaired Against Segregation (UPIAS). That group defined "disability" as "the loss or limitation of opportunities to take part in the normal life of the community on an equal level with others due to physical and social barriers" (UPIAS, 1976). On this definition, disability in effect loses its grounding in biological dysfunctions in the individual and becomes entirely a matter of the social reception of perceived human difference. Disability is a disadvantage resulting from discrimination and related invidious and unjust social responses. Although both the interactive and radical models are sometimes referred to as "the social model" of disability, we will attempt to avoid terminological confusion by reserving that term for the more radical model, using the term "interactive" for the moderate model.

The very idea of HRQL is deeply problematic on both models. For the interactive model, it is difficult or impossible to assess the separate contribution of health or impairment to quality of life, even if we had a generally accepted definition of health or impairment. As one of our contributors contends, apportioning causal responsibility between health and nonhealth factors, or between impairment and environment, is unavoidably arbitrary and ad hoc. A proponent of the social model would claim that there is nothing, or almost nothing, to apportion – that impairment (if not health) has little to do with quality of life, except in serving as a marker for discrimination and oppression. For this reason, quality of life is not meaningfully or significantly related to impairment (if not to health), except through social processes that deny people with disabilities adequate resources and power. On both models, then, the notion of HRQL has very limited utility and may seriously exaggerate the role of biology in personal, social, and political destiny.

Moreover, both models recognize that the social processes that contribute so greatly to the "burden of disability" treat impairment as a dichotomous social marker. Even if biomedical impairment should be understood as a matter of degree, the processes of stigmatization and exclusion impose a sharp dichotomy. Nowhere is this dichotomy so apparent as in prenatal testing, where the presence or absence of a single genetic or chromosomal fact about the zygote or fetus dominates the judgment of its life prospects, determining whether it will be brought into the world. One of our contributions focuses on this aspect of prenatal testing, arguing that this uncritical, excessive reliance on a single characteristic reproduces the stigmatization of people with disabilities at the level of reproductive choice.

It is difficult to underestimate the social impact of the reconceptualization of disability on the legal, political, and scientific landscapes. A person's inability to perform certain actions, or to participate fully in certain social roles such as parent, student, or employee, is now treated as, in part, a consequence of deliberately or negligently exclusionary social attitudes, practices, and policies. Much of the disadvantage that people with impairments experience is now attributed to disabling barriers thrown up by institutions and by social attitudes; their activity and participation are limited by these phenomena, not by their impairments. The disability rights movement, and its reconceptualization of disability, have helped to put into place countless laws, programs, and policies that have improved the legal status and public perception of disabled individuals in many countries of the world.

Nevertheless, the growing use of prenatal testing to make reproductive decisions, and of HRQL measures to assess the cost-effectiveness of health interventions, seems to many in the disability community to threaten these gains. As we noted earlier, there are two aspects to this concern. One is practical: that these trends in reproductive and health care decision making will cause tangible harm to people with disabilities – depleting their communities, reducing their political impact, worsening their health care, increasing their stigmatization. The other concern is conceptual and ethical, or expressive: that the appraisal of lives with disabilities as having categorically, or even presumptively, lower quality is inconsistent with the understanding of disability that now informs enlightened legislation and social policy. This tension may be disturbing even if its practical impact on individuals with disabilities is contained or mitigated. It is this concern that the present volume addresses.

II

In section I of this Introduction, we discussed the close links between the debates over the measurement of health and quality of life, the practice of prenatal testing for impairments, and the modeling of disability as an interaction between an impairment and an unaccommodating environment. These connections have not, with few exceptions, been closely examined, in part because they fall between the established disciplines of health methodology and economics, on the one hand, and the fledgling field of disability studies, on the other. In particular, moral issues about health measurement and prenatal testing have rarely been discussed in the same setting, or by the same people.

This volume brings together two important literatures. One concerns the role of well-being and quality of life in social policy, particularly health policy. Among the main themes of this literature are the competing conceptions of quality of life and well-being employed in different contexts, and the relevance of individual and aggregative measures of quality of life to health care decision making (e.g., Nussbaum and Sen, 1993). The second literature addresses the ethical and social issues raised by preconception and prenatal testing for disability (e.g., Parens and Asch, 2000). An emerging theme of this literature is the significant role of assumptions about the quality of life of people with various disabilities. Critics of prenatal testing tend to dispute those assumptions and question their relevance to the decision about whether to continue a pregnancy; defenders of prenatal testing tend to defend both the assumptions and their relevance.

Until recently, these two literatures have been largely isolated from each other. While references to quality-of-life measures in health policy can occasionally be found in articles on prenatal testing, and vice versa, few scholars have written about both, or compared the two domains in a systematic way. And while people with disabilities, and disability scholars, have played a dominant role in the debate over prenatal testing, they and their perspectives are not adequately represented in many recent collections of work on health policy and quality-of-life assessment. The lack of contact between these two literatures is disturbing for two reasons. First, it has meant that the perspectives of people with disabilities, and disability scholars, have been largely absent from the mainstream academic and professional debate on quality of life and health care resources, a debate that has had a significant impact on actual health policy. Second, it has restricted the comparison of the conceptions of well-being invoked and challenged in the two domains of health policy and reproductive decision making, a comparison that should enrich the discussion in both areas.

The Contents of This Volume

The first several chapters in the volume focus on the relationship of health, disability, and quality of life. Wachbroit begins by distinguishing clinical from policy uses of health assessment measures. Clinicians are usually interested only in disease-specific health assessments or quality-of-life measures. But measures designed for policy use are typically generic, so as to be able to yield comparisons and rankings of widely different diseases. Wachbroit argues that many of the objections to health assessment measures do not raise problems for disease-specific measures and clinical uses, but rather for generic measures and their policy uses. These problems include not only the conceptual and mathematical difficulties involved in assessing the contribution of health to well-being, but also moral concerns that the reliance on such methods in health care policy making will sidestep or undermine democratic control of important decisions about resource allocation.

Whereas Wachbroit raises a concern about democratic procedures and the policy uses of health assessment measures, Silvers launches a more radical critique. She claims that such uses typically rest on a monolithic view of health as a resource, asset, or commodity, one whose distribution affects and is affected by considerations of justice. She maintains that this view is an oversimplification, ignoring the many ways in which individuals value health and its consequences for well-being. The extraordinary variety of ways in which people can flourish suggests a comparable variation in the impact of abnormal functioning, an impact that people with normal functioning, notably health professionals, are notoriously poor at gauging. She contends that the distorting effects of treating health as an indispensable practical good will be greatly exacerbated by the growth of predictive genetic testing in the coming generation, exposing previously hidden health deficits in a large portion of the population. Silvers urges that health be viewed not as a good with instrumental value for almost all forms of human flourishing, but as an intrinsic good, one that, like art, will have radically different values when assessed from different standpoints.

Brock has a much more positive view of the use of health assessment measures, even though he is reluctant to use overall quality-of-life assessments in public policy contexts. Indeed, he argues that, on the basis of such health assessments, parents are morally *required* not to give birth to a seriously disabled child when the alternative of giving birth to a less disabled or nondisabled child is available at no great cost. The argument is not based on any particular measure of health or health-related well-being, but rather on the claim that any acceptable measure must in large part be objective – it cannot be a measure solely of an individual's feelings or self-assessment. On any plausible objective measure, Brock claims, people with serious disabilities will, on average, rate lower, even if we make liberal assumptions about the success of adaptation. Brock maintains that his conclusion about reproductive policy does not imply that existing disabled people should receive lower priority in the allocation of health care resources based on the lower utility expected from the extension of their lives. In allocating scarce lifesaving resources, the right of people with disabilities to equal treatment overrides any concern about reduction in net utility.

Amundson strongly rejects Brock's conclusions by challenging the conceptual framework on which they rest. He denies the possibility of any objective element in health or quality-of-life assessment, rejecting the claims that biological abnormality captures something objective in nature and arguing that the distinction between overall quality of life and health-related quality of life is mere ideological gerrymandering. Furthermore, he challenges the widely shared presumption that impairments – such as dysfunctional limbs or sense organs – reduce the quality of life. When they do, he claims, the fault lies with the environment – for example, wheelchair inaccessibility – and not with the biological condition itself. Amundson acknowledges that his arguments are based on the Social Model of disability, a model for which he admittedly doesn't argue, but one that he presents as a critical ideological corrective to the prevailing Medical Model, which attributes those disadvantages solely to biology. He holds that health assessments, at least as standardly understood, reflect an unjust bias against people with disabilities.

Nord agrees that quality-of-life assessment should be a subjective measure, but he doesn't share Amundson's radical dismissal of objective measures. Nord argues that even if people's feelings of euphoria or judgments of their own well-being are not infallible indicators of their quality of life, going beyond subjective measures in quality-of-life assessment carries too great a risk of cultural bias. Nord doesn't directly defend the policy uses of health and quality-of-life assessment measures; rather, he maintains that many of the problems with, and objections to, their use arise from equivocation or confusion about what such measures mean, and about what purposes they should serve. He illustrates this point by reviewing some of the history of the development of QALY and DALY measures, showing how the distinct concepts of (1) the worth of a person with a health condition, (2) the well-being experienced by that person, and (3) the desirability of preventing that condition have very often been conflated by those who develop HRQL measures.

The remaining chapters in the volume examine the assumptions about disability and quality of life that inform specific areas of policy and practice and the consistency of those assumptions with the moral equality of people with disabilities.

McMahan argues that a reasonable pluralism about well-being may support both the prenatal decision to prevent the birth of a child with impairments and the postnatal judgment that life with such a child is rich and rewarding. Reasonable values about how one wants to live may inform a prospective preference for no child over an impaired child, and the consequent use of prenatal testing and selective abortion to satisfy that preference. But equally reasonable values may inform the retrospective preference for an impaired child over no child, a preference expressed by most parents of children with impairments. There are an indefinite number of ways in which people can flourish. Even though not all of these ways are consistent with each other, there is no inconsistency in shifting over time and experience from one reasonable set of values or way of living to another. Although McMahan recognizes that the parent of an impaired child might reasonably prefer that child to an unimpaired one on the basis of deep attachment, he is doubtful that any set of reasonable values could underwrite a preference for an impaired child over an unimpaired child.

Asch and Wasserman also doubt that any reasonable values could underwrite a preference for an impaired over an unimpaired child. But they doubt as well that any reasonable values could support a preference for an unimpaired over an impaired child – at least a preference strong enough to compel selective abortion. This is not because there are no inherent disadvantages in having an impairment, or in raising a child with one, but because such disadvantages, realistically appraised, rarely provide prospective parents with a morally adequate reason to exclude a child with an impairment from their family. They argue that such exclusion typically results from a narrow focus on the impairment rather than on the future child who will bear it, a focus sharpened by the technology of prenatal testing. This eclipsing of the whole by the part characterizes the stigmatization faced by existing people with disabilities, and it may give them grounds for concern or for offense. Asch and Wasserman maintain that for this reason, the selectivity displayed by parents who abort for impairment is harder to defend *ex ante* than McMahan suggests and harder to reconcile with the moral equality of people with disabilities than Brock claims. They argue that such selectivity is incompatible with the most appealing conceptions of parenthood and family, and with the ideal of unconditional love that informs those conceptions. They urge greater pluralism about the ways in which parents and families can flourish, a pluralism that regards the rearing of most impaired children as potentially no less rich and rewarding than the rearing of other children.

Tom Shakespeare would probably not be persuaded by either McMahan or Asch and Wasserman. He doubts that there are conclusive arguments for or against the morality of selective abortion, and he believes that there are circumstances in which individuals may reasonably choose to have or forego prenatal testing for impairment, or choose to abort or carry an impaired fetus. But just because of the moral latitude individuals enjoy, and the moral uncertainty they face, society should scrupulously protect autonomy in decisions about prenatal testing and termination. Like Asch and Wasserman, he finds that stereotypes, overgeneralizations, and dubious assumptions about the impact of impairments on quality of life shape decisions about testing and termination. But he believes the more important bias occurs at the institutional level, and that the debate over prenatal testing tends to place too much emphasis on individual decision making. Just because of the importance and difficulty of the choices that individuals must make, society has strong obligations to ensure that those choices are knowing and voluntary. In order to do so, it must provide adequate accommodation and support for children with disabilities and their parents, unbiased media portrayals of lives with disabilities, and balanced information about raising children with disabilities for parents making decisions about whether to test or terminate. Reviewing the relevant social science literature, Shakespeare concludes that society fails dismally in all three areas.

Bickenbach exposes some of the problems in the policy uses of health measures that Wachbroit addresses on a more theoretical level. He analyzes the assumptions about health, disability, and quality of life made in the assessments of population health and of national health systems. He argues that in using one of the most influential measures of HRQL, the health-adjusted life equivalent, to rate national health systems, the World Health Organization belies its avowed commitment to equality in several ways: by taking cost-effectiveness as its ultimate standard for rating health systems, by ignoring inequalities among ethnic and socioeconomic groups, and by assigning the extension of lives with impairments lower priority based on a flawed methodology for assessing the impact of impairments, one that relies solely on the judgments of health professionals. Bickenbach identifies an apparent dilemma for the construction of health measures: they must either locate the burden of health conditions entirely in the individual, which is unfair or misleading, or they must take account of social and environmental contributions to that burden, thereby ceasing to be measures of health performance or attainment. He concludes that if policy makers are to take equality in health care seriously, they should explore alternatives to health measures and to the kind of cost-effectiveness analysis that employs them, alternatives such as the "benchmarks of fairness" scheme proposed by Norman Daniels and his colleagues.

Despite their differing emphases and conflicting judgments, our contributors develop common themes. Several of them scrutinize alleged conceptual and empirical links between impairment and well-being, and between health and well-being. Most claim that those links are more tenuous or complex than is often supposed. Asch, Wasserman, and Shakespeare, for example, argue that reproductive decision making in its present social context is shaped by unjustified or overbroad generalizations about the impact of impairments on well-being, ignoring the highly variable effects of different impairments in different settings. These stereotypes shape both the decisions of individual parents about whether to test for impairments prenatally, and the collective decisions of society to develop and promote such tests. Shakespeare argues for pluralism regarding the goods of health, maintaining that the impact of different diseases on different people may not be reducible to a single value expressed in quality-, disability-, or health-adjusted life years. McMahan argues more generally for reasonable pluralism about what makes a life go well.

Several of the contributors pose significant challenges to the assumptions underlying the measurement of health and health-related quality of life. Some, notably Wachbroit, Silvers, Amundson, and Bickenbach, do so explicitly; others, such as McMahan and Shakespeare, do so implicitly. If there is what Rawls has called "an irreducible plurality of reasonable conceptions of the good," and therefore of individual well-being, it may not be possible to achieve the full ordering presupposed by many measures of health and quality of life. If the impact of health on well-being depends on an individual's environment and social circumstances, it may not be possible to assess *health-related* quality of life without holding the environment constant – an impossible task. And if health measures attempt to take into account all of the environmental and social factors that affect the "burden" of disease and disability, they will cease to be measures of health in any conventional sense of that term.

Even though these common themes and challenges do not constitute a consensus on the interlocking issues of health assessment measures, genetic testing, and disability policy, they offer a clear introduction to what is at stake, practically, conceptually, and ethically. We hope that this volume succeeds in persuading scholars, advocates, and policy makers of the value of examining any of these issues in the context of the other two.

NOTES

1. The notion has also been adopted by rehabilitation professionals as their primary therapeutic concern, and it has sometimes been called the "cornerstone" of health promotion and other public health endeavors (Brown, Renwick, and Nagler, 1996). Quality-of-life assessments are now widely used in making a variety of clinical and administrative decisions (Patrick and Erickson, 1993).
2. Some might be concerned that the WHO definition refers to "well-being" rather than to "quality of life." Many writers, including some of our own contributors, use the two terms interchangeably; others distinguish them, often in conflicting ways. For example, some writers treat well-being as inherently subjective or experiential and quality of life as a more objective, inclusive, or comprehensive notion; others do just the reverse. It is not the purpose of this Introduction to propose or argue for any particular analysis

21

of quality of life or of well-being, and hence for any particular claim about how they relate to each other. Pre-analytically, the two terms are often used interchangeably without confusion, and we will follow this practice here for expository convenience, except when discussing literature that proposes or assumes a difference between the two terms.

3. In one of the few theoretical attempts to draw a line between health-related and non-health-related quality of life, it has been argued that the difference can be marked only contingently, in terms of which factors can be expected to be directly affected by health care interventions (Spilker and Revicki, 1996). This criterion is arguably circular, since it depends entirely on what is meant by a "health care intervention." The classification that results from applying this criterion is also counterintutive. Thus, Spilker and Revicki identify a person's coping strategies as non-health-related, although developing these strategies is, presumably, a central goal of many mental health interventions. Even more controversially, they deny that air- and water-quality improvements are health-related, which would come as a surprise to any public health professional or agency.

4. The gap between of the diagnostic signs of biomedical disfunctioning and the vast panoply of individual and social functioning that people engage in led to an interest in refining the notion of functional status. As early as the mid-1970s, the WHO, seeing the need to more systematically classify levels of human functioning, began work on what was eventually published, in 1980, as the *International Classification of Impairments, Disabilities, and Handicaps*. The ICIDH was essentially a terminological classification, the aim of which was to set the stage for a consistent, international language of human functioning, the first step in the development of assessment instruments.

5. Most of the industry-leading quality of life instruments intended for general use – the McMaster Health Index Questionnaire, Sickness Impact Profile, Nottingham Health Profile, and the MOS Short Form Health Survey, to name a few – were developed in response to the increasing public focus on health promotion. The items selected in these instruments were often lifted from instruments that were already in widespread use and had good psychometric properties. During the 1980s, other approaches were taken to broaden the pool of items, in the hope of better capturing a more inclusive sense of quality of life. For example, in the development of its own instrument, the WHOQOL, WHO relied on iterative drafts provided by an international and interdisciplinary panel of experts who used a modified Delphi consensus-shaping process (WHOQOL Group, 1994). In a few instances, developers supplemented professional opinion with interviews with lay people – some with chronic health conditions, others without.

REFERENCES

Albrecht, G. L., and Devlieger, P. 1999. "The Disability Paradox: High Quality of Life against All Odds." *Social Science and Medicine* 48: 977.

Amundson, R. 1992. "Disability, Handicap, and the Environment." *Journal of Social Philosophy* 9: 105.

Anspach, R. 1979. "From Stigma to Identity Politics: Political Activism among the Physically Disabled and Former Mental Patients." *Social Science and Medicine* 13: 765.

Asch, A. 2003. "Disability Equality and Prenatal Testing: Contradictory or Compatible? (Symposium, Genes and Disability: Defining Health and the Goals of Medicince)." *Florida State University Law Review* 30: 315–41.

Asch, A. 2000. "Why I Haven't Changed My Mind about Prenatal Diagnosis: Reflections and Refinements." In E. Parens and A. Asch (eds.), *Prenatal Testing and Disability Rights*. Washington, DC: Georgetown University Press, pp. 234–58.

Asch, A. 1999. "Prenatal Diagnosis and Selective Abortion: A Challenge to Practice and Policy." *American Journal of Public Health* 89 (11): 1649–57.

Battin, M. 2003. "Euthanasia and Physician-Assisted Suicide." In H. LaFollette (ed.), *The Oxford Handbook of Practical Ethics*. Oxford: Oxford University Press, pp. 673–704.

Bickenbach, J. E., Chatterji, S., Badley, E. M., and Üstün, T. B. 1999. "Models of Disablement, Universalism and the ICIDH." *Social Science and Medicine* 48: 1173–87.

Bowling, A. 1997. *Measuring Health: A Review of Quality of Life Measurement Scales*, 2nd ed. Buckingham and Philadelphia: Open University Press.

Brock, D. 1993. "Quality of Life Measures in Health Care and Medical Ethics." In Martha Nussbaum and Amartya Sen (eds.), *The Quality of Life*. Oxford: Clarendon Press, pp. 95–132.

Brock, D. W. 1995. "The Non-Identity Problem and Genetic Harms – The Case of Wrongful Handicaps." *Bioethics* 9 (3/4): 269–75.

Brown, I., Renwick, B., and Nagler, M. 1996. "The Centrality of Quality of Life in Health Promotion and Rehabilitation." In R. Renwick, I. Brown, and M. Nagler (eds.), *Quality of Life in Health Promotion and Rehabilitation: Conceptual Approaches, Issues, and Applications*. Thousand Oaks, CA: Sage.

Bury, M. 1987. "Social Aspects of Rehabilitation." *International Journal of Rehabilitation Research* 10 (supp. 5): 25.

Day, H., and Jankey, S. G. 1996. "Lessons from the Liberature." In R. Renwick, I. Brown, and M. Nagler (eds.), *Quality of Life in Health Promotion and Rehabilitation: Conceptual Approaches, Issues, and Applications*. Thousand Oaks, CA: Sage.

Deyo, R. A., and Patrick, D. L. 1999. "Barriers to the Use of Health Status Measures in Clinical Investigation, Patient Care, and Policy Research." *Medical Care* 27 (supp. 3): S254.

Driedger, D. 1989. *The Last Civil Rights Movement*. London: Hurst.

Duster, T. 1990. *Back Door to Eugenics*. New York: Routledge.

Francis, L., and Silvers, A. (eds.). 2000. *Americans with Disabilities*. New York: Routledge.

Gill, T. M., and Feinstein, A. R. 1994. "A Critical Appraisal of the Quality of Quality-of-Life Measurements." *Journal of the American Medical Association* 272: 619–26.

Griffin, J. 1993. "Commentary on Dan Brock: 'Quality of Life Measures in Health Care and Medical Ethics.'" In Martha Nussbaum and Amartya Sen (eds.), *The Quality of Life*, Oxford: Clarendon Press, pp. 133–9.

Griffin, J. *Well-Being: Its Meaning, Measure, and Moral Importance*. Oxford: Oxford University Press, 1986.

Huether, C. A. 1983. "Projection of Down's Syndrome Births in the United States 1979–2000, and the Potential Effects of Prenatal Diagnosis." *American Journal of Public Health* 73: 1186–9.

Huether, C. A. 1990. "Epidemiological Aspects of Down Syndrome: Sex Ratio, Incidence, and Recent Aspects of Prenatal Testing." *Issues and Reviews in Tetralology* 5: 263.

Imrie, R. 1997. "Rethinking the Relationships between Disability, Rehabilitation, and Society." *Disability and Rehabilitation* 19: 263.

Kuhse, H., and Singer, P. 1985. *Should the Baby Live? The Problem of Handicapped Infants*. Oxford: Oxford University Press.

Kuppermann, M. E. Gates, and Washington, A. E. 1996. "Racial-Ethnic Differences in Prenatal Diagnostic Sex Use and Outcomes: Preferences, Socioeconomics, or Patient Knowledge?" *Obstetrics and Gynecology* 87: 675–82.

Lippman, A. 1991. "Prenatal Genetic Testing and Screening: Constructing Needs and Reinforcing Inequities." *American Journal of Law and Medicine* 17: 15–50.

Lubetkin, E. I., Sofaer, S., Gold, M. R., et al. 2003. "Aligning Quality for Populations and Patients: Do We Know Which Way to Go?" *American Journal of Public Health* 93: 406.

McDowell, I., and Newell, C. 1991. *Measuring Health: A Guide to Rating Scales and Questionnaires*. New York: Oxford University Press.

Murray, C. 1996. "Rethinking DALYs." In C. Murray and A. Lopez (eds.), *The Global Burden of Disease: A Comprehensive Assessment of Mortality and Disability from Diseases, Injuries, and Risk Factors in 1990 and Projected to 2020*. Geneva: World Health Organization, pp. 1–98.

National Committee on Vital and Health Statistics. 2001. *Classifying and Reporting Functional Status*. <www.ncvhs.hhs.gov/010617rp.pdf>.

National Digitial Archives of Datasets. 1996. "Data for Health Authorities Boundaries at April 1996 (PHO-A4.1B). Down's Syndrome: Diagnoses and Outcomes in the Period 1994 to 1996. (Data from the National Down Syndrome Cytogenic Register)." <http://ndad.ulcc.ac.uk>.

Nord, E., Arnesen, T., Menzel, P., and Pinto, J. L.. 2001. "Towards a More Restricted Use of the Term 'Quality of Life'." *Quality of Life Newsletter* 26.

Nussbaum, M. 1990. "Aristotelian Social Democracy." In R. B. Douglass, G. Mara, and H. Richardson (eds.), *Liberalism and the Human Good*. New York: Routledge.

Nussbaum, M. 1992. "Human Functioning and Social Justice: A Defense of Aristotelian Essentialism." *Political Theory* 20: 202–46.

Nussbaum, M. 1998. "The Good as Discipline, the Good as Freedom." In D. Crocker and T. Linden (eds.), *Ethics of Consumption: The Good Life*

Justice, and Global Stewardship. Lanham, MD: Rowman and Littlefield, pp. 312–41.

Nussbaum M., and Sen, A. (eds.). 1993. *The Quality of Life.* Oxford: Claredon Press.

Parens, E., and Asch, A. 2000. "The Disability Rights Critique of Prenatal Genetic Testing: Reflections and Recommendations." In E. Parens and A. Asch (eds.), *Prenatal Testing and Disability Rights.* Washington, DC: Georgetown University Press, pp. 3–43.

Patrick, D. L., and Erickson, P. 1993. *Health-Status and Health Policy: Quality of Life in Health Care Evaluation and Resource Allocation.* New York: Oxford University Press.

Patrick, D. L., and Erickson, P. 1993. "Assessing Health-Related Quality of Life for Clinical Decision-Making." In S. R. Walker and R. M. Rosser (eds.), *Quality of Life Assessment: Key Issues in the 1990s.* Dordrecht and Boston: Kluwer Academic Publishers.

Purdy, L. 1996. "Genetics and Reproductive Risk: Can Having Children Be Immoral?" In his *Reproducing Persons: Issues in Feminist Bioethics.* Ithaca, NY: Cornell University Press.

Roan, S. 2004. "Safer, Easier, Prenatal Testing." *Los Angeles Times*, February 9.

Safilos-Rothschild, C. 1970. *The Sociology and Social Psychology of Disability and Rehabilitation.* New York: Random House.

Sagarin, E. (ed.). 1971. *The Other Minorities: Non-ethnic Collectivies Conceptualizd as Minority Groups.* Toronto: Ginn.

Scotch, R. 1984. *From Goodwill to Civil Rights.* Philadelphia: Temple University Press.

Scotch, R. 1989. "Politics and Policy in the History of the Disability Rights Movement." *The Milbank Quarterly* 67 (supp. 2): 380.

Sen, A. 1980. "Equality of What?" In S. McMurrin (ed.), *Tanner Lectures on Human Values I.* Salt Lake City: University of Utah Press.

Sen, A. 1993. "Capability and Well-Being." In Martha Nussbaum and Amartya Sen (eds.), *The Quality of Life.* Oxford: Clarendon Press, pp. 30–53.

Spilker, B. (ed). 1996. *Quality of Life and Pharmacoeconomics in Clinical Trials,* 2nd ed. Philadelphia: Lippincott-Raven.

Spilker, B., and Revicki, D. A. 1996. "Taxonomy of Quality of Life." In B. Spilker (ed.), *Quality of Life and Pharmacoeconomics in Clinical Trials,* 2nd ed. Philadelphia, Lippincott-Raven.

Sumner, L. W. 1996. *Welfare, Happiness, and Ethics.* Oxford: Clarendon Press.

Union of the Physically Impaired Against Segregation. 1976. *Fundamental Principles of Disability.* London: Union of the Physically Impaired Against Segregation.

Verbrugge, L. M., and Jette, A. M. 1994. "The Disablement Process." *Social Science and Medicine* 38: 1.

Walker, S. R. 1993. "Industry Perspectives on Quality of Life." In S. R. Walker and R. M. Rosser (eds.), *Quality of Life Assessment: Key Issues in the 1990s.* Dordrecht and Boston: Kluwer Academic Publishers.

Wasserman, D. 2001. "Philosophical Issues in the Definition and Social Response to Disability. In G. Albrecht, K. D. Seelman, and M. Bury (eds.), *Handbook of Disability Studies*. New York: Sage, pp. 219–51.

Wegner, J. 1983. "The Anti-discrimination Model Reconsidered: Ensuring Equal Opportunity without Respect to Handicap under Section 504 of the Rehabilitation Act of 1973." *Cornell Law Review* 69: 401.

WHOQOL Group. 1994. "Development of the WHOQOL: Rationale and Current Status." *International Journal of Mental Health* 23: 24

World Health Organization. 1980, 1993. *International Classification of Impairments, Disabilities and Handicaps*. Geneva: World Health Organization.

World Health Organization. 2001. *International Classification of Functioning, Disability and Health*. Geneva: World Health Organization.

Wright, B. 1983. *Physical Disability – A Psychosocial Approach*, 2nd ed. New York: Harper and Row.

Zola, I. 1989. "Toward the Necessary Universalizing of a Disability Policy." *The Milbank Quarterly* 67: 401.

Chapter 1

Assessing Quality of Life

Clinical versus Health Policy Uses

ROBERT WACHBROIT

INTRODUCTION

The cruel quip "The operation was a success but the patient died" expresses a common anxiety that medicine's criteria of success may be too narrow. Fixed on the goal of removing or ameliorating the symptoms – if not correcting the underlying physiological abnormality – medical practice can sometimes seem professionally inattentive to the impact that a particular disease or treatment may have on a patient's well-being beyond the specific signs and symptoms of the disease. In response to these concerns there has been, at least since the 1970s, growing clinical attention to and research on the use of so-called quality-of-life (QOL) measurements to inform treatment decisions.

Hundreds of these QOL instruments are currently available, many of which are finely tailored to specific diseases or sets of symptoms (McDowell and Newell, 1996). They typically consist of identifying a set of outcomes or consequences arising from a particular disease – physical or emotional functioning, patient self-perceptions and experiences, social limitations, and so on. This set can be called the QOL profile of the disease. Through a method of scoring that is determined to be both reliable and responsive, the disease and the various treatment options are evaluated in terms of their impact on each of the concerns identified in the profile. For example, ambulatory oxygen might well relieve the symptoms of someone suffering from a lung disease; nevertheless, its impact on the patients QOL profile – its effect on his daily activities, how he feels about himself, and so on – might well indicate that carrying a tank of oxygen around results in a lower quality of life and so, arguably, is not the best treatment for this patient's condition.

Assessments of quality of life are also made in the area of health policy, but these typically involve a different sort of calculation and measurement. Such measures are closer to utility measures, often expressed as a single number. Their use is not so much to evaluate clinical options as to enable cost-benefit or cost-effectiveness calculations. They are not disease-specific, precisely so that comparisons between diseases are possible – for example, is the standard treatment for diabetes more cost-effective than the standard treatment for coronary artery disease?

The assessment and use of quality of life in health policy is far more controversial than its assessment and use in clinical care. Part of the reason for this difference lies in the mathematical challenges of constructing a measure of quality of life that is not disease-specific. Part of the reason also lies in the problems with justifying the policy use of quality-of-life measures. I will try to present some of these difficulties, arguing that they indeed pose serious objections for policy uses but not for clinical uses of QOL assessments. Although the distinction is not often made between quality-of-life assessments as used by clinicians and medical researchers and such assessments as used by public health professionals – such as epidemiologists, as well as health economists and health policy makers – we shall see that it needs to be more widely acknowledged.

HEALTH-RELATED QUALITY OF LIFE

An immediate problem arises with any attempt to use (or design) a quality-of-life or well-being measure as a health assessment tool. Health, while extremely important for well-being, is plainly not the only matter that can affect well-being. Economic status, family dynamics, employment opportunities, number of friends, and so on can all significantly affect well-being. While we would expect that a person's well-being would rise or fall as that person's health improved or declined, other factors can easily obscure or confound these shifts. For example, we can easily imagine two people suffering from the same disorder; one has consequently lost his job, whereas the other retains his job and enjoys generous support services. Changes in their quality of life are hardly reliable assessments of changes in their health. Indeed, poorer health can sometimes result in better quality of life or well-being. A common illustration of this possibility is flat feet. Consider two people, alike in all respects except that one has flat feet. We can easily imagine circumstances in which the one with flat feet is thereby ineligible for military service and so enjoys a better quality of life than the one with normal feet.

The standard response to this problem is to relativize it: our interest is not in quality of life but rather in *health-related* quality of life (HRQL). But this response only identifies the problem. How is HRQL to be defined, and can it be measured? One challenge lies in making health-relatedness not appear to be arbitrary. The pain that results from a particular disease can affect well-being and would be reflected in HRQL; however, the job loss that results from that same disease can also affect well-being but would not be reflected in HRQL. Why is the pain health-related but the job loss resulting from the disease not health-related? The distinction can't be based on the "immediacy" or "directness" of the consequence, since the pain could be delayed and the job loss could be immediate. It can't be based on whether the consequences are socially dependent, since HRQL is often taken to include social limitations and psychosocial considerations. Saying that we are interested only in the health consequences of a disease or disorder plainly just labels the issue and so does not answer the question.

Some might dismiss this challenge as being merely of theoretical interest. Even if we have difficulty articulating the principles that distinguish health consequences from nonhealth consequences, we have little difficulty, aside from some possible borderline cases, distinguishing these two consequences in practice. Such a reliance on (unprincipled) intuitions may seem defeatist or even subversive, since part of the reason for employing HRQL measures is surely to replace intuitions about who is more or less healthy – seat-of-the-pants assessments of health – with principled judgments and precise calculations. Nevertheless, I would like to put this problem to one side. Even if it can be adequately addressed – and I've said nothing to indicate that it cannot be – the idea of HRQL faces more daunting objections.

THE SEPARABILITY OF HEALTH[1]

In order to calculate HRQL, we need to determine the impact of health on well-being or quality of life. The logical way to proceed would be to identify the various components of health, determine the impact of each of these components, and then combine the results. For example, let us call a "health profile" the particular assessments of the various components that comprise a person's health status. Among the elements of a person's health profile would be such things as the person's visual acuity and hearing level. We could determine the impact of that person's health on his well-being by determining the impact of that particular level of visual acuity (hearing, etc.) on well-being and then combining these various impacts. The combination would not be a simple summation, since some of the components of health – the elements of a person's health profile – may interact with each other, as in the case of co-morbidities, and so would not be independent variables.

The problem with this procedure is that many health components affect well-being only in conjunction with various nonhealth factors, many of which can vary considerably from person to person. The impact on well-being of a particular level of visual acuity, for example, will depend upon such things as the number of books the person has. Presumably, the more books an individual has, the more impact a sudden loss of sight would have on that person's well-being. But people differ greatly in the number of books they own and in the importance they attach to them. Thus, two people with the same health profile but in different environments (i.e., faced with different nonhealth factors) – or even the same person at two different times and environments – can yield different answers to the question of how that state of health affects well-being.

The significance of this observation – sometimes expressed by saying that health is not a separable component of well-being – can be gauged by examining three types of assessment reflecting HRQL: (1) an assessment of a particular health state; (2) an assessment of the health of a population or group of people, sometimes called a "summary health measure"; and (3) an assessment of the health of an individual. Let me discuss these in turn.

The inseparability of health indicates that we cannot state what impact a particular health condition has on well-being. We cannot, for example, determine the affect that diabetes has on well-being, because the impact that diabetes-affected eyesight has on well-being will vary with environment. We should therefore be skeptical of published lists of *the* quality-of-life assessments of different health conditions – for example, Murray and Lopez (1998). We must conclude that such calculations either have restricted the identified health consequences to those with little environmental interaction or, perhaps only implicitly, have designated some particular environment or set of nonhealth factors as standard or canonical (calculating the impacts of the health components accordingly) or performed some sort of averaging over a range of environments. But any of these options surely needs to be justified. Do we include books in the environment? If so, how many and why? Lack of justification in the specification of the nonhealth factors translates into an arbitrariness in the resulting health assessments.

The situation looks more promising if we are consider assessing a particular health condition in a population. If the environmental and other nonhealth factors vary little within the population, then a health assessment could be calculated – but two important qualifications must be noted. First, the restriction to populations with roughly uniform environments is not trivial. We can easily define "artificial populations" that have relatively uniform or fixed nonhealth factors, but it is not clear that such populations are relevant or interesting for health policy purposes. It probably matters little if we can construct a population having the right characteristics by taking a few people from different regions of the planet. The resulting group might not constitute a body over which a health policy could be framed – because, for example, the group was subject to too many diverse and conflicting political jurisdictions. It is an empirical question whether populations relevant for health policy – such as national populations or important subnational populations – can satisfy the requirement of having only small variations in nonhealth factors. (This of course assumes that we understand what "small variations" means. Should the relevant variation be in the number of books, the size of books, the type of books, etc.?) If we consider the United States, with its wide diversity, it is not at all obvious that there are any interesting subpopulations in the country that are sufficiently uniform in nonhealth factors. Think of how nonhealth factors – such as the number of books, the number of videos, and the number of paintings – vary with region, with socioeconomic status, with age, with profession, and so on.

Second, the resulting HRQL for that health condition must be understood as being relativized to that particular population (with its roughly uniform environment). We shouldn't be surprised if the effect of diabetes on the HRQL of a group of struggling farmers in southern India is different from the effect of diabetes on the HRQL of a group of successful professionals in urban New York, assuming that each of these populations is characterized by fairly uniform environments. And with this relativization come constraints on what we can meaningfully compare. We cannot say, for example, whether, in terms of its impact on well-being, lung cancer is worse than coronary artery disease without specifying the nonhealth factors. In some environments a particular type

31

of lung cancer will be worse, in other environments the identical type will not be.

If we shift our attention to the case of assessing the health of an individual – or the effect of a specific disease on the HRQL of a particular person – the matter is much simpler. Indeed, the first qualification is not even applicable, since we are usually dealing with only one environment or set of nonhealth factors. And we can determine whether lung cancer is worse than coronary artery disease because the comparison is specific to an individual. Moreover, insofar as an individual's nonhealth factors change little over time, we can make approximate comparisons over a brief time span. Nevertheless, even if we confine ourselves to assessments of individuals, the next argument raises further problems.

THE INDETERMINACY OF HEALTH

The idea of HRQL seems to presuppose the existence of something that corresponds to total or overall health. Mathematically, we can represent overall health as a function of the various health components. In order to keep the exposition simple, let us suppose there are only two health components: visual acuity and hearing level. Thus, we can represent health as a two-place function:

$$\text{Health} = H(\text{eyesight, hearing}).$$

Making some plausible assumptions – that H yields a real number between 0 and 1, that some of the health components vary continuously, and so on – we get the result that, for any given value of overall health, we cannot determine the values of the specific health components that constitute that health state. This conclusion reflects the lesson from elementary algebra that you cannot calculate the value of two (or more) variables with only one equation. The nonexistence of a function inverse to H, which would take a particular value of overall health as input and yield unique values for eyesight and hearing, means that in some cases

$$H(\text{eyesight}_1, \text{hearing}_1) = H(\text{eyesight}_2, \text{hearing}_2)$$

even though

$$\text{eyesight}_1 \neq \text{hearing}_2 \text{ and } H(\text{hearing}_1 \neq \text{hearing}_2).$$

(For the mathematically alert: I am intentionally conflating variables and their values in order not to complicate the notation. Nevertheless, the meaning should be clear.)

The problem raised in the previous section was that the impact of a health state on well-being depended upon environmental and other nonhealth factors. The response was to restrict such calculations to single or uniform environments and to relativize HRQL accordingly. The argument of this section points to a problem that exists even if we restrict ourselves to a single environment. Regardless of how we determine overall health from a given health profile – recall that the assumptions were mathematically minimalist – different health profiles can yield the same overall health. In such cases, even though different health profiles could have different impacts on well-being, this difference could not be captured using overall health as our input, since overall health is the same for both profiles. Using the above illustration, even though the health profiles (eyesight$_1$, hearing$_1$) and (eyesight$_2$, hearing$_2$) would have different impacts on well-being, no well-being function using H as a variable could capture that difference.

The conclusion of this argument, in other words, is that the impact of (overall) health on well-being is indeterminate. It might be useful to compare this conclusion to the earlier problem of characterizing HRQL. In order for an assessment of quality of life or well-being to be a health assessment, we need to restrict our attention to that part or aspect of quality of life that health affects. But, according to the argument just presented, the impact of health (as opposed to the components of health) on well-being is indeterminate or not well defined. The idea of HRQL cannot be taken literally.

One response to this problem is, of course, to jettison the concept of overall health and confine discussion and calculations to the impact of health profiles or specific health components. This would mean replacing HRQL with something even more finely grained – diabetes-related quality of life, for example, or eyesight-related quality of life. As we will see, it may be easier to accommodate such a replacement in clinical uses of quality-of-life assessments than in policy uses.

GENERIC VERSUS SPECIFIC

The arguments we have discussed so far present a greater problem for health policy makers, public health administrators, health economists, and so on – those who want to use quality-of-life measures as generic assessments of health – than they do for clinicians, who want to use such assessments to evaluate and monitor the treatment of specific patients. In order to see this, we need to say more about these different uses.

For health policy, the primary purpose of using quality-of-life measures is to determine how bad a particular disease or disability is in comparison to other diseases or disabilities. While it may not be clear whether lung cancer is better or worse than coronary artery disease, we might nevertheless be able to determine which is worse as far as HRQL is concerned. If we hold that the aim of health policy – to maintain or improve the population's health – should be understood to mean that HRQL is to be maintained or improved, then assessing health conditions in terms of HRQL would provide a common metric by which we could rationally set priorities – in research, in funding, in public services, and so on. We could determine whether lung cancer has a more devastating impact on HRQL than coronary artery disease and use that information to help justify the priority to be placed on responding to lung cancer.

Advocates of this use of HRQL measures often assert that such calculations are not intended to dictate health policy priorities. While HRQL assessment is an important factor, it is not the only consideration policy makers must keep in mind. For example, priority in biomedical research funding should reflect not only the severity of the diseases being investigated but also the relevant research opportunities (has some important breakthrough recently been made on which further research can build?), the implications for basic research, and so on. Nevertheless, while HRQL assessments do not dictate policy, its advocates believe that they shift the burden of proof in health policy: even though HRQL assessments do not decide health policy priorities, the burden is on people who want to set them differently to explain why.

A more ambitious use of HRQL assessments would be to employ them in cost-effectiveness evaluations. Not only does HRQL provide a basis for comparing the impacts of different diseases, it could also be used to calculate the efficacy of various treatment programs or policy options. Lung cancer might be worse than diabetes, as measured by HRQL, but a particular program for diabetes might result in more improvement in HRQL per dollar than any existing program for lung cancer. This doesn't mean that health policy should pursue the goal of cost-effectiveness. Some theories of justice – for example, those that place a special priority on those who are worst off – would argue against a strict adherence to cost-effectiveness. Nevertheless, many would argue that it is irresponsible to ignore cost-effectiveness.

An even more ambitious use of the idea of HRQL assessment would be as a basis for comparing health policy concerns to those in other areas of public policy. We would need to extend HRQL assessment to quality of life assessment more generally and then calculate the impact of non-health interventions in these terms. In this way, we could compare the significance of different policy issues – health, education, transportation, and so on – and thus rationally set policy priorities. We'll have more to say about this ambition later.

Regardless of the level of ambition, the core use of HRQL in health policy is to compare diseases or health conditions. For that purpose, we need generic HRQL measurements; anything more specific would undermine or limit comparability. Nevertheless, we are blocked by the separability argument if we want to compare health conditions independently of any nonhealth factors; we are blocked by the determinacy argument if we want to compare health conditions independently of any specific component of health.

For the clinician, the primary reason to employ quality-of-life measures is to supplement the standard physiological indicators of a particular disease in the monitoring and guiding of treatment and care. While lung disease often means reduced lung capacity or shortness of breath, it can also result in chronic fatigue and emotional frustration (e.g., pervasive anxiety about breathing). These broader consequences of a disease – its affect on the patient's quality of life – are important to note for the practice of good medicine. When no cure is available, these measures can inform care by identifying the scope of the patient's needs. When treatment options exists, these measures can help to identify which option would be more comfortable, more responsive to the patient's needs, more satisfying, and so on. Only in those situations where we have a standard treatment that brings about a complete cure do quality-of-life considerations lose some of their importance. Presumably, by curing the disease we thereby effectively respond to the associated quality-of-life considerations. (Of course, the trauma of a disease can sometimes extend beyond the cure or elimination of the disease. For example, some women whose breast cancer has been surgically cured nevertheless continue to suffer from a diminished self-image.)

Even though the medical literature often refers to these assessments and measures as "quality-of-life" or "health-related quality-of-life," they are actually far more specific to the disease at issue (Guyatt et al., 1997). Determining how well the patient maneuvers visually in her environment is not usually part of an assessment of the impact of lung cancer on quality of life, though it usually is part of an assessment of the impact of diabetes on quality of life. (To avoid tedious circumlocution, I will continue to use the terms HRQL etc., though we should bear in mind that the HRQL instrument for lung cancer may, or should, be quite different from the HRQL instrument for diabetes.)

It is probably no coincidence that the interest in HRQL assessments in medicine has occurred roughly at the same time as the scrutiny and criticism of medical paternalism. While much of the concern about paternalism is based on an appreciation of the need for respecting the patient's autonomy, it is also based on an acceptance of the idea that deciding what is good for the patient was not entirely a medical matter based on physiological considerations alone. It is important to think about treatment decisions in the larger context of the patient's values, concerns, tolerance for risk, psychological state, and so on. And the patient is typically the best judge of these matters. HRQL measures cannot replace the patient's deliberations, but they can inform them. We would expect that a patient would want to know the impact of alternative treatments on HRQL, if such information were available, before making a decision about which treatment to undergo. HRQL instruments in medicine could be useful in informing patients.

It is clear, therefore, that the clinical uses of HRQL do not need to engage in the comparisons that the arguments of the previous section have found so problematic. The clinical use of HRQL is concerned with determining the burden of a particular disease on a specific individual. What clinical reason would there be for comparing this burden with the burden that a very different disease generates, or with the burdens that people in very different circumstances suffer? Determining the burden of a particular disease on a specific individual need not abstract, neglect, or average out the impact that nonhealth factors or different overall health states can nevertheless have on the same burden.

IS HRQL IMPORTANT FOR HEALTH POLICY?

If we believe that health policy should be based on HRQL measurements, then the preceding arguments are not so much objections as challenges or difficulties that must be addressed or worked around. At worst, the arguments are paradoxes – seemingly valid arguments against the possibility of doing what we otherwise know quite well can and should be done. If the arguments are therefore to serve as persuasive objections, we need to examine the need for HRQL measures in health policy. Does health policy become arbitrary or irrational without such measures?

It might be useful to contrast health policy with education policy on this matter, because in other contexts much is made of the apparent similarities between the two. Many people have argued for the importance of health care, for the demand for universal access, for the tie between health care and justice, and for the role that access to health care plays in ensuring equality of opportunity by saying, in effect, that the justification for the corresponding claims in education are generally accepted and that health is not fundamentally different from education with regard to these matters (Guttmann, 1981; Daniels, 1985; Pogge, 1989). It is as important to have a healthy citizenry as to have a well-educated citizenry; it is as unjust to deny health care to the poor as to deny education to the poor; there is as much reason for a right to health care as there is for a right to education.

When we look at education policy, we see a field awash in concerns about measurement and assessment. The aptitude and knowledge of students, both individually and collectively, are constantly measured, as well as the performance of schools, school districts, education programs, and even educational tests themselves. Educational needs, successes, and failures are indicated by using various specific aptitude and achievement measures. Furthermore, professionals in education policy are of course aware of the importance of education for well-being. Nevertheless, measurements of the impact of education on quality of life or well-being have not been developed and are not used in education policy. (There have been several studies on the economics of education and its impact on human capital, but that is a different matter. See, for example, Hanushek and Luque [2001].) There is no doubt that arts education and science education affect well-being, and in very different ways, but no one has argued that decisions regarding the allocation of resources between these two should be informed by QOL measurements. No one has claimed that education policy should be informed by measurements of well-being.

Nor do other areas of public policy – national security, transportation, commerce – appear to use or need measures of well-being to assess policy needs or programs. Unless health policy is confused or misguided in using HRQL measures, one of two conclusions must follow. Either (1) other policy areas should nevertheless develop appropriate measures of well-being, because their ability to identify and prioritize needs and to assess programs and developments would be improved by using such measures, or (2) health policy is unique – in its subject matter or mission – and therefore, unlike other public policy areas, needs to use such measures.

There is not much that can be said about (1) at this level of generality. A certain kind of doctrinaire utilitarian (or, what is often the same thing, a certain kind of welfare economist) might maintain on principle that other areas of public policy would be improved if they were informed by well-being measures. But given the controversy over utilitarianism, such a claim would not, on its own, be very persuasive. A more convincing argument would have to proceed by examining the details of particular policy areas on a case-by-case basis. What would a measurement of related well-being look like for national security or transportation, and how could it shape budget priorities or the choice between weapons systems or the decision to fund Amtrak? Should a "QOL impact statement" be attached to every policy proposal? It is difficult to believe that there would be much motivation to conduct such an examination, especially when we note the lack of consensus among health policy theorists themselves over which well-being measure to use. Policy professionals have little reason to be impressed with the use of well-being measures in health policy.

Can a case be made for (2)? Is there something unique or special about the mission or subject matter of health policy that requires the development and use of well-being measures? One might claim, for example, that health is much more intimately connected with well-being than any other policy area. This assertion is encouraged by looking at the WHO definition of health: "Health is a state of complete physical, mental and social well-being and not merely the absence of disease or infirmity" (WHO, 1946). According to this definition, a measurement of health should amount to a measurement of well-being. Appealing to this definition, however, won't help as a justification for the widespread use of measures of well-being in health policy. Because health is linked so strongly and completely with well-being, it becomes difficult if not impossible to identify any aspect of an individual's life or well-being that is not a matter of health. The WHO definition stretches the concept of health beyond our ordinary understanding and beyond anything that is associated with medicine: it's not clear why medicine should be more important to health, so understood, than economics, education, or politics, for "health" becomes just another word for well-being. Narrowing the terms of the definition of health to health-related well-being is obviously circular. For this and other reasons, the WHO definition has been widely criticized and rejected. No one – not even, apparently, WHO itself, in its recent efforts in investigating the "burden of disease" or defining and assessing health – takes it seriously (Salmon et al., 2003).

A different approach turns not so much on a definition of "health" as on a definition of "health policy." The subject matter of health policy just is the impact of health on well-being. Although something like this approach may be operating, at least implicitly, in some discussions of health policy, it cannot be defended when presented so explicitly, since it begs the question: instead of an argument, we are given a definitional assertion. It hardly demonstrates that health policy has a special concern with well-being, since it doesn't show why, for example, education policy isn't defined as the impact of education on well-being.

Our examination of whether health policy, as opposed to other public policy disciplines, has a special or greater concern with well-being has so far yielded negative results. But perhaps this doesn't matter. If the use of HRQL assessments in health policy is helpful, that may be justification enough for their use.

It may well seem odd to object to the use of HRQL in health policy given the apparently modest role that advocates assign to it. As we noted, no one, except a few ideological utilitarians, believes that HRQL assessments should *determine* health policy. The common position is that HRQL assessments and calculation should *inform* but not dictate health policy decisions. How could one object to that?

The problem is what we could call the "transparency problem." Health policy, like any public policy, reflects not only the facts and probabilities, as best as they can be ascertained, but also values. Whereas the facts and probabilities might be matters for the experts, the values that shape public policies should be open to the public. We require, therefore, that health policy, at least as far as its values are concerned, be transparent. It should be clear what values are shaping policy, so that if there are important public disagreements or shifts in judgment, the appropriate adjustments or corrections can be made in accordance with our political institutions. That is to say, health policy must be responsive to the public's values, suitably informed and mediated through appropriate and accepted political processes.

Health policy, when determined or even only informed by HRQL assessments, significantly departs from the requirement of transparency. If HRQL assessments were little more than epidemiological statistics – such as infant mortality rates or incidence levels of a particular disease – they probably would not present a problem for transparency. But, as we have seen, HRQL assessments are typically more than that. It is generally acknowledged, even by advocates of the use of HRQL assessments in health policy, that these assessments are value-laden at several points. Deciding which consequences of a health condition are sufficiently important to be included in a health profile will typically involve value judgments. Assigning numbers to particular health components and giving them relative weights in a calculation will also be based on value judgments. For example, one health assessment tool will add a weighting on evaluations of particular health conditions that depends upon the age of the individual, reflecting a judgment that the earlier in life one contracts a disease, the more burdensome it is. Another health assessment tool will weigh matters differently, reflecting a judgment that a disease is less burdensome if it is contracted at the beginning or at the end of life than it would be if contracted during the middle years, when one is more productive. And yet another tool might not apply any age weighting at all, reflecting an egalitarianism regarding the burden of disease – the idea that we shouldn't distinguish between the ten-year-old, the forty-year-old, and the seventy-year-old as far as the assessment of a particular health condition is concerned. The problem is not that these value judgments are incorrect or without justification – indeed, they are sometimes explicitly acknowledged and argued for (Murray, 1996; Nord, 1999). The problem is that when health policy is informed by valued-laden HRQL assessments, it ceases to be transparent. The values that shape the HRQL assessments also affect the subsequent health policy. These values will, however, be less accessible than the public values informing the health policy, because, by being embedded in HRQL assessments, they come under the guise of expert judgments regarding health states. They are therefore not presented as values for the public to deliberate upon. Whether our health policy should place special emphasis on youth should be an explicit political decision, publicly deliberated, and not an implicit decision made by experts.

One might reply that transparency is not important as long as the values embedded in HRQL assessments are correct (or accurately capture the values of society). But this amounts to claiming that democratic *procedures* and the *process* of public deliberation are not important – only the results are important. (Compare that idea to this defense of medical paternalism: if we were certain about what the patient would choose, then there would be no need for informing her or obtaining her consent.) It is doubtful that advocates of HRQL assessments in health policy would want to advance such an antidemocratic view.

This problem of transparency need not be much of an issue in clinical uses of HRQL assessments because of the requirement for informed consent, according to which the patient's medical decisions are made by the patient based on conversations with the physician. If, for example, the physician presents the patient with two treatment options, saying that one has been shown to be associated with a better quality of life, the patient can ask, and the physician should make clear, what these assessments of quality of life mean in this specific case. If age weighting was used in an assessment, the patient can be so informed and decide whether to accept or reject it. But the sort of back-and-forth conversation between the patient and the physician that can inform the patient of implicit values in health assessments is not feasible at the level of public policy.

In the end, the worries about transparency may well be more important than the earlier technical problems about separability and determinacy. Not only does this touch upon the point of determining HRQL in health policy, rather than using particular methods for these determinations, but it captures, I believe, part of the reason why the use of HRQL in health policy has attracted such widespread criticism and concern. Some worry that in using HRQL assessment, something is being slipped pass them. They may be right.

NOTES

This paper is based on a series of papers written during the course of NIH grant Ro1-HG01979. I am grateful to David Wasserman for urging that I gather the main points into one essay and for his advice.
1. The argument in this section is a reformulation of Broome's (2002).

REFERENCES

Broome, John. 2002. "Measuring the Burden of Disease by Aggregating Well-Being." In Christopher J. L. Murray, Joshua A. Salomon, Colin D. Mathers, and Alan D. Lopez (eds.), *Summary Measures of Population Health: Concepts, Ethics, Measurement and Applications*. Geneva: World Health Organization, pp. 91–113.

Daniels, Norman. 1985. *Just Health Care*. Cambridge: Cambridge University Press.

Guttmann, Amy. 1981. "For and Against Equal Access to Health Care." *Milbank Memorial Fund Quarterly – Health and Society* 59: 542–60.

Guyatt, G., Naylor, D., Juniper, E., Heyland, D., Jaeschke, R., and Cook, D. 1997. "Users' Guides to the Medical Literature XII. How to Use Articles About

Health-Related Quality of Life." *Journal of the American Medical Association* 277 (15): 1232–7.

Hanushek, Eric A., and Luque, Javier A. 2001. "Efficency and Equity in Schools around the World." Research report available at <http://www.worldbank.org/education/economicsed/research/econseries/hanushek.pdf>.

McDowell, Ian, and Newell, Claire. 1996. *Measuring Health: A Guide to Rating Scales and Questionnaires*. Oxford: Oxford University Press.

Murray, Christopher J. L. 1996. "Rethinking DALYs." In Christopher J. L. Murray and Alan D. Lopez (eds.), *The Global Burden of Disease*. Cambridge, MA: Harvard University Press, pp. 1–98.

Murray, Christopher J. L., and Lopez, Alan D., eds. (1998). *Health Dimensions of Sex and Reproduction: The Global Burden of Sexually Transmitted Diseases, HIV, Maternal Conditions, Perinatal Disorders, and Congenital Anomalies*. Cambridge, MA: WHO/ Harvard University Press.

Nord, Erik. 1999. *Cost-Value Analysis in Health Care: Making Sense out of QALYs*. Cambridge: Cambridge University Press.

Pogge, Thomas. 1989. *Realizing Rawls*. Ithaca, NY: Cornell University Press.

Salomon, Joshua A., Mathers, Colin D., Chatterji, Somnath, Sadana, Ritu, Ustun, Bedirhan, and Murray, Christopher J. L. 2003. "Quantifying Individual Levels Of Health: Definitions, Concepts And Measurement Issues." In Christopher J. L. Murray and D. B. Evans (eds.), *Health Systems Performance Assessment: Debates, Methods, and Empiricism*. Geneva: World Health Organization, pp. 301–318.

World Health Organization. 1946. *Constitution of the World Health Organization*. Reprinted in Arthur L. Caplan, H. Tristam Engelhardt, Jr., and James J. McCartney (eds.), *Concepts of Health And Disease: Interdisciplinary Perspectives*. Reading, MA: Addison-Wesley, 1981, pp. 83–4.

Chapter 2

Predicting Genetic Disability while Commodifying Health

ANITA SILVERS

I. IS HEALTH A RESOURCE?

Is health a crucial resource for succeeding in everyday life? Public health policy makers speak as if this were so, both for individuals and for the community as a whole.[1] As a World Health Organization document states: "Health is therefore seen as a resource for everyday living. . . . it is a positive concept emphasizing social and personal resources. . . ."[2] And a Canadian government report explains: "Health is thus envisaged as a resource which gives people the ability to manage and even to change their surroundings."[3]

It seems obvious to them, first of all, that citizens whose health is, or is likely to be, compromised are unfortunately (and possibly inequitably) limited in their pursuit of deserved opportunities and ends. Second, the presence or prospect of numerous citizens whose health is, or is likely to be, unusually compromised likewise seems obviously to limit a society from the collective realization of desirable social conditions and goals. This way of speaking about health commodifies it. On this conception, health resembles wealth. For individuals who possess it, health is a personal asset that enables productive interaction with the people and things that surround them. Its value, therefore, is instrumental. For societies, citizens' health is treated as a collective asset that is instrumental for achieving the general good.

Further, this way of thinking about health transforms it into a good that may be allocated to some individuals at a loss to others. Health, in other words, becomes a conveyable product. In order to pursue this way of thinking about health, we have to shape our conception of it to serve discussions about its proper distribution. Health thereby takes on the countenance of a transferable material asset.

A consequence, as we shall see, is that states of health or health conditions are depersonalized and abstracted from how particular individuals are mindful of them. Claims about the value of specific states of health are detached from the varying standpoints of those who experience them. For this approach requires us to answer questions about whether distributing health to recipients of type A rather than recipients of type B makes better use of it. In order to render such comparisons, we must conceptualize what is being allocated – namely, health states – as commodities that preserve their identities independent of the individuals to whom they are allocated. Only by so doing can we presume it possible to demonstrate which, among alternative assignments of the commodity to different patients, is the allocative pattern that constitutes the most productive and effective instrumentality for distributing health.

Thinking of health as a resource subject to public distribution in this way calls for making comparative judgments about the instrumental value that various distributive patterns can realize. Is it preferable, for instance, to elevate the health of a small number of chronically ill and disabled individuals when the health of a larger number of normal individuals can be maintained for roughly the same cost? The prospect of resolving policy questions such as these has stimulated industrious investigative efforts that have come to pervade discussions of justice in health care policy.

In this chapter, I raise questions about the intelligibility, propriety, and serviceability of attempts to do so. I begin by considering what prompts such thinking. The core of this position lies with our intuitions about the symbiosis of health and justice: health is said to be an enabler of justice, and justice, in turn, is seen as facilitating the acquisition of health. In what follows, I sketch out the fundamentals of this position.

Next, I consider an interpretation that introduces stronger claims about the ties between health and justice by presuming that health is a commodity. Commodifying health invites us to think of chronically ill and disabled people as posing a special allocation problem. I argue that the source of the problem lies not in the difficulty of formulating an adequate distributive principle, but instead in the very idea of creating public allocative schemes for distributing health. This problem, which is conceptual rather than normative, plagues us whether we cast health as a public resource, or as a personal one that the state intercedes to allot. In comparing both public and personal distributions of health, retrospective, contemporary, and prospective perspectives on health's disruptions and diminutions cannot help but be elided, so as to obscure the evidence for comparative assessments.

These conceptual problems may be tolerated, but at a price. In the next two parts of the chapter, I examine some of the costs of casting health as a resource – that is, of considering it in instrumental terms. In section III, I explore ramifications of designating health as a public asset. In sections IV and V, I identify methodological problems with casting health as a personal asset. Regardless of whether commodifying health aims at serving public or private ends, I contend that by doing so we impede rather than advance justice.

One answer to this complaint is that practical justice is a matter of trade-offs. Schemes that do best for most citizens may fail to do best for everyone equally. So inequitable treatment may be justified if the distributive principles involved provide that no one does worse than if they were not applied, while deserving people do better than they would otherwise. In section VI, I consider this defense of biased allotments of health. Predictive genetic testing, I argue, makes it much more difficult to contain the injustice occasioned by commodifying health.

It would be rash to argue that health is never properly thought of as a resource. There are some contexts in which we reasonably may expect it to be. For example, businesses that employ on-site medical professionals to treat workers' illnesses and injuries, or to provide preventative health care programs, may reasonably focus this "benefit" on preventing or treating conditions that impede worker productivity. Rational employers may offer these health care programs to reduce absenteeism and keep skilled workers on the job. In this context, workers' health is valued by the employer as a resource that contributes to the business's productivity.

On the other hand, a society should not relate to its citizens as a business relates to its workers: citizens are not tools of the state, and healthy citizens are not valuable for reasons similar to those for valuing well-maintained, strong tools. Trading off different citizens' allotments of health is a process that cannot help but injure justice. Better to fall back into a framework in which we acknowledge health's value to be preeminently intrinsic. Health care justice should be based on people's direct and personal experiences of the value of being healthy, or not healthy, rather than on suppositions, speculations, and extrapolations about who will make the most effective use of health assets.

II. DO HEALTH AND JUSTICE CONVERGE?

Influential justice theorists long have thought that health is a good with a special moral status. They are convinced that citizens need their health in order to benefit from, and to contribute to, the practice of justice. This conviction suggests that it is only just for the state to underwrite their attaining and preserving it. Health therefore seems good for justice, and justice likewise seems good for health.

This association of health and justice is no recently introduced view. At least since the time of the Greeks, the value of citizens' having fit bodies and minds has seemed obvious to many people. From this conviction, however, further questions arise. One line of inquiry considers whether, or to what extent, individuals should achieve good health in order to participate in the state's exercise of justice. A complimentary series of questions explores whether, or to what extent, the state should facilitate individual citizens' attaining good health, both as an instrument that enables pursuit of the state's own material ends and as a component of its obligation to treat them justly.

States have various powers to advance their citizens' health. Concomitantly, states might actively or passively injure people's health (for example, by exposing them to radioactive waste or by failing to regulate sanitary food preparation), or they might actively or passively disregard people's health (for example, by denying some people health benefits that are provided to everyone else, or by establishing health benefit programs that do not serve all people equitably). Injustice is manifested in the state's denial or neglect of important benefits such as health to those who need and deserve them.

Without committing to any specific theory, either of health or of the just state, we can expect that in desirable societies more citizens who can benefit will have access to the material resources needed to achieve and sustain good health than in unjust states. Broadly, just states promote the good of citizens equally, while unjust states ignore the good of the many and serve only the few. In this light, we may anticipate that just states will be disposed to pursue broad public health initiatives, seeking to improve conditions for all types of citizens, while unjust states will focus on health issues of importance only to the most influential citizens, if they cultivate public health at all. Similarly, just states will promote equity in health care research. For example, in a just state, principles regulating drug development and testing will provide that therapies benefit women as much as men. Further, therapies for illnesses prevalent in minority populations will be sought with energy comparable to what is devoted to the illnesses of populous or powerful populations.

As justice is good for health, health also is good for justice. The idea here is that health facilitates each citizen's flourishing as a contributing member of society. Individuals fortunate in their health are productive and thereby add to the assets of the community. Moreover, they neither restrict other people's opportunities nor reduce other people's welfare by spreading illness or by requiring extraordinary allotments of resources or care.

In order to discover where fundamental agreement about health and justice may lie, we so far have sketched the relation between health and justice in the very broadest strokes. In doing so, we carefully have not committed to any specific theory of justice, or of health. So far, the account outlined here is compatible with many different principles for achieving equality, and with many different understandings of justice. It complies with familiar notions of the mutual facilitation of justice and health without presuming the stronger claims that health is a prerequisite for realizing justice or that, consequently, justice demands the distribution of health,

Yet these stronger claims are routinely advanced in contemporary discussions about health and justice in philosophy and public affairs, as if they also were intuitive.[4] For example, one of the most influential writers on this subject, Norman Daniels, comments that there is a "surprising convergence between what is needed for our social and political well being and for our mental and physical health."[5] This overlap, he believes, signals an alignment of personal and public interests in regard to health. The convergence suggests to Daniels both that there is a public interest in maintaining and restoring individuals' personal health, and that programs for serving this public interest offer citizens private benefits as well. In principle, distributive health schemes should have no problem in commanding the consent of the governed, for a just public scheme that complies with collective ends will equally advance the private ends of individual citizens.

It is not difficult to slip into thinking of each citizen's good health as an asset not only for herself but for the state as well. Daniels points out that to do so is compatible not only with his own analysis of justice, but with antithetical analyses as well.[6] Daniels' own view focuses on equality of opportunity as the condition that must be satisfied in order to achieve justice. If they are to pursue opportunity, he thinks, people

47

must be healthy. Having health is a prerequisite for people to consider their access to opportunity to be meaningful, for without health, individuals may regard opportunities offered to them as just so many empty promises. Daniels believes it to be a strength of his approach that health's importance in securing equality is acknowledged by views antithetical to his own – namely, by those positions that direct us to equalize outcomes rather than opportunities. For it is hard to see, he thinks, how citizens can be said to have realized equality of welfare unless they are equally fortunate in their enjoyment of health. (Daniels's interpretation should not be taken as veridical: by no means would all welfarists agree to treat health as good mainly because it has instrumental value.)

III. IS HEALTH A PUBLIC ASSET?

Thus, the more effective the arrangements for sustaining individual citizens' health, the better positioned a society may seem to be to achieve collective aims such as justice. Citizens should participate more or less equally in these ends, both in contributing to them and in benefiting from them, and in order to do so they will need to be roughly equal in physical and cognitive functioning, so that they share a level platform of capability for pursuing opportunity and/or taking satisfaction in outcomes. Appeal to biological species-typicality offers such a platform.

Some theorists, such as Daniels, explicitly equate biological typicality with optimal functionality.[7] Others, like Thomas Murray, assume that species-typicality is the mark of whether advantageous physical or cognitive capabilities are fortuitous rather than engineered.[8] (I have commented extensively elsewhere on the mistakes involved in identifying species-typicality as a standard of biological optimality.)[9] We are inclined to label as pathologies health conditions associated with species-atypical limitations of functioning that we perceive as being disadvantageous. Within a framework where health is judged in terms of instrumental value, these states of health are termed disorders and are characterized as ineffective or depleted resources.

Judgments of pathology introduce an embedded standard that presumes, rather then proves, the desirability of species-typicality. When I speak subsequently in this chapter of "chronic pathology," I will mean an enduring anomalous biological condition that does or will occasion non-species-typical functioning that is presumed to be disadvantageous. Some people with chronic pathologies display dysfunctions that currently limit them. Others are currently asymptomatic and in that sense are healthy, but they either previously have experienced a disruption of health (with sequellae), or they are at high risk of doing so in future. Although in principle medicine enables us to attain or maintain species-typical – that is, normal – health, in practice inadequacies of financing or of scientific knowledge constrain success. For individuals with chronic pathologies, species-typical health may be acquirable only through extraordinary expenditures of resources, or may not be attainable at all.

On the applications of justice theory that we have been discussing, increases in physical or mental functionality contribute value to the extent that they are effective instruments for attaining certain personal or public ends. So, for example, it will be valuable to improve a person's health if doing so helps that individual to pursue normal opportunities. To illustrate, a kidney transplant will be valuable to the extent that it frees the patient from dialysis and enables her to work, go to school, be with her family. If no such opportunities are enabled – perhaps because the patient is too old to have access to them – the assets expended to execute the procedure are unlikely to be commensurate with the assets gained as a result of it. In the latter circumstances, even if transplantation improves the patient's health, the justice-theoretical framework does not warrant the expenditure, at least not as a matter of justice.

Policies that obligate us to maintain species-typical health in the population cannot help but direct health-improving efforts away from citizens with chronic pathologies. The primary context for pursuing this strategy has been in relation to deciding how health care policy should treat chronically disabled people. They present a problematic case because their consumption of health care will not increase the communal stock of health. Because illness or accident has irremediably depleted some portion of their health assets, they may become candidates for receiving less health care than other people enjoy.

Chronically disabled people are portrayed, not as especially deserving recipients of health care, but as not even ordinarily appropriate recipients. Justice itself is thought to invite people who are worst off in respect to health assets to accept being worst off in receiving care as well. For, it is argued, all of us, but especially those badly off in health, are best served by living in a just society, even if we are the worst off in that society. Leading public health theorists have proposed that "denying access [to health care] . . . at the expense of the worst off . . . must be adopted to improve the overall level of well-being of the community."[10]

Daniels, for one, argues that injustices such as sharp inequalities undermine civil society, attenuate social cohesion, and magnify mistrust.[11]

These consequences of social injustice are said to be most threatening for people with chronic illnesses or disabilities, for their depleted capabilities make them more than usually dependent on the trustworthiness of other people and the stability of social conditions. In order to deploy existing resources most effectively, we should place them in the service of the normal people on whom society depends. People who will be difficult or impossible to return to species-typicality are better relegated to dependence on assistance from normal people. (Individuals who have received rehabilitative services or who lack diagnoses identifying an organic cause, but nevertheless are dysfunctional, are likely to be dismissed as malingerers.) The alternative – allocating more and more health care in the wild hope that something, sometime, will work – is contraindicated both because resources would be diverted from more effective uses and because, for these patients, there is little prospect of benefit that would justify incurring the risks of continued medical intervention.

Such citizens may be thought to be treated justly despite their being denied equitable services for their health. Despite their inferior treatment by a health care system that advances the general health at their expense, they are said to be better off than they would be in a society less effective in promoting a population with good health. Fostering social stability and trust by directing resources to improve the general health may be claimed as a beneficial strategy for people who currently are unhealthy or who are at high risk of depletion of their health resources in future. The security afforded by social conditions of stability and trust would seem to be of comfort to individuals experiencing limited capability now, or who face such a future. In the same spirit, treating chronically ill and disabled people dissimilarly by giving the rest of the population priority for health services may be defended as necessary for the former group's own interests. In order to sustain a society with a population sufficiently healthy to take care of them, they may have to relinquish their own group's consumption of health services. Public investment in their health cannot elevate it sufficiently to make it a more worthwhile asset than the equivalent investment made in the health of normal people. Yet, the argument goes, there is no injustice because even though normal people do better under this scheme, people with chronic pathologies do no worse. They may be less healthy than they would be under other schemes, but their security and general support is no worse, and perhaps better, than it would otherwise be.

In sum, then, although policies that focus on maintaining the general level of health at or above species-typicality may do so by directing health care resources away from people with chronic disabling conditions, they may be supposed necessary to sustain a society that best serves the interests of the disabled. This conclusion is challenged, however, if we ask whether chronically ill and disabled people's dependency is itself a product of their marginalization by such policies. For one thing, the degree to which they are dependent may vary with the degree of health they can maintain. Persons crippled by certain forms of multiple sclerosis may, for instance, remain more independent than they would otherwise if they receive expensive therapies to mitigate acute episodes. Further, a medical system that focuses on restoration to species-typical functioning prompts complacence about the exclusionary effects of framing social organization with the expectation that people will function normally.[12] The influence of such a system may encourage retaining inflexible employment, education, transportation, communication, and other environments that are intolerant of species-atypicality in people's bodies and minds.[13] Finally, by extrapolation, members of the group could be expected to forswear health levels necessary for their own lives, or the lives of future people like them, in order to promote social security and stability threatened by a burdensome number of people in extended dependence.

Considerations like these cast strong doubt on claims about the justice of systems that allot health assets to people who are, or who can be, species-typical, at the expense of people who will never comply with this standard. Such defenses of inequity presume that the governed will find it just to distribute health so as to maximize its effectiveness as a resource for social and political well-being and so will consent to this distributive scheme. As we have seen, however, strategies that maximize the instrumentality of health may not command broad assent, for individuals may not believe the public interest to be congruent with their own. In this regard, systems that identify effective health with species-typicality advance the interests of the species-typical, but beg questions of justice for anomalous individuals.

IV. IS HEALTH A PERSONAL ASSET?

So far, we have been concerned with the idea that health is a public resource and therefore should be allotted so as to maximize its effectiveness in promoting collective goods. We could abandon this line of thought, however, while continuing to suppose that health has mainly instrumental value. For we could distribute health on the basis of its most effective contributions to individuals' welfare or well-being. If health's value is instrumental, distributing it so as to secure the most individual well-being maximizes value.

Distributing health so as to maximize individual well-being requires us to commensurate health care outcomes so as to learn who will profit more, and who less, from various medical interventions. We can pursue such a program, however, only if we can make comparative judgments about the effectiveness of species-typical, and chronically pathological, health on well-being. In order to do so, scales of quality of life or successful living have been devised to measure the presumed reductions in well-being associated with the depletion of health. There are at least two distributive purposes for which these scales of well-being are applied.

One is to determine how much or how little well-being particular health care interventions produce, in order to decide which among competing treatments or programs will be most productive for an individual or group. Here health care outcomes are assessed retrospectively on the basis of evidence of their past effectiveness in order to decide which interventions to continue or expand, or to abandon. What is judged here is the propriety of the intervention, based on evidence of its past success or failure. There is nothing unusual or problematic about this kind of empirical assessment. When we ask whether a support program has improved developmentally disabled clients' quality of life, in order to decide about renewing the program's funding, or whether a surgical or a pharmaceutical approach to treating heart disease results in a better quality of life, the basis of judgment can be made clear. We can agree on objective criteria, such as clients' becoming employed or patients' returning to employment. When we recommend courses of action based on these assessments, we can make clear what benefits or losses each choice has been found to bring.

The second use for quality-of-life measures is to identify which among competing individuals or groups who might receive a particular health care intervention will enjoy the greatest increase in well-being. Here outcomes are assessed prospectively, on the basis of the future worthiness of the prospective recipients, in order to decide which among them to select. What is judged here is the suitability of the patient to be a beneficiary, not the suitability of an intervention for a preselected beneficiary. Why can't we simply survey subjects and compile the reports of their experiences of health? We then could use this information to project which types of people make the best use of health – for whom, that is, health most effectively facilitates well-being.

One problem will be whether our subjects are reporting retrospectively – based on their previous experience of the health state – or prospectively, based on how strenuously they would seek or avoid the health state. A prospective outcome is a different kind of object of knowledge, and is the object of a different kind of knowledge, than a retrospective outcome. Unlike retrospective assessments, prospective assessments of the worthiness of various individuals to be healthier are not straightforwardly empirical, because they do not simply emerge from, and rest on, evidence of past effectiveness.

We often exaggerate how difficult something will be before we experience it. People who have never driven in the heart of a metropolis, or eaten sushi, or skydived, are convinced of the unpleasantness of these activities. They may even feel the discomfort viscerally, shuddering at the prospect. Later, when we find them inching forward through the intersection, or slurping down shooters, or calmly toppling with their parachutes from the airplane's door, they cannot recall what it was that so concerned them. Yet in rating the attractiveness or repulsiveness of these experiences, people who don't have any direct experience of them claim the same epistemological standing as those who do.

Correlating states of health and well-being by surveying what people think about them runs into a similar difficulty. Sighted people notoriously overestimate the disruptiveness of being blind because they can only speculate about it. In order to scale well-being on the basis of reports about the impact of health conditions, we must know whether all respondents are assessing the same thing. But assessments of health conditions a person has experienced and of health conditions a person expects to experience do not weigh the same thing. The former refer to experienced fact, the latter to supposition and speculation.

Suppose a subject is asked to rank the importance to well-being of various states of health. For instance, she is asked about the degree to which various health limitations – deteriorating sight, obesity, bipolar dsease, diabetes – decrease well-being. Is she weighing the experience of these conditions retrospectively and intimately, based on her own experience of them? Or prospectively and apprehensively, because she is predicted to be susceptible to them? Or does she think of these conditions only as pertaining to others in an abstractly distanced or depersonalized way? Reporting from such varied standpoints results in judging quite different things.

This difficulty extends beyond the conflation of retrospective and prospective, or of intimate and distanced, standpoints. For example, Christopher Murray[14] reports that the burden of blindness generally is weighted differently in different scenarios by nondisabled people when they make forced choice assessments, even though they are assessing what seems to him to be the same thing. If the choice is between extending the life of 2,000 blind people or of 1,000 seeing people, most nondisabled people choose to benefit the larger group. In this choice, the burden of disability doesn't seem to discount the value of people's lives.

However, the majority of nondisabled people will also choose to expend resources so that sight is restored to blind people rather than using the resources to give the same number of seeing people an extra year of life. In this choice, Murray thinks, eliminating the burden of disability appears to raise the value of people's lives. He believes it is inconsistent to judge this way. But it is not. Murray fails to distinguish between the burden of blindness and the burden of life with blindness. It is consistent to think that being blind is a burden, an obstacle that one must constantly work to overcome, but that being alive while blind is not a burden, regardless of the challenges associated with being blind.

Analogously, being poor usually is a burden, but we do not conclude that it is better not to live at all than to live in poverty. The different weightings are not inconsistent because different things are being weighed. However subtle the phenomenological differences between experiencing being alive and experiencing a less-than-optimal way of being alive, these invoke different experiential objects. Because the experiential objects being weighted are different, even though both are referred to as "living with blindness," the typical intuitions about the two trade-offs that Murray reports are consistent. Because the two trade-offs weigh very different objects, there is no reason to expect them to yield the same results.

The distinction between burdensome limitations and burdensome lives explains why disability advocates who oppose putting others at risk of being like themselves are not rejecting their own being. This is the case with polio survivors who fought to bar the live-virus vaccine from developed countries' markets because the inoculations that protected many crippled a few. Similarly, thalidomide survivors campaigned for the strictest regulation of this drug.

Menzel and colleagues[15] report findings about preferences consistent with those described here. For instance, asked whether they preferred to allocate resources to mitigate a severe illness a bit or to mitigate a moderate illness considerably, only 11 percent of 150 Norwegian health policy officials gave priority to the moderately ill; 37 percent gave priority to the severely ill, and the rest preferred to divide the resources evenly.[16] In another study, nearly half of the respondents preferred to allocate resources equally between treatments for two illnesses, even though one of the treatments helped patients a little and the other helped patients a lot.

Are these preferences irrational and consequently irrelevant to the rational distribution of health? Menzel and his coauthors believe they are not. These authors take their data to show that, for many respondents, maintaining hope and at least some level of access to treatment has its own high value. They recommend distinguishing between the utility of complying with certain principles and the utility of experiencing certain states of health. Respondents who adopt public or community perspectives will prefer distribution priorities that reflect such policies as adherence to egalitarianism and to the rescue principle of saving those who are worst off. People who take a personal perspective will prefer distribution priorities that are likely to facilitate maintaining the health conditions most important to them.

Assessments made from these perspectives are, of course, relativized to each respondent's experiences and expectations. People who believe, in the abstract, that pain medication during childbirth is an unnecessary and even unhealthy luxury often urgently amend their assessments when experiencing childbirth themselves. People who, in the abstract, rate heroic measures taken on behalf of very low birthweight neonates as rashly risking prolonging a possibly burdensome life often insist on the most aggressive intervention if their own child is very prematurely born.

Assessment procedures that equivocate among different standpoints on the instrumental value of a health state are flawed. They take preferences expressed about one kind of experienced object as evidence of preferences for another, and very different, kind of experienced object without independently correlating these reactions. For example, a person's experiencing herself as cognitively impaired and demented from Alzheimer's is very different from a person's experiencing the probability of her future diminution of capability from Alzheimer's. These assessments of the condition's effect on well-being differ as well, not just in conclusions but also in kind, from those made by a person reacting to the probability of her husband's impairment from Alzheimer's, or to the reality of his being currently impaired, and or to the probability or reality of a stranger's impairment half a world away. We cannot simply extrapolate from the interpretations of third-party observers, whether intimately or distantly involved, to the direct experience of people with chronic pathologies. So we cannot simply compile different people's beliefs about how such a pathology affects well-being.

V. IS THERE AN UNIVOCAL STANDPOINT ON JUDGING HEALTH?

When I experience five one-dollar bills, I experience the amount of money no differently whether the bills belong to me or to you. Further, you and I differ not at all about whether the bills suffice to acquire a coffee at Starbuck's or a diamond ring at Tiffany's. Nor does the money's purchasing power differ depending on who hands it to the cashier.

We presume that there will be an univocal standpoint from which we establish the instrumental value of material assets. I cannot, however, likewise assess the value of your health assets because your health is a resource for you in ways that it can never be for me. Difficulties in finding a univocal standpoint from which to assess health's contribution to well-being should make us wary of the feasibility of transferring our thinking about allocating material assets to the distribution of health care.

If judgments from various standpoints differ, whose should prevail? Murray notes that people who are used to functioning despite an anomalous physical or mental condition rate the quality of life associated with being in that state higher than either individuals at the onset of the condition or individuals unfamiliar with the condition. He goes on to say that weighting the condition from the former standpoint assigns a higher priority to extending the life of individuals with the condition, while from the latter standpoint, interventions preventing or repairing the condition seem more effective than preserving the lives of those already in a state of health that cannot be repaired.

This is not surprising. Of the parties engaged in the assessment, the minority whose lives are at stake believe the elimination of their lives would be the biggest burden, while the majority whose lives are not at issue may find the minority's very existence to be the biggest burden. Murray comments:

[U]sing non-adaptive weights devalues the importance of interventions that extend the life of those living in a health state worse than perfect health. I find this attribute of cost-effectiveness . . . a vexing moral problem. I would like to use the adapted weights for evaluating life-extending interventions and the pre-adaptive weights for evaluating preventive or rehabilitative interventions. Yet, giving up internal consistency . . . would come with a high price. The potential for confusing or conflicting results in burden and cost-effectiveness analysis would be too great.[17]

Murray's verdict about the difference that varying standpoints make in how a health condition is experienced foregrounds the problem of treating health as a distributable resource, even if the purpose of the allocation is to do no more than facilitate citizens' personal well-being. He thinks that reflecting the actual variety of standpoints, voices, and interests in the data used to assess the effectiveness of health care interventions threatens to disrupt the simulation of a univocal standpoint from which to judge the effectiveness of competing allocation policies or patterns. There is political importance to constructing such a standpoint, Murray thinks, for one is needed to facilitate the public distribution of health care.

Of course, if we pay no attention to the disruptive minority of people with chronic pathologies whose preferences express adapted weights, there will be no dissent from the proposition that protecting the unadapted majority from having to adapt to an anomalous health condition more effectively furthers well-being than extending the lives of the minority who have adapted to the condition. But this is far from the objective assessment, free from advocacy driven by special political interests, to which Murray aspires.[18] For, in the absence of an argument that convinces us of their irrelevance, eliminating minority voices is unquestionably inegalitarian. Doing so therefore means rejecting egalitarianism as the principle guiding allocation of the commodity of health. Doing so thus takes on the countenance of a political decision that privileges certain standpoints over others.

Are there strong arguments for accepting some standpoints about the burden of an anomalous health condition over others, when these disagree? Murray acknowledges that the same impairment may be differentially disabling, depending on the environment. The cases he has in mind are ones in which an impairment is more disabling in a technological society than in a rural one, or in an advanced economy than in a simple one. It is well known that mild mental retardation does not disable women in environments in which a woman's role is to clean, cook, and bear children. Murray believes it would be inegalitarian to allocate resources to rich societies, but not to poor ones, in order to prevent mental retardation. Consequently, according to Murray, however the burden of mental retardation is measured, it must be uniform regardless of its impact on people's lives.

"In many cases," Murray says, "allocating resources to avert disability [rather than averting impairment] could exacerbate inequalities."[19] Egalitarianism, he thinks, demands uniformity in assessing the burden of an impairment, lest differences in context suggest that the most privileged are most dependent on exalted functioning. Here he misunderstands the requirements of formal justice, mistakenly imagining that imposing homogeneity is an appropriate means for securing equality.[20] Further, there is nothing inequitable in acknowledging that an impairment is no burden at all when it is not experienced as one.

Indeed, it is more inequitable to treat people as dysfunctional when they actually are not than to refrain from intervening in cases where intervention has little or no benefit. After all, the original point of the exercise was to maximize the benefits of health care interventions relative to their costs. Undergoing an intervention almost always costs the patient some experience of pain and risk. As long as the patient is competent, commensurability demands that the benefit offsetting the patient's cost be measured in terms of the patient's own experience of good. But surely a medical intervention is not experienced as beneficial by individuals who were not dysfunctional prior to it and who are no more functional, relative to their environment, as a result of it. One would have thought it equally obvious that when competent patients do not consider treatments to be benefits, their judgments deserve considerable weight.

Daniels, however, argues to the contrary. He contends that we can resolve the problem posed by people who adapt to disability by agreeing to take equality of opportunity rather than efficiency of outcome as the distributive system's rationale. He thinks our obligation to improve disabled people's health requires us to provide certain kinds of health care for them whether or not they believe this will improve their welfare. He observes that "people with long-standing disabilities will often rank their welfare higher than would other people who are merely imagining life with such disabilities," and he speculates that "perhaps people with disabilities accommodate by adjusting their goals and expectations."[21] However, "even if they are more satisfied with their lives than people without disabilities might expect,"[22] and even if they are decisively determined to be adjusted to and happy in their condition, Daniels thinks they lack the objectively fair share of opportunity that normal or species-typical functioning would provide.

But whether an atypically small opportunity range is unfair depends on whether quality of opportunity is less important than quantity. Too much opportunity can cause suffering, for uncertainty about which possible road to take is a familiar life-spoiler. It is much better to focus successfully on a few fulfilling options than to be torn with indecision in the face of many glittering ones. Being capable of achievement despite a limited option range is better insurance for well-being than being granted a glut of options. This analysis is widespread in eighteenth- and early nineteenth-century literature, where accepting narrowed options is laudably associated with achieving moral control and self-direction and is not dismissed as mere adaptive resignation to an inferior condition.

Parenthetically, it is not clear that the difference between an individual's report of the quality of the life she lives despite her limitations, and others' views of that life, is merely the difference between adaptation and nonadaptation. Imagine an individual who is limited to eating the cuisine of China (because, for whatever reasons, she cannot travel beyond its borders), and who believes that she enjoys a very high quality of gustatory well-being. A French researcher might be unconvinced, because he does not believe dining can be satisfactory without the opportunity to quaff a glass or two of Bordeaux. Like Murray and Daniels, who rationalize disabled people's reports of their high life quality, he believes the Chinese diner to be truthful but mistaken, because she does not regret the unavailability of blissful dining *à la francaise*. It would, of course, be odd to say that the subject has adapted because she reports being eminently satisfied by Chinese haute cuisine, and odd as well to say that she is mistaken in being so satisfied. Surely, the unavailability of French food does not make the best Chinese cooking less exquisite. Gourmets resident in the East and gourmets resident in the West reasonably and objectively differ with respect to the comestibles and potables they consider crucial to their well-being.

VI. WHOSE STANDPOINT SHOULD PREVAIL?

As we have seen, judging the effectiveness of individuals' states of health as resources for their well-being introduces a variety of standpoints. There is little agreement about which dimensions of health, or health-related functioning, are central, or crucial. People with anomalous health histories, health prospects, or current states of health often differ from people who are species-typical, and they differ as well from each other.

In the previous section, we examined several arguments for deferring to the standpoints of species-typical people. All were flawed.

It is, further, epistemologically aberrant to grant precedence to judgments about anomalous health states made by species-typical people over those made by the individuals actually experiencing these health states. Ordinarily, we defer to first-person reports of subjective states. As Martin Milligan points out, many blind people have experienced both sightedness and blindness, while few sighted people have done so.[23] To defer to sighted people, who know less, for assessments about the instrumental disadvantages of blindness rather than to blind people, who know more, appears to violate standard epistemological practice.

This is, evidently, a political rather than an epistemological choice. Species-typical individuals are in the majority. They will always be so, for we take to be typical whatever the biological characteristics of the majority of the species happen to be. By the same token, people with chronic pathologies will be in the minority, for biological anomaly is a necessary (but not a sufficient) condition of pathology.

But how small a minority may they be? Predictive genetic testing promises to identify which individuals are at risk of disadvantageous non-species-typical functioning attributable to biological anomalies. Predictive genetic testing thus identifies individuals and groups whose health assets are likely to be impoverished. Presymptomatic genetic testing can identify persons who are highly likely to become chronically disabled. Among the conditions for which testing can be done are many currently unpreventable and unrepairable ones. Are the interests of individuals with such genetic anomalies also to be deflected in order to improve the overall health of the community? With regard to predictive genetic testing, bioethicist Dan Brock observes:

[P]eople who feel healthy and who as yet suffer no functional impairment will increasingly be labeled as unhealthy or diseased. . . . For many people, this labeling will undermine their sense of themselves as healthy, well-functioning individuals and will have serious adverse effects both on their conceptions of themselves and the quality of their lives.[24]

Brock speaks as if the source of being damaged by labeling or categorization lies mainly in people's psychological inadequacy, their inability to maintain self-esteem. But labeling is first of all a social activity, and labeling by others usually antedates and influences self-labeling. The adverse personal effects of being assigned to the unhealthy classification while one is asymptomatic derive from, and are exacerbated by, the social consequences of such labeling, namely, the exposure to inferior treatment in social interactions, including the programs through which we access health care.

Among the costs of being labeled as at risk for diminution of health are likely to be denial of employment, ineligibility for insurance, and even withdrawal of medical treatment needed to sustain life itself. People labeled as having the Huntington's gene, the Duchenne or Becker dystrophy gene, or the ALD gene (although adrenoleukodystrophy usually becomes symptomatic between the ages of four and ten, there is a variation with onset between twenty and forty) might be assigned low priority for expensive lifesaving treatment for health conditions unrelated to their genetic status. People labeled as having one of the Alzheimer's genes might be denied certain kinds of jobs (for instance, employment as an air controller) because of fears that they might someday jeopardize the public's safety. People labeled as having the genes associated with AMD (age-related macular degeneration), retinitis pigmentosa, Wilson's disease, breast cancer, or cystic fibrosis might be denied employment because of fears that their medical conditions will eventually make them less productive, or they might be denied the medical insurance coverage offered other employees. Prenatal testing is an especially strongly contested application of predictive genetic testing. Here, fetuses labeled as having genes associated with various kinds and degrees of anomalous functioning may be terminated prior to birth.[25]

The list of genetically related health anomalies for which presymptomatic identification could occur is very long indeed. Francis Collins has remarked that "it is estimated that all of us carry dozens of glitches in our DNA." In the first ADA case heard by the Supreme Court, Chief Justice Rehnquist foresaw that the decision, which allows disability discrimination protection to asymptomatic individuals who test positive for a disease, "would render every individual with a genetic marker for some debilitating disease 'disabled' here and now because of some future effects."[26] At least one ADA case specifically alleging genetic discrimination has now been filed with the EEOC: an employee with positive performance evaluations whose employment was terminated after genetic testing revealed that she had alpha 1 antitrypson deficiency.[27]

Collins has testified that citizens are already declining to serve as subjects in genetic research out of fear that they could lose health benefits based simply on their participation. He describes two individuals who have suffered already – one denied a job because he tested positive as a carrier of Gaucher's disease, another who will not be tested for genetic disposition for colon cancer (for which there is a family history) because he fears losing his medical insurance. Collins states: "while genetic information and genetic technology hold great promise for improving human heath, they can also be used in ways that are fundamentally unjust."[28] All these facts suggest that the question of whose standpoint should prevail should not be framed as a choice between the vast majority whose valuations are objective and the small deluded minority with adapted values. Rather, our choice is about whether to obscure or exclude a standpoint that will become familiar to almost all of us at some time in our lives in favor of another standpoint that almost all of us also adopt.

Parenthetically, according to a recent national survey of managed care medical and pharmaceutical directors: "The benefit of performing QoL research is that it examines the patient's perspective on how he or she is affected by a disease and its treatment. This perspective broadens the scope of information on the therapeutic impact of a new agent."[29] According to this study, cost-effectiveness is enhanced when providers take into account patients' personal perspectives on the extent to which treatments improve their quality of life. "If a patient improves his QoL with a therapy, he will likely improve compliance on a higher level. Increased compliance will likely produce . . . reduced costs and better outcomes. It is these reduced costs that will benefit the MCO initially. Improved outcomes and better QoL may keep a patient from switching providers, thus benefiting the physician and MCO."[30] Thus there are clinical and economic reasons, as well as moral ones, for respecting patients' different standpoints and their subjective assessments of their quality of life. (Note that as long as patients' well-being is the standard, clinical, economic, or moral reasons sometimes may recommend intervening with benign treatment or even with placebos even in the absence of evidence of their causal efficacy. This is simply to observe that a reassured asymptomatic patient may extract a lesser cost in medical resources from society and from himself than an anxious asymptomatic patient who is convinced that he is riddled with disease.)

CONCLUSION

In this chapter, I have attempted to show how inapt it is to commodify health. Doing so supposes that there is an univocal standpoint from which to generalize about the effects of health conditions on well-being. But differences in standpoint – for example, the differences among retrospective, contemporary, and prospective assessments of experiencing the same health-related limitation – cannot be fairly elided or accurately abstracted from. The importance of these distinctions, and the problems occasioned by ignoring them, will grow with the increase in prospective assessments triggered by predictive genetic testing (including prenatal testing).

Cases differ because of the many differences in social environment, personal history, temperament, and taste. Indeed, when people are asked to rate various healthful or health-depleted states for purposes of commensuration, it is not even clear how we can know whether they are rating the same things. There is no objective standard for agreement regarding which aspects of people's biological states are central to elevating their quality of life.

Thus, selecting any one among the many standpoints as the definitive one from which to judge the value of alternative allocations of health care cannot help but be a political decision arbitrarily privileging some over other citizens. Because people with chronic pathologies have been a powerless minority, the political pressure to acknowledge their standpoints heretofore has not been great. Predictive genetic testing will increase the known population of this minority by discovering individuals who as yet are asymptomatic, but growth in numbers may not translate into increasing influence.

Over the last decade, liberal political theory has affirmed the importance of assigning equal importance to the values of cultural majorities and minorities. In this spirit, medical professionals are now educated to be sensitive to the cultural backgrounds from which their patients come. Similar arguments can be made for acknowledgement of patients' personal values in regard both to anomalous health states and to functioning in anomalous rather than species-typical modes.

Multiculturalism embraces species-typical states of health and modes of functioning. For multifunctionalism, health has no preeminence as a resource, either for collective productivity or for personal well-being. Health is useful indeed, especially where the social climate favors species-typical over unusual modes of functioning. There are, nevertheless, alternative routes to both functionality and its ends. (See Silvers[31] for further discussion of multifunctionalism, especially with respect to its operation in the allocation of health care in rehabilitation medicine.)

Despite these considerations, readers may be reluctant to abandon thinking of health as the universally crucial resource for the well-being of both individuals and the state. Absent assigning a privileged moral status to health, how can we assure that care for health takes priority over support for other desirable ends? And how can we decide who should receive health care for which nonemergent (that is, chronic) conditions, and what kinds of treatments, without a moral compass to point the way?

In this chapter, I have argued that we are not helped in establishing the importance of health care, nor in distributing it fairly, by thinking of health as instrumental to good lives and good societies. We should instead acknowledge that experiences of the lived quality of any health condition can be as various as those of the contemplated quality of aesthetic objects. Like good and bad art, poor health and good health may absorb the attention of some of us, while others are comparatively oblivious to degrees of difference.

Like enduringly good art, prolonged good health is a good in itself, but one that may be weighed differently when assessed from different standpoints. The benefits of social arrangements that make such goods accessible to those who seek them are well known. Equally well known are the muddles precipitated by attempts to impose abstract rating schemes on objects known primarily through intimate personal experience. The value of being beautiful or having aesthetic value cannot be evaluated through such a scheme.

Nor, I have argued in this chapter, can the value of being healthy. To devise a public process for making health attainable that better accords with our intuitions about where, when, and why it is a preeminent good, we would be wise to fiddle no longer with schemes based on economic models that commodify it. We should start anew to develop a model more sensitive to lived experiences of health by acknowledging the multidimensional influences that health has in our lives.

NOTES

1. "World Health Organization Health Promotion: A Discussion Document on the Concept and Principles" (Copenhagen: World Health Organization Regional Office for Europe, 1984).
2. T. Kue Young, *Population Health: Concepts and Methods* (New York: Oxford University Press, 1998), p. 1.
3. Canadian Department of National Health and Welfare, "Achieving Health for All" (1984), quoted in Young, *Population Health*, p. 2.
4. Commenting on Norman Daniels's claims about the convergence of health and justice, Frances Kamm points out that the direction of causation is important for understanding the correlated data. The data show that better health is associated with higher social class. These data might signify an

injustice if being of higher social class causes people to enjoy better health, but not if having better health causes people to rise in social class. Frances Kamm, "Health and Equality of Opportunity," *American Journal of Bioethics* 1(2): 17–19 at 17.

5. Norman Daniels, "Justice, Health, and Health Care," in Rosamond Rhodes, Margaret Battin, and Anita Silvers (eds.), *Medicine and Social Justice: Essays on the Distribution of Health Care* (New York: Oxford University Press, 2002), pp. 6–23.

6. Norman Daniels, "Justice, Health, and Healthcare," *American Journal of Bioethics* 1(2) (Spring 2002): 2–16 at 5–6.

7. N. Daniels in D. Van DeVeer and T. Regan (eds.), *Health Care Ethics: An Introduction* (Philadelphia: Temple University Press, 1987), pp. 290–325.

8. T. Murray, "Ethical Issues in Human Genome Research," *FASEB Journal* 5(1) (1991): 55–60. Reprinted in J. Arras and B. Steinbock (eds.), *Ethical Issues in Modern Medicine* (Mountain View, CA: Mayfield, 1995), pp. 479–87 at p. 484.

9. Ani Satz and Anita Silvers, "Disability and Biotechnology," in Maxwell Mehlman and Thomas Murray (eds.), *The Encyclopedia of Biotechnology: Ethical, Legal, and Policy Issues* (New York: Wiley, 2000), pp. 173–87; and Anita Silvers, "A Fatal Attraction To Normalizing: Treating Disabilities as Deviations from 'Species-Typical' Functioning," in Eric Parens (ed.), *Enhancing Human Capacities: Conceptual Complexities and Ethical Implications* (Washington, DC: Georgetown University Press, 1998), pp. 95–123.

10. Donald Patrick and Pennifer Erickson, *Health Status and Health Policy* (New York: Oxford University Press, 1993), p. 367.

11. Daniels, "Justice, Health, and Healthcare," p. 7.

12. See Anita Silvers, David Wasserman, and Mary Mahowald, *Disability, Difference, Discrimination* (Lanham, MD: Rowman and Littlefield, 1998), for a lengthy discussion of the ways in which practices framed by the expectation that people shall function in species-typical modes are disabling.

13. Employers' intolerance is not always aimed at individuals with more than usually limited functionality. Some police departments will not hire applicants who meet all their standards but have higher IQs than is typical for the population. They contend that officers who are more than commonly intelligent are not content staying on the job. Mike Allen, "Help Wanted Invoking the Not-Too-High IQ Test," *New York Times*, September 19, 1999, section 4, p. 3.

14. Christopher Murray and Allan Lopez (eds.), *The Global Burden of Disease* (Cambridge, MA: Harvard School of Law, 1996), p. 36.

15. Paul Menzel, Marthe Gold, Erik Nord, Jean-Louis Pinto, Jeff Richardson, and Peter Ubel, "Toward a Broader View of Values in Cost-Effective Analysis in Health Care," *Hastings Center Report* 29(3) (May–June 1999): 7–15.

16. Ibid., p. 9.

17. Murray, "Ethical Issues," pp. 31–2.

18. Ibid., p. 1.

19. Ibid., p. 33.

20. For a nuanced appreciation of formal justice, see Anita Silvers, "Formal Justice," in Silvers, Wasserman, and Mahowald, *Disability, Difference, Discrimination*, pp. 23–146.
21. Daniels, "Justice, Health, and Healthcare," p. 4.
22. Ibid.
23. Brian Magee and Martin Milligan, *On Blindness* (Oxford: Oxford University Press, 1995), p. 49.
24. Dan Brock, "The Human Genome Project and Human Identity," in Robert Weir, Susan Lawrence, and Evan Fales (eds.), *Genes and Human Self-Knowledge: Historical and Philosophical Perspectives on Modern Genetics* (Ames: University of Iowa Press, 1994), p. 31.
25. For a discussion of disability and predictive genetic testing, see Ani Satz and Anita Silvers, "Disability and Biotechnology," in Maxwell Mehlman and Thomas Murray (eds.), *The Encyclopedia of Biotechnology: Ethical, Legal, and Policy Issues* (New York: Wiley, 2000), pp. 173–87.
26. *Bragdon v. Abbot* (1998).
27. Nancy Lee Jones, "Genetic Issues Relating to Discrimination and Privacy," Congressional Research Service Report for Congress, January 24, 2001.
28. Testimony of Francis Collins, M.D., Director, National Institutes of Health Genome Research Institute: United States Senate, Hearing on Genetic Information in the Workplace, July 20, 2000.
29. Bruce K. Crawford, Ellen M. Dukes, and Christopher J. Evans, "The Value of Providing Quality-of-Life Information to Managed Care Decision Makers," *Drug Benefit Trends* 13(7) (2001): 45–52.
30. Ibid.
31. Anita Silvers, "Bedside Justice: Personalizing Judgment, Preserving Impartiality," in Rosamond Rhodes, Margaret Battin, and Anita Silvers, *Medicine and Social Justice: Essays on the Distribution of Health Care* (New York: Oxford University Press, 2002), pp. 235–47.

Chapter 3

Preventing Genetically Transmitted Disabilities while Respecting Persons with Disabilities

DAN W. BROCK

The principal goal of the Human Genome Project and other genetic research is to increase our capacity to prevent or treat human disease. We now devote substantial resources to research furthering the understanding of the genetic basis of various serious disabling congenital conditions. When genes are identified for such conditions, tests can usually be developed that will enable prospective parents to determine their risk of passing on the conditions to their children, or that will determine the presence of the condition in a fetus. Health insurance often supports the costs of this testing. In the future, such testing of a fetus may allow genetic or other *in utero* interventions to prevent the development of the disabling condition, but there is typically a considerable time lag between the development of genetic tests for a congenital condition and therapeutic interventions to prevent or treat the condition. When individuals pursue such testing now, either before or after conception, they typically do so with the intent of avoiding the birth of a child with the condition that is being tested for. This can be done before conception by employing sperm and/or egg donation in order to eliminate the genetic material of the person carrying the genes for the condition; by using *in vitro* fertilization and preimplantation embryo testing; or by avoiding conception altogether. It can be done after conception by aborting an affected fetus and trying again to achieve a normal pregnancy. Physicians who learn that women for whom they are caring are at risk for passing on serious disabling conditions or diseases typically inform them about that risk and the availability of genetic tests for the conditions, and recommend that they obtain the testing. Prospective parents who know or learn that because of factors such as family history or age they are at risk of passing on such conditions or diseases to their offspring often seek to obtain genetic tests with the intent of avoiding the birth of a child with the disabling condition or disease. Thus, at the level of research funding, health insurance coverage, professional practice, and the desires of prospective parents, there is public support for efforts to prevent the birth of children with serious disabling diseases or conditions.

At the same time, in the prioritization of scarce health care resources – either lifesaving resources, such as organs for transplantation and beds in an ICU, or non-lifesaving treatments – a patient would not typically receive lower priority than another patient with similar medical need on the basis of having a serious disability. Discriminating against the disabled patient would typically be viewed as unjust and would probably be in violation of laws such as the Americans with Disabilities Act. Yet if the birth of a seriously disabled child is a bad outcome to be avoided when a nondisabled child could be born instead, then wouldn't it also be a better outcome if a nondisabled patient were given priority over a disabled patient, in particular for scarce lifesaving resources such as organ transplantation or an ICU bed? In each case, a nondisabled person rather than a seriously disabled person exists. And standard measures for evaluating the benefits of health interventions, such as quality adjusted life years (QALYs) and disability adjusted life years (DALYs), do adjust for disabilities such as blindness and mental impairment by assigning a lower value to years of life with than years without such disabilities.

On the face of it, it may seem inconsistent to attempt to avoid the birth of a seriously disabled child while ignoring the presence of serious disability when deciding which lives to extend or save. Many advocates for the disability community would agree that it is inconsistent, and argue that attempting to avoid the birth of a disabled child is as much a case of unjust discrimination against the disabled as giving seriously disabled patients lower priority for lifesaving medical treatments would be. Others may agree that it is inconsistent, but argue that we should not ignore that a serious disability does indeed typically lower a person's quality of life. They believe that our interest in using scarce medical resources to produce the best outcomes requires giving preference to nondisabled patients. Still others may argue that the inconsistency is only apparent. My aim in this chapter is in part to explore the issues involved in deciding whether these two practices are in fact inconsistent. I shall argue that they are importantly different morally, and so not inconsistent; attempting to avoid the birth of seriously disabled children is morally justified, while giving weight to disability in prioritization of lifesaving resources would typically be unjust.

THE CONCEPT OF QUALITY OF LIFE

It may be helpful to indicate at least the broad outlines of the conception of well-being or quality of life that I will be assuming in this chapter, since various claims about the quality of life of disabled persons are often central to these disputes. I cannot fully detail or defend that conception here, but I have written about it elsewhere (Brock, 1993). I shall use the notions of well-being and quality of life interchangeably to refer to an overall assessment of how good a person's life is, how well the life is going. Quality of life is often used to refer to a fully subjective assessment, the person's own assessment of how good his life is. I believe our conception of a good life includes, but is not exhausted by, this subjective assessment by the individual of her life and how happy or satisfied she is with it (Griffin, 1986).

But the subjective level of satisfaction or happiness with one's life is only one aspect of the quality of life, not the whole of it. Besides subjective satisfaction, there are the activities, accomplishments, and personal relations that actually make up that life, that make up what could be called the objective content of the life. If these objective contents are significantly impoverished, then a person's quality of life will be diminished, even if he remains satisfied and happy with his life. To take an extreme case, even if there in fact were happy or contented slaves during the period when slavery existed in this country, their condition of slavery was bad for them and diminished the quality of their lives; being a slave to another is a condition unworthy of an individual capable of being an autonomous human being. A second example is that in many parts of the world today, deep-seated gender bias remains so powerful that many women simply do not form the expectations about career opportunities, independence, medical care, or even nutrition that men in their societies expect for themselves. This leads to a diminished quality of life for women, independent of whether it leads to their having a diminished level of satisfaction or happiness with their lives. While these examples involve injustice, that only shows that being treated unjustly in these ways makes a person's life worse, even if the person is satisfied with how she is being treated.

I have cited activities, accomplishments, and personal relations as examples of objective components of a good life. It is important not to construe these categories in an unduly narrow way that merely reflects the dominant preferences and way of life of the society at the expense of both disabled persons and others who pursue unusual plans of life.

For example, one might argue that a life bereft of any aesthetic experience or appreciation is the poorer for that, but it would be a mistake to believe that inability to have a particular form of aesthetic experience would make a life worse. So a blind person might not be able to experience visual art but could fully experience music or literature; likewise, a deaf person might be precluded from experiencing music but could have an aesthetically rich experience of visual art. Whether disabled or nondisabled, no one can pursue all the valuable forms of activity and accomplishment possible in a life; rather, everyone must choose which particular experiences to pursue.

I assume that another component of a good life is self-determination or autonomy, which I understand here as people's interest in forming, revising over time on the basis of critical reflection and experience, and pursuing their own conception of a good life. It is in the exercise of self-determination, and in having it respected by others, that we take control over and responsibility for our lives and the kinds of persons we become – the capacity for self-determination is a central source of human dignity. It is in part the importance of self-determination in a good life that makes having a reasonable array of opportunities in life important, because without alternative opportunities, significant choice is not possible. Serious disability can have a negative impact on people's lives by significantly restricting their opportunities even if, through adjustment to their disability, their subjective satisfaction with their lives is undiminished. Thus, when I use the term "quality of life" in what follows, I refer to an overall assessment of how good a person's life is, one that includes the person's own subjective assessment of or happiness with his life as well as objective components such as accomplishments, personal relations, and self-determination, including having the reasonable array of opportunities that self-determination requires.

GENETIC TESTING TO PREVENT DISEASE AND DISABILITY

My concern in this chapter is with genetic disease that results in disabilities that are serious but still compatible with a worthwhile life. A few genetic diseases such as Tay Sachs and Lesch Nhyan disease are so devastating, in terms of the suffering and early death that they cause, as to be incompatible with a life that is worth living from the standpoint of the person whose life it is. There is little controversy about genetic testing for these kinds of conditions. The controversy concerns genetic diseases that result in serious disabilities but that still leave the persons who have them with valuable lives well worth living. Examples are Fragile X syndrome, at least in its less severe manifestations, which is the leading cause of inherited mental retardation; Huntingtons disease, a progressive and lethal degenerative neurological disease of midlife onset; cystic fibrosis, a disease of the lungs and pancreas resulting in thick mucous accumulations, chronic infections, and shortened life expectancy; and Leber congenital amaurosis, the leading cause of congenital blindness (genes causing this disease have been identified, but tests for them have not yet been developed). Testing for a serious adult onset condition such as Huntington's disease is complicated by the fact that it occurs only after several decades of normal life, so that there is a significant possibility of therapeutic interventions being developed before its onset in any fetus now tested for the condition. These different examples range from more to less serious, but all are conditions for which genetic testing might be done with the goal of preventing the birth of affected individuals.

There are other minor disabilities with genetic origins, such as cleft palate or very mild elevations of risk for adult diseases, for which few if any would employ genetic testing in the reproductive context; instead, we use medical interventions to ameliorate these conditions and/or expect individuals to learn to live with them. Of course, where the lines separating devastating, serious, and minor disabilities should be drawn is controversial; for example, some would judge blindness to be a minor, not serious, disability, one not warranting reproductive testing to prevent the birth of affected individuals. My concern here is not with precisely where that line should be drawn or whether a particular disability is serious or minor. Indeed, I believe there is no one correct answer to such questions; reasonable people can and do disagree about particular conditions. My concern is with the middle category of genetic diseases and disabilities that most people would consider serious, but neither devastating nor minor. As examples of serious disabilities, I shall use blindness and serious mental impairment or retardation, though recognizing that some would judge blindness to be sufficiently minor to not warrant reproductive testing. The critique of genetic testing that I want to evaluate here is for serious disabilities that constitute substantial disadvantages but that still leave individuals who have them with worthwhile lives.

Is there, then, a sound rationale or justification for public support of genetic testing programs aimed at the prevention of serious disease and disability? In the case of already born individuals, it is relatively uncontroversial that it is morally desirable to prevent their becoming seriously disabled. The Americans with Disabilities Act defines disability as a physical or mental impairment that substantially limits at least one major life activity. On this account, a disability is bad for a person, other things being equal, because it reduces the person's abilities or opportunities to pursue major life activities as compared to what they otherwise would have been, and because it reduces the person's well-being to the extent that it consists in part of successful pursuit of such activities. Serious disabilities tend to make the achievement of some life goals more difficult or less successful and/or to significantly limit the life goals that can reasonably be pursued. Parents would be considered irresponsible and negligent if they failed to act to prevent serious disabilities such as blindness and mental impairment in their children, and child abuse and neglect laws would typically permit the state to intervene to force medical treatment against the parents' wishes, if necessary, to prevent such conditions in their children. Public policy permits competent adults to reject medical treatments that would prevent such conditions in themselves, but it does so in order to respect individuals' rights to self-determination and bodily integrity, their right not to be treated without their informed consent, and not because refusal of such treatment is not usually bad for them and contrary to their interests. Why, then, is there considerable opposition in the disability community and elsewhere to the prevention of serious disability in the prenatal context?

One important response emphasized by members of the disability community to the supposed disadvantage that disabilities represent is to challenge the assumption that the "defect" is in the person rather than the environment (Silvers, 1998). The degree to which a physical or mental impairment in normal function is handicapping or disadvantaging depends both on the individual's physical or mental impairment and on the individual's environment. Society has been made increasingly aware by disabled persons both of the degree to which the social environment has been constructed on the assumption that all people have normal human abilities and capacities, and of the degree to which the disadvantage caused by physical or mental impairment can be reduced or eliminated by changing the environment to better accommodate disabled persons; for example, wheelchairs, access ramps, and special transportation have greatly reduced the disadvantage resulting from impaired physical mobility. In many cases, much or even all of the disadvantage resulting from a disability may come from a failure to make reasonable adjustments in the social environment, adjustments that justice and equality of opportunity morally require. In many cases, the denial of opportunity that persons with disabilities suffer is now so comingled with stigma, social rejection, institutional discrimination, and nonaccommodating environments that it is impossible to fully disentangle the reasons for the lost opportunity. Nevertheless, I assume that serious disabilities such as blindness and serious mental retardation will remain significant disadvantages for common human pursuits even after the goal of achieving reasonable and just social accommodation to disabilities has been reached; they are not "mere" or solely social constructions or socially constructed disadvantages.

Many in the disability community make a second response to the claim that disabilities constitute disadvantages that should be prevented. They argue that their lives are, on balance, no worse as a result of their disability than the lives of nondisabled people, and that it is a mistake to believe that disabled persons have a lower quality of life. A number of studies have shown that disabled persons rate their quality of life higher than nondisabled persons rate it, including their family members and doctors (Sackett and Torrance, 1978; National Association on Disability, 1994). Moreover, we can understand why this is so. First, societal prejudices and stereotypes about disabled persons and their lives remain powerful and strongly influence common beliefs – many of which are false beliefs – about disabled persons and their lives. Second, disabled persons often succeed in reducing or even eliminating the negative impact of their disability on their lives. Christopher Murray has distinguished three processes that typically occur after a person suffers a serious disability (Murray, 1996). *Adaptation* is the process by which a person improves her functional performance through new learning and skill development. *Coping* is the process by which persons adjust and lower their expectations for functioning to reflect their lowered performance, thereby increasing their satisfaction with their level of performance. *Accommodation* is the process by which individuals adjust their life plans and activities to deemphasize or eliminate activities made more difficult or impossible by their disability and substitute activities not similarly limited.

Together, the processes of adaptation, coping, and accommodation can result in a person with even a severe disability accurately evaluating her quality of life as nearly as good, as good, or even better than it was without the disability. Moreover, we know that becoming disabled and going through the process of adaptation, coping, and accommodation

73

in some cases produces insights and character strengths that enrich a disabled person's life in a way and to an extent that would not have been possible by other means. And so when persons with even very severe disabilities claim that their overall quality of life is no worse than that of nondisabled persons, there is often good reason to accept their evaluation as correct. How can this be squared with the common belief that becoming seriously disabled is a misfortune that should be avoided or prevented when possible?

Several points are relevant. One is that although the process of adaptation, coping, and accommodation may enable many persons with serious disabilities to have lives just as good as those of typical nondisabled persons, for other persons with such disabilities this process has only limited or partial success, so that both they and others would rate their quality of life as significantly diminished by their disability. A policy of attempting to prevent persons from becoming disabled must be applied to both sorts of cases, at a point in time when one typically cannot predict whether the disability will result in a long-term lowering of the person's quality of life or not. So far as I know, no one claims that the cases of lowered quality of life resulting from serious disabilities such as blindness and serious mental retardation are outweighed by a sufficiently large number of cases of enhancement in quality of life resulting from such disabilities so as to result in an overall net gain in quality of life for all affected. Indeed, if this were so for particular conditions, it would call into question whether they were properly considered disabilities at all; even if still considered disabilities because they constituted impairments of normal human functioning, they would not be disadvantageous and would warrant the characterization of "differently abled," not disabled. The policy of prevention can thus be justified by the plausible claim that the expected impact on a person's quality of life from a serious disability is negative at the time when preventive efforts must be made, and that what the actual impact will be on the particular individual in question is uncertain or unknown.

A second point is that the process of adaptation, coping, and accommodation, even when fully successful in restoring a disabled person's quality of life to its level before the disability, is often an arduous and burdensome process – for example, it can require lengthy, costly, and difficult rehabilitation. One can reasonably seek to avoid the necessity for that process in order to avoid its burdens, even if one could know ahead of time (which of course one cannot) that it would in the end be fully successful. This can be illustrated by the fact that many disabled persons would still prefer not to have become disabled even if, as a result of adaptation, coping, and accommodation, they rate their quality of life as undiminished from what it had been before they became disabled.

It has been responded, to the concerns both about the burden of a disability itself and about the burdens of the process of adaptation, coping, and accommodation, that everyone's life contains significant burdens and hardships and that it is a mistake to think it is possible or perhaps even desirable to prevent or remove all burdens. Seeking to do so involves a misplaced perfectionism and a fundamental misunderstanding of the human condition. But seeking to prevent serious disabilities need not involve these attitudes. Recognizing that every life will have some share of burdens, misfortunes, and hardships is fully compatible with seeking to prevent them when we can; though each life will have some of them, it is better if each life has fewer rather than more.

Persons seriously disabled from birth do not go through a process of adjusting to having become disabled after having been nondisabled. They simply grow and develop, often taking their disability to be natural in almost the same way that nondisabled persons accept normal, species-typical limitations in function as natural. The burdensomeness of the process of adaptation, coping, and accommodation is then not a reason to attempt to prevent the disability. Nevertheless, if the disability substantially limits a major life activity, then it still limits or closes off an important area of functioning and the activities that such functioning makes possible, even if the person may not "miss" them. For example, if a person has been blind from birth, she may never fully understand the experiences she is missing from not being sighted. Nevertheless, there will be valuable human activities requiring sight that will not be possible for her, or that will be more difficult and less successful without sight, such as visual experiences and the pleasures or work or recreational activities requiring sight, and the potential loss or limitation of those activities in her life may be reason enough to attempt to prevent her disability when that is possible. Even in cases such as deafness, where the deaf community claims that its alternative sign language and the culture it supports are just as rich and functional as the spoken language and culture of hearing persons, there are still valuable human activities, such as the appreciation of music, that are closed off to deaf persons. A concern for the richness of the lives and opportunities of potential persons could justify attempting to prevent congenital blindness or deafness.

A third point is that the effects of the process of coping on the quality of a person's life are complex and problematic. On the one hand, we admire people who realistically adjust their expectations in the face of serious disabilities and "get on with their lives," as it is sometimes put. To realistically adjust one's expectations to one's new situation and to what is now possible for one is considered healthy coping or adjustment, permitting one to be satisfied and happy with more limited functional performance instead of unhappily focusing on one's loss. Since one aspect of quality of life is one's subjective level of satisfaction or happiness with one's life, this process of coping allows one to restore or retain satisfaction and happiness in the face of serious functional limitations or losses. But, as noted earlier, I believe that subjective satisfaction is only one aspect of quality of life. The fact that such satisfaction is not diminished does not always show that a person's overall quality of life is not diminished.

There are, then, good reasons to attempt to prevent persons from becoming disabled that are consistent with recognizing the high quality of life and satisfaction or happiness of many disabled persons. But the critic of genetic testing will not be satisfied by these points. These may be reasons for preventing people from becoming disabled, the critics may grant, but genetic testing is employed not just to prevent disabilities in people but to prevent the creation or existence of disabled people. So the potential for a serious disability is taken not just as a reason to prevent the disability but as a reason to prevent the existence or birth of a person with the disability. It seems to conflate persons with their disabilities, to see persons only in terms of their disabilities, and to embody a social judgment that it is better if persons who would be seriously disabled never exist; for people with disabilities, the practice seems straightforwardly to imply the judgment that it would be better if they had never been born (Silvers, 1998; Asch, 2000). That judgment may be justified in the relatively rare cases of devastating diseases such as Tay Sachs disease and Lesch Nhyan disease, which typically result in death in early childhood and cause severe suffering without compensating benefits for the child. But the vast majority of disabilities, and of conditions for which genetic testing is now available and will be in the future, are not so devastating as to leave the individual with a life not worth living. Instead, they are serious disabilities that constitute substantial limitations and burdens, but that still leave the individual with a life well worth living and glad to be alive and to have been born.

Whereas prevention of disabilities in already existing persons can, for the reasons already outlined, be done for the sake of those persons, aborting a seriously disabled fetus who would have a life well worth living cannot be done for the sake of the fetus or the person that fetus will become. But if it is not done for the sake of the fetus or the person that the fetus will become, then for whose sake is it done? Who is benefited by preventing the disability? Providing an answer to this question will take us into difficult and controversial issues about abortion, the nature of personhood, and the nature of moral principles concerned with prevention of harm, issues that I will not be able to explore fully here. But we can at least attempt to understand how these issues are implicated in this challenge to preventing serious disabilities, and we can try to examine the kinds of positions on these issues that will help to meet the challenge.

ABORTION AS A MEANS OF PREVENTING DISABILITY

First, how are abortion and the nature of personhood implicated in the issue of preventing individuals who would have serious disabilities from being born? Here I use the concept of personhood, or person, as a moral concept to designate a being who has the moral standing that persons are typically accorded in common moral theories – in particular, to designate a being whose life deserves strong moral protections, a being that it would be seriously wrong to kill. Many people, as well as some influential religious traditions, believe that conception, which marks the beginning of the existence of an individual human organism, also marks the point at which the individual becomes a person whose life deserves the same moral protections that are accorded to born persons. Others, who do not believe that an individual at conception is a person, nevertheless locate the onset of personhood early enough in fetal development that it still occurs well before the point at which genetic testing and the abortion of fetuses with serious genetic conditions are typically performed. Call these positions about the nature of personhood the "early person" view. On the early person view, it is correct to see the abortion of a fetus whom genetic testing has shown will have a serious genetically transmitted disease or disability to be morally equivalent to killing a born person who has a similar disease or disability. In each case, one is killing a person with a worthwhile, although disabled, life.

There is virtually universal consensus that it would be seriously wrong to kill persons who want to continue to live simply because they have a serious disability. On the early person view, abortion of a fetus because it has or will have such a disability is no different and equally wrong. Thus, individuals who hold the early person view will see abortion of fetuses because they have or will have disabilities to imply or express the judgment that persons with disabilities may permissibly be killed because of their disabilities (call this the "unacceptable judgment"), and not just the judgment that it would be better if they did not exist. Individuals who hold the early person view will oppose any genetic testing and selection that involves abortion.

It would be a mistake, however, to argue against genetic testing and subsequent abortion on the grounds that it expresses a commitment to the unacceptable judgment. Those who abort seriously disabled fetuses, of course, do not believe that it is morally permissible to kill persons who have similar disabilities; instead, they reject the early person view and deny that fetuses are persons and deserving of the moral protections accorded to persons. Likewise, public and legal policy that permits abortion of disabled fetuses does not imply any acceptance of or commitment to the unacceptable judgment; rather, it reflects the legal view expressed in *Roe v. Wade* that the fetus is not a legal person and that women's right to privacy entitles them to decide during the first two trimesters of pregnancy whether to continue or to terminate a pregnancy (*Roe v. Wade*, 1973). When considering the abortion of seriously disabled fetuses, then, one's view about the personhood of the fetus and the moral permissibility of abortion will affect the relation or difference one sees between aborting disabled fetuses and killing persons with disabilities. But it is of fundamental importance to understand that defenders of prenatal testing and selective abortion reject the early person view and so are not committed to the unacceptable judgment.

Those who hold the early person view morally reject both the unacceptable judgment and the abortion of disabled fetuses. Those who hold that fetuses are not persons, and so that abortion of disabled fetuses is morally permissible, are not thereby committed to the unacceptable judgment, but instead to the denial of the early person view. So, not surprisingly, one's view about whether the fetus is a person – that is, about the moral permissibility of abortion – will affect one's moral assessment of aborting disabled fetuses. Disagreement will be about whether fetuses are persons and the moral permissibility of abortion generally; there is no disagreement about the fact that the presence of a disability cannot justify killing a person. No expressive implications about the moral standing of disabled people that in any way could undermine the wrongness of killing them follow from the positions of those who reject or accept the moral permissibility of aborting disabled fetuses.

It bears emphasis that opposition to genetic testing and selection cannot rest fully on opposition to abortion. In the case of preconception testing, the actions taken to avoid the conception of a disabled fetus do not involve abortion. Nor, in turn, would any question arise in those preconception cases about the implications for the killing of disabled persons.

Many opponents of the selective abortion of disabled fetuses, however, reject the early person view and so do not oppose abortion or charge that the practice implies the permissibility of killing disabled persons. Their opposition to genetic testing and selection does not rest on opposition to abortion. They accept that abortion of a disabled fetus, like steps taken to prevent the conception of a disabled fetus, prevents the creation of a disabled person rather than terminating the existence of a disabled person. But to disabled persons, this practice still seems to have the unacceptable implication, to which understandably they especially object, that it would have been better if they had never been created or born. And yet, as they point out, who would it be better for, since it would not be better for them? And more generally, who is it better for if disabled persons are prevented from coming into existence, since if they do come into existence, they will have worthwhile lives that they are glad to have?

I shall set aside for the moment the possible effects of the disabled person's existence on others, such as the family or the broader society. The potential effects on the parents and other family members of having a seriously disabled child are often the decisive consideration in parents' decisions about whether to bring such a child into existence. Although I shall argue that these are not irrelevant considerations, there is an additional consideration involved in deciding whether it is morally justified to bring a seriously disabled child into existence when one could bring a nondisabled child into existence instead. This is the prevention of the loss of well-being or opportunity that can be caused by the disability itself to the person who has it, not the effects of the disability on others. The core difficulty for this intuitive motivation is what Derek Parfit has called the nonidentity problem (Parfit, 1984).

THE NONIDENTITY PROBLEM AND NON-PERSON-AFFECTING MORAL PRINCIPLES

To fix attention on the general problem in question, which is not restricted to cases of genetically transmitted disease, imagine a case, call it P1, in which a woman is told by her physician that she should not attempt to become pregnant now because she has a condition that is highly likely to result in serious mental retardation in her child. Her condition is easily and fully treatable if she takes a quite safe medication for one month. If she takes the medication and delays becoming pregnant for a month, the risk to her child will be eliminated and there is every reason to expect that she will have a normal child. Because the delay would interfere with her vacation travel plans, however, she does not take the medication, gets pregnant now, and gives birth to a child who is seriously retarded.

According to commonsense moral views, this woman acts wrongly, and in particular wrongs her child by not preventing its disability for such a morally trivial reason, even if, for moral or pragmatic reasons, most people would oppose coercive government intrusion into her decision. According to commonsense morality, her action is no different morally than if she failed to take the medicine in a case, call it P2, in which the condition is discovered, and so the medicine must be taken, after conception and when she is already pregnant. Nor is it morally different from another case, call it P3, in which she fails to provide a similar medication to her born child, if doing so is again necessary to prevent comparable mental impairment in her child. It is worth noting that in most states in the United States her action in P3 would probably constitute medical neglect, and governmental child protection agencies could and would use coercive measures, if necessary, to ensure the child's treatment. This suggests that it might be only because her reproductive freedom, bodily integrity, and right to decide about her own health care are also involved in P1 that we are reluctant to coerce her decision, if necessary, there as well.

As noted earlier, the philosophical problem at the heart of cases like P1, which I have elsewhere called cases of wrongful disability, is the nonidentity problem (Brock, 1995; Buchanan et al., 2000). To avoid misunderstanding, I emphasize that I believe most cases of failure to prevent genetically transmitted disabilities are not wrongful; the woman's action in P1 is, I believe, wrong, but whether other, more realistic cases would be wrong depends on a number of factors that I have discussed elsewhere but cannot pursue here (Buchanan et al., 2000). In cases in which the full morally relevant factors would not make it morally required to prevent the disability, or morally wrong to fail to do so, the question is whether the disability that the child will have constitutes any moral reason at all to prevent it, even if preventing it or not doing so would both be morally permissible. My point now is not to pursue the question of when preventing the disability is morally required as opposed to when the disability constitutes only a nonobligatory moral reason to do so, since the nonidentity problem raises a serious difficulty for either view. For simplicity of exposition in what follows, I shall usually refer to the cases in question as "wrongful disability," but the discussion for the most part applies equally well to the view that the future child's disability constitutes only a moral reason to prevent it, with doing so not morally required and failure to do so not wrongful.

In cases of wrongful disability, the person with the disability still has a life well worth living, whereas in cases of wrongful life the person's condition, with a disease such as Tay Sachs or Lesch Nhyan disease, may be so awful as to make it overall not worth living. As with wrongful life cases, in which the necessary comparison of life with nonexistence is thought to create both philosophical and policy problems, so also in wrongful disability cases do some of the philosophical and policy problems arise from having to compare a disabled existence with not having existed at all. But the nature of the philosophical problems in wrongful life and wrongful disability cases are in fact quite different. The philosophical objections to wrongful life cases center on whether it is coherent to compare an individual's quality of life with never having existed at all – that is, with nonexistence. In wrongful disability cases such as P1, a person's disability uncontroversially still leaves him or her with a worthwhile life. The philosophical problem, as noted earlier, is how this is compatible with the commonsense view that it would be wrong not to prevent the disability, or at least that there is a moral reason to do so.

The special difficulty that the nonidentity problem creates for there being any instances of wrongful disability, or for there being any moral reason to prevent the disability, is that it would not be better for the person with the disability to have had it prevented. Since that could be done only by preventing him or her from ever having existed at all, preventing the disability would deny the disabled individual a worthwhile, although disabled, life. The disability could have been prevented only by conceiving at a different time and/or under different circumstances, in which case a different child would have been conceived, or by terminating the pregnancy, in which case again this child never would have been born, although a different child may or may not have been conceived instead. (This does not assume that personal identity is determined by a person's genes; in case P1, for example, if the woman waits a month to conceive, her child will be the product of a different sperm and a different egg and will be conceived at a different time, something like a sibling of the child she would have had if she had not waited to conceive. On most views of personal identity, and not just on the mistaken view that equates personal identity with genetic identity, this is enough to make the later-born child a different child.) None of these possible means of preventing the disability would be better for the child with the disability – all would deny him or her a worthwhile life.

But if the mother's failure to prevent the disability did not make her child worse off than he or she would have been without the intervention, then her failure to prevent it seems not to harm her child. And if she did not harm her child by not preventing its disability, then why does she wrong her child morally by failing to do so? How could her future child's disability even be a moral reason to prevent it? How could making her child better off, or at least not worse off, by giving it a life worth living, albeit a life with a serious disability, wrong it? It is commonly assumed that a wrong action must be bad for someone, but because her choice to create her child with its disability is bad for no one, she seems to do no wrong. On this view, a wrong action must wrong someone, but she wrongs no one. Of course, there is a sense in which it is bad for her child to have the disability, in comparison to being without it, but there is nothing its mother could have done to enable that child to be born without the disability, and so nothing that she does or omits doing is bad for her child.

So actions whose harmful effects would even constitute seriously wrongful child abuse or neglect if done to an existing child are no harm, and so apparently not wrong, if their harmful effects on a child are inextricable from the act of bringing that child into existence with a worthwhile life! This argument threatens to undermine common and firmly held moral judgments, as well as public policy measures, concerning prevention of such disabilities for children – the woman in P1 appears not even to have a moral reason to take the medicine based in the effects on her child of not doing so, much less any moral responsibility to do so.

The difficulty in our standard moral principles requiring us, or giving us reason, to prevent or not to cause harm, which philosophers have called their person-affecting feature, is that the persons who will suffer the harm if it is caused or not prevented, or who will not suffer the harm if it is not caused or is prevented, must be one and the same distinct individual. Here is an example of a person-affecting harm-prevention principle relevant to the context of preventing genetically transmitted harms:

Person-Affecting Harm Prevention (PA): Those individuals responsible for a child's, or other dependent person's, welfare are morally required (or have a moral reason) not to cause or let it suffer serious and inadequately compensated harm or loss of benefit that they could have prevented without imposing substantial burdens or costs on themselves or others.

For other purposes, this principle would need considerable spelling out, but I use it here only to illustrate the person-affecting feature. For example, it requires one not to cause or to prevent harm or loss of benefit that is not *adequately* compensated. What counts as adequate compensation, and whether that compensation can be to others besides the person harmed, are complex and controversial questions, but I take it that the mother's inconvenience in P3, where an already-born child is affected, is not adequate. I leave open what moral obligations there may be to secure benefits in similar circumstances, since that question is not crucial to the cases of disability prevention. I also emphasize that the weaker version of the principle represented in the parenthetical clause – that such harm prevention is morally good, even if not morally required – is still more plausible and widely accepted.

If the obligation not to cause harm, or to prevent harm, is violated, a distinct child is harmed without good reason, and so the moral wrong is done to that person. Since harms to persons must always be harms to some person, it may seem that there is no alternative to principles that are person-affecting, but that is not so. The alternative is clearest if we follow Derek Parfit by distinguishing "same person" from "same number" choices (Parfit, 1984). In same-person choices, the same persons exist in each of the different alternative courses of action from which an agent chooses. In same-number choices, the same number of persons exist in each of the alternative courses of action from which an agent chooses, but the identities of some of the persons – that is, who exists in those alternatives – is affected by the choice. P1 and typical cases of prenatal disability prevention are same-number but not same-person choices – the woman's choice affects which child will exist. If the woman does not take the medication and waits to conceive, she gives birth to a retarded child, whereas if she takes the medication and waits to conceive, she gives birth to a different child who is not retarded; if a woman uses genetic testing and then aborts a fetus with serious genetic disease, she typically then tries to conceive a normal child instead.

A different way of making the same point is to say that a non-person-affecting principle for the prevention of harm applies not to distinct individuals – cases in which the prevention of harm must make a distinct individual better off than he or she would otherwise have been – but to the classes of individuals who will exist if the harm is or is not prevented (Peters, 1989). Assessing the prevention of harm by the effect on classes of persons, as opposed to the effect on distinct individuals, also allows for avoidability by substitution – an individual who does not suffer impairment if one choice is made is substituted for a different person who does suffer impairment if the other choice is made. A principle applied to the classes of all persons who will exist in each of two or more alternative courses of action will be a non-person-affecting principle, such as:

Non-Person-Affecting Harm Principle (NPA): Individuals are morally required (or have a moral reason) not to let any child or other dependent person for whose welfare they are responsible experience serious and inadequately compensated harm or loss of benefit, if they can act so that, without affecting the number of persons who will exist and without imposing substantial burdens or costs or loss of benefits on themselves or others, no child or other dependent person for whose welfare they are responsible will experience serious and inadequately compensated harm or loss of benefit.

NPA of course also raises all the interpretative issues that I set aside when considering PA. My point is not that all moral principles concerning obligations, or giving us reasons, to prevent harm, or that principles of beneficence and nonmaleficence more generally, should be non-person-affecting. In typical cases of harm where a distinct individual is made worse off, the moral principles most straightforwardly applicable are person-affecting. My claim is only that an adequate moral theory should include as well non-person-affecting principles; Jeff McMahan has called this an encompassing view, which gives independent status to both person-affecting and non-person-affecting principles or considerations, though there are many unresolved issues in how person-affecting and non-person-affecting principles are to be combined in a comprehensive moral view (McMahan, 1998, 2002). But my point here is only that with non-person-affecting principles such as NPA, the nonidentity problem does not stand in the way of there being possible cases of wrongful disability, or a possible moral reason to prevent serious disabilities, in the reproductive context. (I emphasize that I make no claim that a non-person-affecting principle such as the one stated here constitutes a full "solution" to the nonidentity problem; there are many unresolved difficulties that I shall not even note here, much less try to resolve. An important part of that problem concerns principles for "different number" cases, where choices affect how many persons exist as well as the identities of those persons, choices that arise in some genetic testing cases and that are central in population policy. Parfit and others have discussed these problems in population policy, but no one to my knowledge has succeeded in developing principles adequate for the full range of cases and difficulties.)

Some will find the stronger version of the non-person-affecting principle stated here much too strong in what it morally requires. While it may be morally permissible to prevent by substitution the creation of a blind or mentally retarded child, surely these conditions are not serious enough to ever make it morally required. I want to say a bit more about how we can clarify this question of the threshold of moral requirement, even granting that it is and will remain morally controversial. Consider a one-year-old child who develops a medical condition requiring treatment to prevent blindness or serious mental impairment. Are the parents morally required to have the child treated? One can imagine special conditions that might call into question whether they are required to do so, but I would argue that blindness and serious mental impairment are serious enough impairments to ground a moral requirement to obtain treatment for one's child to prevent them in a typical case. And I believe most people would agree.

Are there reasons to treat a preconception or prenatal case of prevention by substitution any differently, on the assumption that no person yet exists in either case? If we accept non-person-affecting-harm-prevention principles, then why should the threshold of seriousness of harm necessary to ground a moral requirement to prevent it be any different here than when person-affecting principles apply, as in the case of the one-year-old child? There are at least two reasons. One is that in the latter case there is a victim of the harm who has a personal moral complaint against the parents, because he is worse off than he would have been had his parents gotten him treatment. In the case of failure to prevent harm by substitution, there is no victim with a personal moral complaint, who has suffered a loss and been made worse off than he otherwise would have been. This is a moral difference between the cases in which person-affecting and non-person-affecting principles apply, but unless there is some further reason to reject non-person-affecting principles, the difference does not seem important enough to greatly change the threshold of harm necessary to ground a moral requirement to prevent it, since the diminishment of well-being or opportunity is the same in each case. A second difference is that in the prenatal case where prevention will require abortion and trying again to have a normal child, even parents who believe that abortion is morally permissible may view it as unfortunate and requiring a weighty justification, and/or they may have already formed an attachment to the fetus, so that aborting it could still exact deep emotional and psychological costs on them. This could justify not preventing the harm because it cannot be done "without imposing substantial costs" on the parents, but that is a different matter than the question of whether a harm is serious enough to the potential child to justify a moral requirement to prevent it in the absence of those burdens. In at least some prenatal cases, these burdens will not be significant, and they will also not be significant in preconception cases that do not involve abortion. There is, of course, room for considerable reasonable disagreement about what impairments, even in the case of the one-year-old child, are serious enough that parents are morally required to seek treatment to prevent them, but my argument is that the standard should not be substantially different in prenatal testing cases of prevention by substitution. However, the greater burdens typically imposed on parents to prevent the harm in prenatal cases, especially when abortion is necessary, mean that often it will not be morally required to prevent a specific harmful condition in prenatal cases that involve preventing the birth of the child, whereas it would be morally required to prevent that condition in the case of a born child. Of course, for parents who hold the early person view and so believe all abortion to be seriously wrong, the prevention of a serious disability will never be a sufficient reason to justify the use of abortion.

How does appeal to non-person-affecting principles of beneficence and nonmaleficence answer the question, for whose sake should a person with a serious disability compatible with a worthwhile life not be created when a nondisabled person could be created instead? It is important to understand that adopting non-person-affecting principles such as NPA amounts to a rejection of the need for an answer to that question. Such principles reject the assumption or principle that for an action to be wrong, it must wrong someone, or that for it to be bad, it must be bad for someone. Failure to act to prevent the conception of the child with a serious disability in case P1 is wrong, but it is bad for no one and wrongs no one – it is not bad for the child born with the disability, because that child has a worthwhile life and could not have existed without the disability. There is no victim of the woman's action in P1, nor is there anyone with a personal moral grievance against her – though, of course, there is a child who exists with a disability. Nor need it be the case that anyone else is made worse off by the woman's action in P1. While non-person-affecting principles in effect reject the need for an answer to the question, for *whose* sake should a disability in cases like P1 be prevented, we can answer for *what* sake or reason the disability should be prevented by not creating the child with the disability when a nondisabled child could be created instead. It is for the sake of a world with less diminishment of well-being or limitation in opportunity that the woman should take the medication and wait a month before conceiving.

THE GOAL OF ELIMINATING SERIOUS GENETIC DISEASES AND DISABILITIES

Is there anything morally problematic about a public policy that seeks to prevent and ultimately eliminate serious genetically transmitted disabilities? Other public policies requiring the use of seat belts and motorcycle helmets, for example, have the goal of reducing nongenetic harms. Of course, the goal of eliminating genetically transmitted disabilities is unlikely ever to be realized. Many parents or potential parents will not know that they are at risk of transmitting such disabilities and so will not test for and detect them when they are present. Others who know they are at risk may not test for the genes in question because they reject the measures – such as egg or sperm donation, IVF, and abortion – necessary to prevent transmission of the condition. Others may simply be prepared to accept what nature or God grants them in offspring. But a public policy that supports testing programs, encourages their use, and funds the tests through health insurance or other means seems to represent public endorsement of reducing the transmission of such disabilities, even if elimination is not a realistic goal. One reason for support of such a policy was noted earlier – it is for the sake of producing a world with less diminishment of well-being or opportunity, and it is hard to see why that is a morally problematic goal.

Nevertheless, there are legitimate concerns about the effects that the goal of reducing or eliminating disabilities may have on disabled members of society or on society generally. One concern is that reducing the number of persons with a particular disability will reduce their effectiveness in bringing social and political pressure to obtain needed support and other social services and accommodations. The extent to which this is so is an empirical question about which it is difficult to be confident. While smaller numbers will likely reduce the visibility and political force of a particular disability group, they also reduce the aggregate extent and cost of needed services. But even if success in reducing the prevalence of a serious disability would have negative effects on those with the disability who remain, that would be a morally troubling reason for not attempting to prevent disabilities that constitute serious disadvantages. It would be analogous to arguing that we should not try to reduce smoking in order to prevent diseases such as cancer and heart disease because that could reduce the effectiveness of advocacy groups in obtaining research into those diseases and services for persons who have them. In each case, this would be to deliberately use the preventable suffering of some persons without their consent for the benefit of other persons.

A second concern is that even though serious disabilities may usually be bad for the individuals who have them, the world would nevertheless be a worse place without people with disabilities in it. It is undeniably true that people with disabilities have achieved much of value for themselves, others, and society generally. However, there is often little reason to believe that they could not have achieved such things even if they were not disabled, or that other, nondisabled persons could not have achieved such things instead. In some cases, however, persons' disabilities may have played an essential role in their achievements – by directing their efforts along particular lines, by building character strengths in the overcoming of their disabilities, and so forth. But I believe it remains true that for the entire class of people who suffer a serious disability it is, on balance, a burden, even if for some individuals it turns out to be a benefit for them, for others, or for society. Since we cannot know ahead of time who will be in which group, then not to prevent the disability for the sake of those benefits would seem to impose a larger sacrifice or burden on many for the sake of a smaller benefit for some disabled persons or for society. Moreover, there is no way in which those who will be burdened could consent to the sacrifice imposed on them for the sake of others – though, were that possible, they likely would consent to the sacrifice being imposed on them for the sake of others, since the alternative for them is not ever to have existed. However, this possibility is telling only against applying person-affecting, as opposed to non-person-affecting, principles to the case. Not preventing the disabilities for this reason seems wrongly to use some persons without their consent for the benefit of others, and also to violate non-person-affecting harm-prevention principles.

Those who are born with serious disabilities compatible with a worthwhile life will in fact be glad that they were born; if their disability could have been prevented only by preventing them from existing, they will not complain of being born with their disability. But again, that is only relevant to the application of person-affecting principles of harm prevention, not to the non-person-affecting-principles supported here. Others without the disability who would be created instead would be equally glad to have been born, and their having been born instead would have the added non-person-affecting benefit of producing less diminishment of well-being or opportunity in the world.

The fact that it is non-person-affecting principles that correctly capture the moral concern in cases of prevention of genetically transmitted disease and disability helps to make clear the way in which the concern to prevent that transmission is a judgment not about the person with the disability but only about the disability itself. As I noted earlier, if the transmission of the disability is not prevented, the child born with it is not a victim of its mother's action with any grievance against her for not preventing the disability; that child could not have existed without the disability and so would not have been better off had the disability been prevented. No false claim is made that the disability should have been prevented for the sake of the child with the disability – that would not have been better for the child. It is only in the few cases of true wrongful life – such as Tay Sachs or Lesch Nhyan disease, where the disease is so awful as to make the child's life not worth living – that it should be prevented for the sake of the child. Nor is the aim that that child not exist, as some disability rights proponents have claimed when they argue that supporting the prevention of genetically transmitted disabilities implies the judgment that they should never have been born. As the non-person-affecting-principle stated here makes clear, the action should be done for the sake of less diminishment of well-being or opportunity in the world; our action is aimed at the disease and its bad effects, not at the person who will experience them if it is not prevented. Standard person-affecting harm-prevention principles, on the other hand, make clear why once a person does exist, we are not committed to wanting her not to exist or to denying her further life. Despite a person's serious disability, once she exists her life is a good to her, and it would be a serious harm and wrong to her to take it from her.

Jeff McMahan has expressed doubts about whether we can distinguish between a judgment about the person with the disability and a judgment about the disability itself in the way I suggest here. He writes: "Suppose we think that ugliness is impersonally bad, or makes the world worse. Can we hold that and avoid implying any judgment about the people who are ugly? If we require plastic surgery to eliminate ugliness, can we claim that our action is aimed only at the ugliness, not at the people who are ugly?" (personal correspondence). Now, McMahan is certainly correct that if ugliness (or pain) is impersonally bad, that will imply some judgments about people who are ugly (or in pain), but the question is whether it implies unacceptable or objectionable judgments.

We might say to the person, "Your ugliness or pain makes the world worse than if you were not ugly or in pain. Being ugly or in pain is also worse for you. However, as a person, a self-determined agent, you have a right to continue to exist with a life you find worthwhile, whether or not you are ugly or in pain. Since your ugliness and pain are, in different ways, essentially yours, you have a right to decide whether to try to eliminate them." McMahan's example of ugliness is different from mine of pain, because the ugly person might believe that his ugliness is so deep a part of his self-conception and of others' conception of him that he would not change it now, even if he also grants that it would have been better had he not been ugly. So we would have good reason not to require that he undergo plastic surgery to eliminate his ugliness, and also to understand his deciding not to do so. The undesirable properties of ugliness and pain are properties of him, and so he should be entitled to decide whether to eliminate them.

How would prenatal cases, such as P1 and P2, be different? At that point, the ugliness or pain are only potential properties of a potential person – either of a person who would be conceived, as in P1, or of an individual who exists but has not yet developed into a person, as in P2. There are more realistic examples. A woman undergoing IVF may have two embryos, only one of which will be implanted, and must choose whether to implant one who is apparently normal or the other who will develop a serious disability. In neither P1- or P2-type cases involving ugliness or pain, nor in the IVF case, do any of the individuals in question have a right to be born or to exist. In each of the three cases, the world will be worse, all else being equal, if the choice is to bring into existence the person who will be ugly, or in pain, or seriously disabled, and each of those individuals will be worse off than the individual who could have been brought into existence instead. At this stage, none of the potential persons yet exist; the judgment implied by the choosing to create the persons who would not be ugly, or in pain, or seriously disabled is that, if you are to create a person, it would be better to create a person who is not ugly, or in pain, or seriously disabled than to create one who is.

A final source of concern about the goal of reducing or eliminating disabilities is that it is part of a broader pressure toward normalization, conformity, and intolerance of difference (Silvers, 1994). These are indeed legitimate and serious concerns. Society benefits greatly from those who are "different" and who pursue a different path in life, and it is important not to lose their achievements and their "experiments in living." The concern about normalization, conformity, and intolerance of difference obviously is much broader than the question of preventing disability, and avoiding them probably depends only to a limited extent on the issue of preventing disabilities. The question is whether not preventing serious and preventable disabilities is necessary for effectively resisting pressures for normalization, conformity, and intolerance of difference. This is an extremely complex issue that is controversial and highly uncertain, but two points seem to me to limit the force of this concern. First, most diversity, nonconformity, and valuable experiments in living seem to arise not from disability but rather from other factors present in both nondisabled and disabled persons. Second, the diminishment of well-being or opportunity usually caused by serious disability supports a strong presumption that it should be prevented. There should be strong evidence of the benefits resulting from the presence of disabled persons in resisting normalization, conformity, and intolerance of difference to justify not preventing serious disabilities. I believe the necessary evidence does not now exist.

THE SOCIAL AND ECONOMIC COSTS OF GENETIC DISEASES AND DISABILITIES

An additional reason why society may legitimately wish to reduce or prevent the transmission of serious genetic diseases or disabilities is the costs of health care and other services that are needed to treat them so as to ensure equality of opportunity for persons with them and to reduce the burdens on other family members that having a seriously disabled member sometimes imposes. Individuals' health care costs are to a substantial extent externalized to the society at large (in the case of government health insurance programs) or to other members of an insurance pool (in the case of private health insurance). As a result, these broader groups have an interest in reducing or avoiding these costs when that can be done by prevention of conditions needing treatment and other services. That interest is a legitimate interest on which those broader affected groups can reasonably act, but of course it does not follow that anything they might do to prevent those costs would be morally justified. In all cases of serious genetically caused disease and disability, these broader groups have an economic interest in cost-effective education programs that make people aware of available genetic testing and the various steps that can be taken, either before conception to avoid the risk of transmission of the disease or condition, or after conception to avoid the birth of an affected child. They also have a moral reason to support such programs for the sake of a world with less diminishment of well-being or opportunity, although, as my earlier discussion of the nonidentity problem showed, this moral reason is not for the sake of the children who would be born with the disability.

I have discussed elsewhere the nature and moral importance of a woman's reproductive freedom, which is typically at stake in possible interference with her choices about whether to prevent genetically transmitted disease to her potential offspring, as well as the factors that affect the strength of her moral obligation or responsibility to prevent such transmission; the relevant factors are multiple and complex, and I shall not repeat that discussion here (Brock, 1994; Buchanan et al., 2000). I have concluded that the intrusion on reproductive freedom of most means necessary to prevent such transmission, the wide range of reasonable disagreement about which cases of failure to prevent such transmission would be cases of wrongful disability, and the nature of the disabilities that can now be prevented together provide a compelling case against using any state interference or coercion, such as the criminal law, to enforce prevention of wrongful disability against the wishes of the potential parents. The decision should be left to the individual parents. But even if the social and economic costs to others do not justify their imposing coercive measures on potential parents in order to prevent those costs, those others may be justified in supporting educational programs that inform potential parents about the means of preventing serious genetically transmitted disease and disability, and that encourage them to use those means to do so. It bears emphasis that those costs do not diminish at all our moral responsibility to ensure the provision of needed health care and other services to persons who are born with or who acquire serious disabilities; that is simply a distinct issue from whether there is a legitimate reason for those who would incur the costs to try to avoid them by encouraging the prevention of serious genetic diseases and disabilities. Persons who are born with or who acquire serious disabilities do not thereby have any lesser moral status or worth than persons without them, and they have the same moral claims to health care and other supportive or rehabilitative services that are needed to protect their well-being or to ensure them the equality of opportunity that all persons deserve.

Consider two other examples of public programs designed to encourage particular groups not to procreate, in part because of the social costs to others of their doing so. We now have a variety of programs aimed at discouraging teenage pregnancies, particularly in the case of single mothers. The motives for these programs are multiple, but they certainly include the social costs that these teenage mothers impose on others, as well as the belief that the children of single teenage mothers would usually receive a better start in life if their mothers waited to get pregnant until they were older and better able to provide for their children. Notice that this concern for the child when the intent is to postpone childbearing is typically subject to the nonidentity problem discussed earlier, and the appropriate moral principles that apply to it will be non-person-affecting principles. Both the financial and child-centered concerns seem legitimate concerns when they would not deny, but only delay, realization of the young girl's procreative interests.

Different programs discouraging the bearing of children have sometimes been aimed at the poor, often with the same sorts of reasons offered for them – the financial costs imposed on society by these children and the inferior start in life that children of the poor have vis-à-vis the children of better-off parents. But these programs, unlike those aimed at single teenage mothers, are deeply discriminatory and unjust, not only because the poverty of poor persons is itself usually unjust, but also because they would deny poor persons the realization of their interests in procreation. The non-person-affecting principle stated here would not apply to these programs aimed at the poor because most of the poor cannot become nonpoor, and because if we encouraged them to act in accordance with it by declining to procreate so that nonpoor parents could have a child instead, this would impose very severe and undue burdens on them by denying them the possibility of pursuing their procreative interests. Societal concern for the social costs imposed when genetically transmitted disease is not prevented and when prevention would not deny prospective parents the realization of their procreative interests is like programs aimed at single teenage mothers, not like those aimed at the poor.

THE RELEVANCE OF DISABILITY IN RESOURCE ALLOCATION AT THE END OF LIFE

I have tried to show how social support for the prevention of genetically transmitted disabilities in accordance with non-person-affecting harm-prevention principles need not imply morally objectionable attitudes or judgments toward persons with disabilities; it implies negative attitudes toward the disabilities themselves, not toward the persons with them. Nevertheless, it does imply that when we can act so that the same number of persons will exist, but so that the persons who do exist will experience less diminishment of well-being or opportunity, we have a moral reason to do so and sometimes can even be morally required to do so. And I have argued that serious disability will usually reduce a person's overall quality of life. Why, then, does this not imply that at the other end of life, when we must prioritize patients for scarce life-sustaining treatments such as organ transplantation and intensive care, or prioritize health programs for financial support, we should also choose the alternative that will result in less diminishment of well-being or opportunity by giving preference to a nondisabled over a seriously disabled patient? Doing so would result in a world with the same number of persons, but with less diminishment of well-being or opportunity. Here again, it might be said, there is no negative judgment about the person with the disability, only a negative judgment about the disability itself and its effects. A commitment to cost-effectiveness in the use of limited health care resources to maximize health benefits seems to favor the nondisabled candidate for the scarce life-sustaining treatment (Brock, 2000). Why would it generally be wrong to do so – as I believe it indeed would be – and is that consistent with what I have said here about the prevention of genetic transmission of serious disabilities by giving preference to the creation of a person without a serious disability over creation of a person with a serious disability?

It seems initially plausible to many that we should use scarce medical resources to produce the greatest medical benefit possible. Since medical benefits are typically understood to be preserving or extending life and preserving or improving the quality of life, medical benefits are often measured in units such as QALYs that incorporate both of these kinds of benefits. Suppose a nondisabled patient and a patient with a disability such as blindness are both in need of a scarce lifesaving treatment – say, a liver transplant. If blindness reduces health-related quality of life, extending the blind patient's life will produce, other things being equal, fewer QALYs than extending the nondisabled patient's life for the same period of time; providing the transplant to the nondisabled patient will produce greater medical benefits. Why might it nevertheless be wrong to prefer the nondisabled patient for this reason?

One reason is that we know that through the process of adaptation, accommodation, and coping, many persons with serious disabilities overcome their disabilities and have just as high-quality lives as persons without disabilities. This suggests that typical measures of health-related quality of life employed to calculate QALYs are often poor measures of overall quality of life. In many contexts, what health care can affect is patients' health and health-related quality of life, and we focus on the capacity of different interventions to improve health and health-related quality of life. What a person does with her health in pursuit of her overall life plan, how she uses her health-related quality of life in the service of improving her overall quality of life, is up to her and not the province or concern of medicine. But when we are selecting or prioritizing patients for life-sustaining treatment, we cannot justifiably say that our only concern is with their health-related quality of life and that it is up to the patients what they do with that health-related quality of life in the service of their overall quality of life or life plan. We are then selecting between lives – deciding who will live and who will die – which suggests that if quality of life is relevant to that selection, it should be the overall quality of life of the patients, not their narrower health-related quality of life.

Measures of overall quality of life, however, are deeply controversial and have a substantial subjective component, which makes us rightly reluctant to use them at all in public policy contexts and, in particular, reluctant to use judgments of others' quality of life that conflict with those persons' judgments of their own quality of life. While there may be some rough agreed-upon standards for health and health-related quality of life, there is far less agreement about standards for comparing people's overall quality of life. It is important to understand that the problem here is twofold. First, when prioritizing patients for life-sustaining treatment, it seems that if quality of life is relevant, it should be the overall quality of the life that is relevant, not merely health-related quality of life that patients are then free to use as they see fit in the service of their overall quality of life. Second, any standards for the evaluation of overall quality of life would be deeply controversial, subjective, and problematic.

Let us set this problem aside, however, and assume either that a health-related quality of life measure is appropriate for measuring the benefits of life-sustaining treatment or that we have an unproblematic and uncontroversial measure of overall quality of life. Consider a case in which, on either measure, the presence of a serious disability reduces a patient's quality of life, so that, other things being equal, fewer QALYs would be produced by sustaining that disabled patient's life than by sustaining a nondisabled patient's life; and assume that the disabled patient would strongly prefer not to be disabled. What would be the moral objection to preferring the nondisabled patient to the disabled patient in order to produce a greater benefit in QALYs? The disabled patient might argue that part of what it means to recognize the equal moral worth of persons is to treat them as having equal moral claims to having their basic needs, including their important health care needs, met. This is consistent with recognizing differences in the importance or urgency of different health care needs, and of the different health care needs of different persons, but it is not consistent with giving different weight to the same health care needs of different persons because of other differences between them distinct from their health care needs. Whether one has a disability that reduces one's quality of life, but is unrelated to one's health care needs, is such a morally irrelevant factor. To give the disabled patient lower priority for a life-sustaining treatment such as a liver transplant is to unjustly discriminate against him on the basis of his disability, and such an action would be both morally unjust and prohibited in law by the Americans with Disabilities Act (Brock, 2000).

Moreover, the disabled patient might argue that just like the nondisabled patient, she will lose everything – her life – without the transplant; both patients need the transplant to sustain life itself. She might grant that she would prefer not to be disabled and would be willing to make significant sacrifices or assume significant burdens or costs to remove her disability, if that were possible. She might also grant that she would prefer and be prepared to sacrifice more to obtain a life-sustaining treatment that would also remove her disability than to obtain a life-sustaining treatment that would still leave her disabled. She might, finally, grant that her quality of life is not as good as it would be if she were not disabled, nor as good as the nondisabled patient's quality of life. Nevertheless, her disability cannot be cured, and so she might reasonably urge that her life as a disabled person is just as valuable or dear to her as the nondisabled person's (admittedly better) quality life is to him. Given that her disabled life is the best life that she can have, she values it just as much as the nondisabled patient values his life; she would be willing to sacrifice just as much to preserve her life as the nondisabled patient would be willing to sacrifice to preserve his life (Brock, 1988). Even if the nondisabled person, and the nondisabled person's life, were also more instrumentally valuable to others or to society, to prioritize patients on the basis of their social value or their instrumental value to others is to fail to recognize their equal moral worth or intrinsic value as persons. Our moral aim in providing health care should principally be to benefit the person in need of care, and there is no basis for assuming that the good of her life to the disabled patient is less than the good of his life to the nondisabled patient.

Sometimes the effect of a serious disability may be also, or instead, to reduce the life expectancy of the disabled person. Suppose that two patients with end-stage liver disease – one of whom has a disability, unrelated to her liver disease, that shortens her life expectancy, and the other of whom is otherwise nondisabled – are competing for a single scarce liver for transplantation. Here again, all other things being equal, fewer QALYs will be produced by transplanting the liver to the disabled patient than to the nondisabled patient, though here that is because the disabled patient is expected not to live as long with the transplant, even if, while alive, her quality of life would be the same as that of the nondisabled patient. I believe that the same kinds of moral objections grounded in fairness that apply against disadvantaging the disabled patient because of her lower quality of life apply equally here against disadvantaging her because of the shorter life expectancy caused by her disability. Notice that if she were to be given lower priority for the scarce life-sustaining treatment either because her quality of life is lower or because her life expectancy is shorter as a result of her disability, then she would be being discriminated against or disadvantaged *because of* her disability, even though the disability is unrelated to her need for, or the effectiveness of, treatment.

I should add that I am not claiming that the degree of benefit – for example, in QALYs – should receive no weight in selection of patients for scarce life-sustaining treatment or in health care resource prioritization more generally. My point is only that there is a reason grounded in fairness not to do so in a way that disadvantages disabled persons. Concerns for fairness and utility must be balanced when they conflict. The role of disability in resource prioritization is complex, and I will not pursue the complexities here, much less the broader moral issues in health care resource prioritization (Brock, 2004). The question here is only whether there is any inconsistency in the attitudes, assumptions, and principles appealed to in the prenatal prevention of disability, even when that involves preventing potentially disabled individuals who would be disabled from coming into existence, and the rejection of disability as relevant in the prioritization of patients for scarce life-sustaining treatment. I have tried to show that there need not be. In each context, it is acknowledged that serious disabilities are, all else being equal, undesirable disadvantages. In the prenatal context, support for their prevention is for the sake of preventing the diminishment of well-being and opportunity that they cause, as the non-person-affecting principle shows. The practice of prevention, and the non-person-affecting principle that supports it, reflect a negative attitude toward disabilities but not toward persons with disabilities. The practice of prevention of disability in the prenatal context implies no judgment about persons with disabilities, because in the prenatal context I am assuming that no person yet exists who has the disability. (This would not be correct if one assumed that postconception but prenatally, a person does exist. I have argued that on that assumption, abortion to prevent the disability the fetus has or will later have is not morally justified, but here only because abortion would then be wrong independent of the presence of a disability in the fetus.)

In the context of prioritizing life-sustaining treatments for existing patients, on the other hand, the necessary judgments are about particular existing persons. We should avoid giving weight in this context to the effects of disabilities on patients' quality or length of life, because that would imply that these effects and the disabilities that cause them reduce the value of the treatments and of the lives they sustain. This would conflict with the equal moral worth of persons on one plausible interpretation of what that concept, at least in part, means. The fundamental point of difference between the prenatal practice of prevention of serious genetically transmitted disabilities, even when that can be done only by preventing the person who would have the disability from coming into existence, and the prioritization of life-sustaining treatment for disabled versus nondisabled patients, is that in the former case, no persons exist who are affected by the act of prevention (setting aside possible side effects for already existing disabled persons), whereas in the latter case, persons with disabilities do exist who will be affected by the resource prioritization; their equal moral worth must be respected, and they must not be wrongly discriminated against on the basis of their disabilities.

NOTE

I want to acknowledge with gratitude the detailed written comments I received on an earlier draft of this chapter from Adrienne Asch, Jeff McMahan, Robert Wachbroit, and David Wasserman. The chapter benefited greatly from their help, although all would still disagree to varying degrees with the positions I take in it.

REFERENCES

Asch, A. 2000. "Why I Haven't Changed My Mind about Prenatal Diagnosis: Reflections and Refinements." In E. Parens and A. Asch (eds.), *Prenatal Testing and Disability Rights*. Washington, DC: Georgetown University Press.

Brock, D. W. 1988. "Ethical Issues in Recipient Selection for Organ Transplantation." In D. Mathieu (ed.), *Organ Substitution Technology: Ethical, Legal and Public Policy Issues*. Boulder, CO and London: Westview Press, pp. 86–99.

Brock, D. W. 1993. "Quality of Life Measures in Health Care and Medical Ethics." In A. Sen and M. Nussbaum (eds.), *The Quality of Life*. Oxford: Oxford University Press, pp. 95–132.

Brock, D. W. 1994. "Reproductive Freedom: Its Nature, Bases, and Limits." In David Thomasma and John Monagle (eds.), *Healthcare Ethics: Critical Issues for Health Professionals*. Gaithersburg, MD: Aspen Publishers, pp. 43–61.

Brock, D. W. 1995. "The Non-Identity Problem and Genetic Harm." *Bioethics* 9: 269–75.

Brock, D. W. 2000. "Health Care Resource Prioritization and Discrimination against Persons with Disabilities." In L. Francis and A. Silvers (eds.), *Americans with Disabilities: Implications for Individuals and Institutions*. New York: Routledge, pp. 223–35.

Brock, D. W. 2004. "Ethical Issues in the Use of Cost Effectiveness Analysis for the Prioritization of Health Care Resources." In T. Tan-Torres et al. (eds.), *Making Choices in Health: WHO Guide to Cost-Effectiveness Analysis*. Geneva: World Health Organisation.

Buchanan, A. E., Brock, D. W., Daniels, N., and Wikler, D. 2000. *From Chance to Choice: Genes and Social Justice*. Cambridge: Cambridge University Press.

Griffin, J. 1986. *Well-Being*. Oxford: Clarendon Press.

McMahan, J. 1998. "Wrongful Life: Paradoxes in the Morality of Causing People to Exist." In J. Coleman and C. Morris (eds.), *Rational Commitment and Social Justice: Essays for Gregory Kavka*. Cambridge: Cambridge University Press.

McMahan, J. 2002. *The Ethics of Killing*. Oxford: Oxford University Press.

Murray, C. J. L. 1996. "Rethinking DALYs." In C. J. L. Murray and A. D. Lopez (eds.), *The Global Burden of Disease*. Cambridge, MA and Geneva: Harvard School of Public Health and World Health Organization.

National Organization on Disability. 1994. *National Organization on Disability/ Louis Harris Survey of Americans with Disabilities*. New York: Louis Harris and Associates.

Parfit, D. 1984. *Reasons and Persons*, Oxford: Clarendon Press.

Peters, P. G. 1989. "Protecting the Unconceived: Nonexistence, Avoidability, and Reproductive Technology." *Arizona Law Review* 31 (3): 487–548.

Roe v. Wade, 410 U. S. 113 (1973).

Sackett, D. L., and Torrance, G. W. 1978. "The Utility of Different Health States as Perceived by the General Public." *Journal of Chronic Diseases* 31: 697–704.

Silvers, A. 1994. "Defective Agents: Equality, Difference and the Tyranny of the Normal." *Journal of Social Philosophy* (twenty-fifth anniversary special issue): 154–75.

Silvers, A. 1998. "Formal Justice." In A. Silvers, D. Wasserman, and M. Mahowald (eds.), *Disability, Difference, Discrimination*. Lanham, MD: Rowman and Littlefield, pp. 13–145.

Chapter 4

Disability, Ideology, and Quality of Life

A Bias in Biomedical Ethics

RON AMUNDSON

The central philosophical concepts regarding disability were constructed not by philosophers but by disability rights activists. Only recently have these concepts received attention in the philosophical literature. This chapter will argue that an important discussion in biomedical ethics is biased against the civil rights interests of people with disabilities because of the failure of philosophers to come to terms with the disability rights movement. Quality of life is conceived in a way that directly conflicts with the Social Model of disability, and the conflict is deeply rooted in biomedical ethical discussion. One particular application will be discussed: the reduction of health care for disabled people because of their allegedly low quality of life.

1. TWO MODELS

A defining characteristic of the disability rights movement is a particular explanation of the disadvantages experienced by disabled people. Disadvantages are explained as effects not of biomedical conditions of individuals but of the socially created environment that is shared by disabled and nondisabled people. This environment (it is said) is so constructed that nondisabled people are privileged and disabled people penalized. Disability is a social problem that involves the discriminatory barriers that bar some people but not others from the goods that society has to offer. For this reason, the view is often called the Social Model of disability. It contrasts with the traditional view, sometimes termed the Medical Model, according to which disability is a problem of individuals whose biomedical conditions disadvantage them. On the Medical Model, disadvantages are natural and inevitable outcomes of simple biomedical facts. Reductions of these natural disadvantages can be accomplished only by individual cures (changing the biomedical facts) or by charitable donations intended to compensate the victims of disability for their inevitable and pitiable conditions. The Social Model depicts disability as a problem experienced by a class of people, a problem that is caused by social organization and that can be remedied by social change. The Medical Model is an individualistic rather than a social theory. Disabilities are properties of individuals, and remedies (e.g., cures, rehabilitations, charitable donations) are meted out one individual at a time.

The 1990 Americans with Disabilities Act is an outgrowth of the disability rights movement and the Social Model of disability. Patterned after earlier civil rights laws, it treats discrimination as a cause of disadvantage and mandates equal treatment (often in the form of equally accessible environments) as its solution. The ADA has given very wide publicity to the problem of disability. But the Social Model that underpins the ADA has not been as widely understood or accepted, and many people who accept the goals of the ADA still tacitly assume the Medical Model of disability. This chapter will examine one of the manifestations of the Medical Model in contemporary biomedical ethics. It will do so from the perspective of the Social Model. The concept of quality of life (QOL) is entwined in many issues of biomedical ethics. I will try to show that prominent discussions of the QOL of disabled people reveal an unjustified and unexamined commitment to the Medical Model of disability, and for that reason a bias against the interests of disabled people. This is not a simple factual error, of course. The treatment of QOL is embedded within a well-articulated framework of literature involving prominent ethicists and other philosophers. All of these people display a sophistication in philosophical ethics that far exceeds my own. I am a philosopher and historian of biology, a disabled person, and a disability activist. I come to this discussion as an activist, representing a perspective that I consider poorly understood among biomedical ethicists.

The reader may consider the Social and Medical Models to present a false dichotomy, each attending to only one aspect of disability. This may be true, but I will make no attempt to reconcile them here. Academic attention to the problem of disability is barely a decade old. The hopes for a global theory of disability are even dimmer than the hopes for global theories of race or gender. The disability rights movement, like the civil rights movements for women and for "racial" minorities, will require significant retooling of our conceptual categories. A decade is not enough.[1]

The Medical and Social Models of disability are ideological, as explanations of social disadvantage often are.[2] My claim that they are ideological amounts to the following. Each model presents an account of the causal relations that hold between disability and other phenomena. The causal accounts at first look like other causal explanations – like the gravitational explanation of the tides, for example. The causal accounts involve or entail the identification of various phenomena as *natural* or *unnatural*, and as *inevitable* or *contingent and changeable*. On closer inspection, it can be discovered that the contrasting causal accounts of the same phenomenon (here disability) serve or harm the interests of different groups of people. A causal account that depicts a social phenomenon as natural and inevitable (or changeable only at great cost) works to the advantage of the people who benefit from the phenomenon, and to the harm of the people who are hurt by the phenomenon. When the same phenomenon is depicted as artificial and changeable, the reformist interests of those harmed by the phenomenon are served. My goal in this chapter is not to argue for the correctness of the Social Model. Rather, I will show that important bioethical discussions presuppose its falseness, and assume the correctness of the Medical Model. This unexamined assumption produces a bias against the goals of the disability rights movement within the practice of biomedical ethics.

2. DISABILITY AND QOL: THE STANDARD VIEW

The Standard View is that disabilities have very strong negative impacts on the quality of life of the individuals who have them. This view is widely held by nondisabled people, both in popular and in academic culture. The Standard View is confronted by a fact that I will term its Anomaly: when asked about the quality of their own lives, disabled people report a quality only slightly lower than that reported by nondisabled people, and much higher than that projected by nondisabled people. Both the Standard View and its Anomaly have been robustly demonstrated in a number of studies. Disabled and nondisabled people have very different assessments of the quality of disabled people's lives.

Many factors are commonly assumed to lower one's QOL. Poverty, the loss or the lack of loving relationships, thwarted ambitions, and frustrated hopes are all assumed to reduce QOL. Some of these are contingently related to disability, as they are to other causes. But disability itself holds a privileged position in the catalog of QOL reducers. The life badness that is assumed to follow from disability goes beyond the badness that comes from the partial and contingent associations that disability has with loss of love, loss of income, and so on. In other words, disability is conceived to have a *surplus badness*, over and above its specific and identifiable affects. It is assumed to be categorically bad, bad beyond its contingent effects, bad to the bone, butt-ugly bad. I will argue that the surplus badness attributed to disability comes not from a rational appreciation of the consequences of disability itself, but from the stigma that disability carries, both in popular and in academic culture. In other words, the Standard View is an *expression* of the stigma of disability. It is not (as it presents itself to be) an estimate of the objective consequences of impairments.

I am interested in the Standard View for three reasons, two of them specific and one generic. The first reason is that the Standard View generally devalues the lives of disabled people. It enforces the "pity" aspects of the Medical Model that disability rights advocates find so objectionable, and thereby obscures the civil rights basis of the disability rights movement. The second reason is that under certain theories of health care rationing, the supposed low QOL of disabled people can imply that they have less claim on health care than nondisabled people do. This is a concrete example of the harm that the Standard View can cause. The third, generic reason is that the Standard View is well integrated within the literature of biomedical ethics. Its flaws are reflected in a wide range of philosophical discussions of disability.

But isn't the Standard View refuted by its Anomaly? Hardly anyone thinks so. Disabilities are so stigmatized that reports to the contrary from the stigmatized group itself are almost universally discredited or ignored. The comedian Jerry Lewis represents the Muscular Dystrophy Association in its charitable appeals. For over a decade, he has been strongly condemned by disability activists for his demeaning depiction of disabled people as pitiable wretches and partial people, in desperate need only of charity and cures. In response to activists' claims that they don't want pity, Lewis recently replied, "If you're paraplegic and in a wheelchair and you don't want pity, stay in your house!" (CBS *Morning Show*, 2001).

Some scholars are more thoughtful than Mr. Lewis about the Anomaly. But they are no less resistant to modifying the Standard View in light of it. This is, I believe, because of the Standard View's close integration with other important concepts in the literature. In sections 3, 4, and 5, I will discuss and critique a constellation of views and concepts that forms the academic context for the Standard View. Sections 6 and 7 will then discuss and critique how the Standard View itself is defended. Sections 8 and 9 examine the use of the Standard View to justify health care priority penalization for disabled people. Section 10 discusses the Anomaly itself (actual reports from disabled people, at last). It also suggests a way in which a low assessment of the QOL of disabled people might be empirically grounded.

3. THE LINKS: NORMALITY, OPPORTUNITY, AND QOL

Within current biomedical thinking, the Standard View of QOL and disability is tied into a well-articulated set of views involving the notions of biological normality and the importance of a wide opportunity range for quality of life. The area includes important work by Christopher Boorse, Norman Daniels, and Dan Brock. The work is founded on Boorse's concept of what he calls "species typical function." Despite the statistical-sounding term "typical," Boorse's concept is of the *normal* functioning of members of a species (not just the most common or usual functioning). Boorse claims that the distinction between normal and abnormal function is an empirically grounded implication of biomedical science, not a prejudice of human observers. In effect, normal and abnormal function are distinct natural kinds. Impairments (the biological aspects of disabilities) are objectively and scientifically defined as species-abnormal functionings (Boorse, 1977).

Boorse's claim is empirical, not normative. Nevertheless, it is very widely cited in the normative literature. His apparently moderate claim about biology supports normative consequences in the work of Norman Daniels, Dan Brock, and others. Daniels uses Boorsian normality to explain the moral importance of health care. On Daniels's view, the importance of health care is to maintain normal function – that is, to avoid disease and impairment. Normality is important because of its essential connection to opportunity. Species-abnormal functioning reduces the "normal" opportunity range, while health care maintains and restores species-normal functioning, thereby protecting opportunity (Daniels, 1981, 1985). Brock then argues that a "normal" wide opportunity range is a necessary condition for a high quality of life (Brock, 1993, 1995, 2000).

The objective normality of biological function was inferred from biomedical science. The linkage from Boorse to Daniels to Brock completes an argument, apparently founded on biological fact, that people with impairments will (must?) have a low quality of life. High QOL is dependent on wide opportunity range, which is dependent on biological normality, which is an objective fact of the natural world.

I believe that this chain of reasoning is flawed at every step. Boorse's contribution misrepresents biomedical science. Daniels's step embodies the prejudices of the Medical Model of disability, and so its shortcomings. Brock's contribution shares Daniels's commitment to the Medical Model, and in addition assumes an epistemologically privileged knowledge of others' lives that is unjustified by the facts.

4. CRITIQUE OF NORMAL FUNCTION (BOORSE)

Intuitive as it is, Boorse's reification of the normal/abnormal distinction is not implied by modern biological theory. I have argued this claim in detail elsewhere, and will outline my concerns here. (See Amundson, 2000 for details.) On Boorse's view, we should expect natural species to be composed of members that have a narrow range of functional variation, forming a bell curve with steep sides. In fact, information from a wide range of biological disciplines can be seen to challenge this sharp distinction between normal and abnormal function. A wide range of functional variation is to be expected. First, evolutionary biology does not imply functional uniformity as an outcome of evolution. Indeed, functional variability is a basic assumption of Darwinian natural selection. Second, the facts of developmental biology do not imply conformity among species members. Developmental plasticity and functional adaptation should lead us to expect variation, not strict conformity, in the functional organization of the bodies of species members. Third, many empirical studies of anatomical and physiological diversity in humans show a wide range of variation, too wide for a supposed "normal range" to be neatly designated. Fourth, genetic studies of various kinds indicate enough genetic diversity in humans and most other species to allow a wide range of function, even ignoring the developmental plasticity that allows identical genotypes to divergently adapt into distinct phenotypes. Functional uniformity may be Henry Ford's ideal of industrial mass production, but it is not a scientific discovery about the biological world.

On my view, Boorse's reified concept of *normal function* can be compared to the historically reified concept of race. In years past, the dominant scientific view was that the traditionally named human races (Caucasian, Negroid, etc.) designated biologically real categories of humans. This view has been abandoned; racial categories no longer have scientific validity. This is not to say that human variation does not exist. Of course it does, and some of the variation (hair color and texture, etc.) is statistically correlated with the traditionally named races. But when we take *all* human variation into account, the distribution of variation does not match the races. The naming of races was a social and economic phenomenon that simply did not match up with biological facts. The same (I say) is true of the normal/abnormal distinction. There is a great range of functional variation among humans, as there is among the members of any species. The variation is so great, and so multidimensional, that the belief in an objective dividing line between normal and abnormal is just as scientifically untenable as a dividing line between Caucasian and Negroid. Biology shows us that we must learn to deal with variation on its own terms and resist the temptation to prematurely categorize. History shows us that premature biological categories sprout constantly from social prejudices about the "true nature" of human beings. When I say that the concepts of race and biological normality are *reified*, I mean that they are falsely conceived to reflect real, objective aspects of the natural world, determinable by biological science. Instead, they reflect social strategies for the management of human diversity.

5. CRITIQUE OF THE DEPENDENCE OF OPPORTUNITY ON NORMALITY (DANIELS)

So I doubt the scientific basis of "normal function" from the start. But I will consider the subsequent steps on their own terms, and set aside my skepticism about normal function. Even if reified normal function existed, Daniels's inference that abnormal function inevitably reduces opportunity range presupposes without argument the correctness of the Medical Model of disability. The Social Model asserts that the opportunities lost to impaired people come from environmental design, not from biology itself. People with atypical *modes* of functioning (e.g., people who read with Braille, communicate using American Sign Language, or travel in wheelchairs) can nevertheless function at a high *level*, at least if the environment poses no obstacles to them. Nevertheless, these atypical modes are stigmatized. The assumption that unusual functional modes *necessarily* reduce one's opportunity is itself a manifestation of that stigma (Silvers, 1998). The very purpose of the ADA is to remove the barriers to opportunity that disadvantage these "abnormals." To assume that "normal opportunity range" is available only to a certain narrow range of body types is to assume that the Social

Model is false and the ADA fruitless. The notion that discriminatory barriers to opportunity are unavoidable facts of nature is no more justified in the case of disability than it would be in the case of racial or sex discrimination.

To be sure, a philosopher could cleverly define "opportunity" so narrowly that certain impairments limit them by definition – complete paraplegics by definition do not have the "opportunity" to walk, or blind people to see. But the same trivialization could be applied to sex and race. African Americans lack the "opportunity" to be white, and women the "opportunity" to sire children. But this is just obfuscation. Whether any of these "lacks" (nonwhiteness, nonsiring, nonwalking, nonseeing) restricts employment, the freedom to live where one chooses, or one's social status depends on the social structures in which they are embedded. The assumed "naturalness" of the linkage of normality to opportunity harms the interests of disabled people, just as the linkage of race and sex to opportunity has been harmful to other disadvantaged groups. The claim by disability rights advocates that they are being *unfairly* discriminated against must be met head on. The notion that opportunity is *by definition* out of the reach of disabled people is rightly rejected by them, just as the same claims were rejected by women and minorities.

6. THE STANDARD VIEW AND "OBJECTIVE" QUALITY OF LIFE (BROCK)

Dan Brock discusses the quality of life in the context of the work of Boorse and Daniels. In series of papers beginning in the early 1990s, he acknowledges the Anomaly but does not consider it an important challenge to the Standard View. He sometimes presents the Standard View as a definitional truth. "Serious disabilities or handicaps will, by definition, typically reduce a person's quality of life" (Brock, 1995: 179). "[S]ince disabilities by definition under the ADA substantially limit one or more major life activities, they will reduce an individual's health-related quality of life" (Brock 2000: 226–7). According to the ADA definition, disabilities limit one or more major life activities. Why must we assume that unlimited major life activities are *by definition* required for a high QOL? Walking and seeing are often given as examples of major life activities. It might be argued that it is a matter of empirical fact that limitations in walking and seeing are associated with lower QOL. This would require empirical data about the correlation. Brock offers no data of this sort. The language of the ADA makes a semantic link only between disability and limitations, not between limitations and re-duced QOL. Brock is assuming some additional conceptual connection. I suggest that this conceptual connection is the Boorse/Daniels linkage between biological normality and "normal" opportunity discussed ear-lier. With the right kind of philosophical account, empirical evidence can appear irrelevant.[3]

In order to explain the Anomaly (and by the way protect the Standard View from refutation), Brock distinguishes between subjective and ob-jective QOL. Subjective QOL is how happy or satisfied one is with one's life. Objective QOL is how well one's life is *really* going. "To be satis-fied or happy with getting much less from life, because one has come to expect much less, is still to get *less* from life or to have a less good life" (Brock, 1993: 309). Reports of high QOL from disabled people are merely subjective.

What are the objective aspects of QOL? In the 1993 paper, Brock dis-cusses with approval an instrument called the Health Status Index (HSI). One of the scales on the HSI is said to judge the "mobility" of the in-dividual. The highest ranking is 5, for those who are able to use public transportation alone. Someone who requires assistance to use public transportation is scored 4, and someone who needs assistance to go out-side scores 3. Brock refers to this sort of scale as measuring "functions of the 'whole person'" (Brock, 1993: 298). The mobility measurement is conceived as a biomedical attribute of the individual being measured. A low mobility score constitutes a part of the objective basis on which the person's QOL is judged as objectively low, whatever the person's subjective opinion about that life.

Is "mobility" as thus measured a biomedical attribute of the indivi-dual? The slightest acquaintance with the Social Model of disability will show that the answer is no. Imagine a set of identical triplets, sis-ters with paraplegia who use wheelchairs and who live in different cities. The first lives in an inaccessible building and needs assistance to go outside. The second lives in an accessible building, but in a city in which public transportation is not wheelchair-accessible. The third lives in an accessible building in a city with accessible public transportation. These three score 3, 4, and 5 respectively on the "mobility" measure, even though they are biomedically identical. It is utter confusion to at-tribute their scores to their biomedical condition. The least mobile (call her Sister 3) is biomedically identical to the most mobile (Sister 5). The difference in mobility scores is caused by differences in environmental barriers. Blinkered by the Medical Model of disability, Brock and the

HSI present "mobility" as a measure of biomedical traits of individuals. It is not.

The same example illustrates the flaw in Daniels's identification of biological normality with opportunity range. The three sisters are biomedically identical, and so equally "abnormal" by Boorse's criteria. But Sister 5's opportunities are immensely broader than Sister 3's. This demonstrates that individual normality does not determine opportunity. The HSI "mobility" scores do measure something, but what they measure is not a biomedical characteristic of the sisters. As the Social Model shows us, it is the accessibility of their respective environments.

7. THE HAPPY SLAVE AND THE HAPPY HICK

In 1993, Brock explained the Anomaly as a mere effect of the lowered expectations of disabled people, and in 1995 he presented the Standard View as a definitional truth. In later papers, he has recognized that disabled people might accommodate their goals to their opportunities without necessarily *lowering* their expectations. But even with this less-belittling possibility, Brock remains committed to the Standard View and dismisses the Anomaly as reflecting subjective rather than objective QOL. Recent endorsements no longer appeal to specific definitional truths (i.e., disability defined as QOL-reducing). His intention is more generally to articulate *our concept of a good life*. This concept, according to Brock, contains both subjective and objective factors, and the objective factors include the absence of significant disabilities.

I am not at all sure what kind of evaluation standards are appropriate to an analysis of "our concept" of QOL. Social critics, after all, claim that some of society's dominant concepts are flawed and objectionable. A correct account of a flawed concept has great charms to those who do not recognize the flaw. Is such an account good because it is true to the concept, or bad because the concept is flawed? A correct account of "our concept of race" to white Americans in the 1830s would surely have included innate variations in intellectual and moral capabilities among races. So I am tempted simply to grant Brock the correctness of his account of the Standard View as "our concept of QOL" and go on to critique that concept itself. The fact that it's "our concept" doesn't make it right. However, Brock does not merely assert the accuracy of his account. He gives one argument for it, involving the example of the Happy Slave. I will therefore examine the extent to which the Happy Slave example supports the Standard View.

If a slave happened to have a high degree of subjective satisfaction with his life, would we be compelled to agree with him? Would we agree with those oppressed women in sexist societies who experience their lives as having high quality? Brock says that we would not. Slavery and oppression reduce the quality of life even for those of the oppressed who do not subjectively recognize the fact. In order to be able to judge that an oppressed person is mistaken about the quality of his or her own life, we must be able to distinguish between subjective and objective QOL. Since we already need to use the objective/subjective QOL distinction to deal with the Happy Slave example, that same distinction can be deployed on the Anomaly.

I am willing to accept the coherence of the distinction between objective and subjective QOL as exemplified by the Happy Slave. But the epistemic status of this kind of judgment about other people's lives is far from sturdy. The logical coherence of objective QOL is a necessary but not a sufficient condition for the correctness of the Standard View. In addition to a proof of coherence, Brock needs evidence of *truth*. At best, the Happy Slave implies only coherence but not truth. It shows that logic alone does not prohibit a third-person judgment of QOL that differs from the judgment of the subject. But something more than logic is needed to warrant specific judgments. How are we to separate judgments that are objectively grounded from those that merely express one's prejudices? Separating the wheat from the chaff requires more than logic. It requires epistemology.

The Happy Slave case is effective because its epistemological credentials are built into the case. We (the third-person judges) can understand a slave's failure to recognize an injustice or a social alternative that outside observers (like us) can perceive. We recognize oppression, and the possibilities of liberation, in ways that slaves and women in sexually oppressive societies do not. Our superior knowledge allows us to trump their subjective judgments with our objective ones. But not all judgments are made from such high epistemic vantage points. The epistemics of the Happy Slave case cannot be extrapolated to every other case in which we want to pass judgment on someone else's life.

Take, for example, the Anomaly. The disabled subjects in these studies know full well their own impairments. They are able to describe in detail the day-to-day difficulties that they can cause, and they realize (sometimes with amusement) that nondisabled people assume them to have a low QOL (Albrecht and Devlieger, 1999). Many acquired their impairments late in life, and so have lived both with and without impairments.

By contrast, most members of the nondisabled public have never experienced life with a significant impairment, and know about impairment only through its social stigma. Who is judging from ignorance? On what grounds does Brock favor the opinions of nondisabled over disabled people, when the issue is itself the QOL of disabled people? The Happy Slave is presumed to be ignorant of the delights of freedom. What ignorance burdens disabled people, and why is it so much greater than the ignorance of the nondisabled majority? Does the advocate of the Standard View really want to claim that nondisabled people *know better than* disabled people what the different lives are like?

Come to think of it, the answer is obvious. *Of course* the advocate of the Standard View wants to claim this. The testimony of disabled people about their lives has been dismissed in favor of that of nondisabled "experts" for a very long time, as historians have documented (Longmore and Umanski, 2001). The real question is this: *when* nondisabled people claim to know better than disabled people what the different lives are like, why should they be believed? Why should the opinions of nondisabled people be epistemologically privileged over those of disabled people?

Judging the lives of others is epistemologically hazardous, even if irresistible. The life of a pious person, or an urbanite, or a parent of a large family is bewildering to me. I gossip and joke about it when I'm with like-minded people. I would never voluntarily exchange my situation for that of a person in any of those categories. Even so, it would be presumptuous of me to claim that the quality of one of those lives is merely subjectively high, and that on objective grounds (known to me and my like-minded friends) it is low.

People who live in rural areas are called *hicks* by some urban people who feel themselves to have superior lives. (Why would anyone give up the symphony just to breathe clean air?) The happiness of hicks is regarded as merely subjective by the sophisticates who judge them. Some of the more reflective sophisticates (some college professors, for example) might realize that their feeling of QOL superiority over hicks is not really an objective judgment trumping a subjective judgment. It is merely one person's subjective judgment clashing with another person's. The Happy Slave example illustrates the coherence of objective judgments on the quality of other peoples' lives, using a plausible case of a correct judgment. But it gives us no hints about how to tell correct judgments from mere prejudices. The Happy Hick exemplifies mere prejudice in a logically similar judgment.

The Standard View is very widespread. Is that because of the superior knowledge of nondisabled people about the lives of disabled people? Or is it merely a reflection of the stigma of disability? The Happy Slave has nothing to tell us. The fact that we *can* trump subjective QOL judgments with judgments *that we believe* are objective does not mean that we are correct when we do so. When our "objective" judgments happen to match our own social prejudices, that coincidence alone should make us wary about our own objectivity. The Happy Slave example gives no epistemological support to Brock's judgment that he can make better judgments than disabled people about their QOL. In the absence of a genuine epistemological basis, it's just a conflict between subjectivities.

Nevertheless, the mere coherence of the objective/subjective distinction does leave open the possibility that a legitimate epistemological basis might be found for an objective assessment of the QOL of disabled people. Some of the following considerations lead us further in that direction.

8. PENALIZING HEALTH CARE PRIORITIES BY QOL

This section will discuss one application of the Standard View of disability and QOL to health care policy. The particular application is not one that the philosophers so far discussed have endorsed. In fact, Dan Brock specifically rejects it (Chapter 3, this volume). But the case does show that the Standard View can be a direct and tangible threat to disabled people. The notion of *quality-adjusted life years* (QALYs) is common in discussions of health care rationing and prioritization. If health care funds are prioritized to maximize QALYs, then funding for people with low QOL should receive a lower priority for the same kinds of care than funding for people with high QOL. On this approach, the Standard View would entail lower levels of health care for disabled people than for nondisabled people.

This section will discuss one particular justification of the policy of health care priority penalization for disabled people. I will term this the Menzel Criterion, because of its expression in a paper by Paul T. Menzel, though he may not endorse this use (Menzel, 1992).[4] The Menzel Criterion states, roughly, that priority considerations that are applied to nondisabled people can be justly applied to disabled people as well. A criterion would be unjust only if it were applied to disabled people but never applied to nondisabled people. This is a very weak criterion, in that a policy that satisfies it may be unjust in many other ways. I do not believe that priority penalization satisfies even this weak criterion, but it fails in an interesting way. The failure is revealing about the Standard View. Here is how the Menzel Criterion would apply to QALY priority penalization of disabled people.

Let us use the term "discrimination" in a morally neutral sense, so that some cases of discrimination are just and some are unjust. Unjust cases of discrimination are those in which it is directed against a member of a "protected class," a class of people against whom discrimination has been practiced for social reasons unrelated to the legitimate goals of some activity. If one is hiring a carpenter, discrimination against people who are unskilled carpenters is not unjust. This is true even if the unskilled carpenter happens to be a woman, a member of a protected class. It is unjust to refuse to hire the woman only if her sex rather than her carpentry skill is the basis of the decision not to hire. An employer could defend against a complaint of unjust hiring practices by showing that other women with higher carpentry skills were hired, and that men who had skills comparable to the complainant were not hired. This would demonstrate that discrimination was based on skill level rather than protected class membership, and so was not unjust.

Health care discrimination might be defended in the same way. Suppose a member of an ethnic minority were refused a heart transplant on the grounds that the operation had a low probability of success. Suppose the decision were challenged as unfair discrimination against an ethnic minority. The decision could be defended by showing that other members of the minority whose probability of success was higher did receive the procedure, and that nonminority patients whose probability of success was similar to the patient's were also refused the procedure.

Consider disability in place of minority status. If some feature X that happens to correlate with disability reduces a patient's ranking in health care prioritization, but the priority judgments are made on the basis of feature X and not based on the disability status per se, then it could be argued that the discrimination is just (if discrimination on the basis of X is otherwise just). Evidence that the priority rankings were based on X rather than on disability could come from that fact that disabled people who do not have trait X are not priority penalized, and that nondisabled people who do have trait X are priority penalized.

Does the use of the Standard View together with QALY health care rationing pass the Menzel Criterion? If people with equal QOLs are treated equally by the scheme, then low QOL rather than disability is the discriminatory factor. Are the advocates of QALY calculations willing to apply the same standards to nondisabled people with low QOL that they apply to disabled people?

It doesn't matter whether objective or subjective QOL measures are used for this purpose. A workable system would probably require the use of objective measures. (Although it is entertaining to imagine a government bureau of sadness detectives, whose job is to unmask unhappy patients who were only *pretending* to be happy in order to increase their health care coverage.) By the line of reasoning so far discussed, the primary objective measure of QOL is range of opportunity. Discriminating against disabled people because of their narrow range of opportunity passes the Menzel Criterion only if nondisabled people are penalized by reduced opportunity range in the same ways as disabled people.

If disability penalization is replaced by narrow-opportunity-range penalization, who else would suffer? Brock mentions in passing two examples of opportunity reduction from sources other than disability. "In the absence of a disability, many of us undergo more-limited changes of this sort as a result of changes in opportunities which accompany such major life changes as a move from city to rural life, taking up a very different occupation, and so forth" (Brock 1995: 183). How much opportunity loss is experienced by a person with urban aims and goals who is forced by contingencies to live in a rural environment (or, for that matter, vice versa)? How much is lost in a major unwanted job change – or, for that matter, in long-term unemployment? How much opportunity loss is associated with unwanted pregnancies? with family illnesses? I do not know, but neither does the advocate of QALY rationing. The most obvious and dramatic cause of opportunity loss is surely poverty. Children born in poverty have an extremely low range of opportunity. Is this a reason to cut back on health care for poor people?

I do not claim that disabled people as a class have a wider opportunity range in today's world than the other classes of people just cited. I simply don't know. But neither do the advocates of QALY health care rationing. I submit that the public at large would not tolerate the lowering of health care priorities for people with a reduced range of opportunities *who are not disabled*. I therefore conclude that the use of the "objective" measure of opportunity range in the priority penalization of disabled peoples' health care fails to satisfy the Menzel Criterion. It does not apply equally to disabled and nondisabled citizens. Opportunity loss is a smoke screen hiding the real grounds for discrimination – the stigma attached to disability itself. Opportunity losses *can only* be socially accepted as justifications for priority penalization if they are sustained by disabled people. This practice does indeed discriminate unfairly against people with disabilities – it discriminates against them *only because* they are disabled.

I must repeat that the Menzel Criterion is a very weak criterion of justice, and social policies that pass it might well fail on other grounds. Even this low hurdle is too high for the policy of QALY priority penalization for disabled people.[5] I will now discuss one higher hurdle, a hurdle that I believe would block priority penalization for disabled people even if the Menzel criterion were satisfied. This criterion would disallow practices that perpetuate an existing injustice, even if they did so in a way that satisfied the Menzel Criterion.

9. JUST AND UNJUST QOL REDUCTION

One problematic feature of QALY criteria for prioritization is that they are insensitive to the causes of reduced QOL. Intuitively, one might think that unjust reductions in life quality might receive a different treatment than just ones. Perhaps a naïve assumption is being made that all of the influences on QOL are matters of fortune, undeserved by the recipient but not unjust. But suppose that reduced QOL arises from social oppression. If we use opportunity range as the operationalization of QOL, it would be easy to argue that women and African Americans have significantly lower opportunity ranges in the United States with respect to both employment and freedom from harassment. Could these very real opportunity losses be used to justify reduction in health care priority? I seriously doubt it – at least not without strong resistance from the affected groups.

Why haven't QOL reductions been discussed as a factor in health care prioritization for *nondisabled* people? I suspect that it is because opportunity losses due to sex or race are seen as unrelated to health care, while the same reductions are seen as a health care issue when they coincide with disability. This is simply another begging of the question in favor of the Medical Model and against the Social Model of disability. According to the Social Model, the opportunities lost to disabled people are taken away by unjust and discriminatory social barriers, not by biomedical conditions. Similar social barriers disadvantage women and racial minorities. If we are unwilling to penalize women and racial minorities for the QOL consequences of the discrimination they experience, it is unjust to penalize disabled people for the same consequences.

The concept of *health-related* quality of life (HRQOL) is sometimes used in this context. This use of HRQOL as a substitute for QOL is simply the gerrymandering of social problems into medical ones. If disability is defined as a health-related problem, then the QALY advocates can use health care priorities as a stick to beat disabled people. The same treatment would not be tolerated with respect to sex or race. Consider again the three sisters. They are biomedically indistinguishable, but they differ immensely in their HSI-defined "mobility." The opportunity restrictions experienced by Sister 3 (the least mobile) are caused not by her biomedical condition but by her inaccessible surroundings. This fact is merely disguised by referring to her "health-related quality of life." Sister 3 is already penalized by her inaccessible environment. To compound the penalty by cutting her health care because of her inaccessible environment would surely be unjust.

I submit that a policy of priority penalization for people whose low QOL stems from social oppression could not be socially negotiated. (Surely the wretched medical treatment of slaves in the American South prior to emancipation is in no way excused because they had a low QOL anyway.) I further submit that a policy of priority penalization based on "objective" factors such as reduced opportunity range could not be negotiated so long as it was applied without discrimination. For these reasons, I conclude that the application of these penalties to disabled people is based *only on their stigmatized status*, and not on their alleged low QOL.[6]

The outcome of this discussion is not entirely negative. Notice that I have been comparing objective QOL measures for both disabled and nondisabled people. I have not been relying on subjective reports alone. This opens the possibility for an empirically grounded and epistemologically respectable comparison of disabled and nondisabled QOL. Such a comparison might replace the subjective (nondisabled person's) intuition that disability *must* reduce QOL. Some details about the subjective QOL reports of disabled people (the Anomaly) will suggest some possible avenues of study.

10. DETAILS OF THE ANOMALY

Let us now consider some details of the various surveys relating to the QOL of disabled people. One pair of correlations is especially interesting (Fuhrer et al., 1992; Bach and Tilton, 1994; Nosek, Fuhrer, and Potler, 1995). First, within categories of impairment (e.g., spinal cord injury, polio paralysis), the reported QOL of disabled people does not statistically correlate with the severity of their impairment. But it does correlate with measurements of what the World Health Organization (WHO) used to label "handicap." (The WHO has since revised this vocabulary, but I will retain it because it was used in the cited research.)[7] WHO handicap refers to the extent to which a disabled person is able to fulfill the social roles that are considered normal for the person's age, gender, and culture. Aspects of handicap that were measured in these studies included reduced social integration, reduced "occupation" (spending time in ways typical of one's peers, as in employment or homemaking), and reduced mobility. As we saw in the earlier discussion of the HSI, mobility is not a characteristic of an individual. Rather, it is the interactive effect of a person's physical abilities and the environment in which the person lives. As seen in the case of the three sisters, WHO handicaps vary greatly among people with identical impairments.

The correlation of reported QOL with WHO handicap rather than with degree of impairment shows that the self-perceptions of disabled people are not reflected in the Standard View. Subjective QOL did not track the degree of disabled people's impairments ("abnormalities"), but rather the accessibility of their environments whatever their impairments happened to be. People who were unable to occupy themselves appropriately, to maintain social contacts, and to move about in their community had a lower QOL. People who were able to do these things had a higher QOL.

Consider again the way the WHO defined "handicap": a person is handicapped when the person has impairments *and* the person is unable to fill certain the usual social functions. Let us call those social functions the *social correlates* of WHO handicap. Notice that the social correlates apply to many people who are not disabled. Many nondisabled people lack mobility, are unemployed, and are socially isolated. Those people would probably report a low subjective QOL, just like people who have WHO handicaps. People who are able to spend their time in culturally appropriate ways (e.g., in employment, domestic activities, and recreation), who have strong social ties, and who can move throughout their community are happy. People who satisfy the WHO social correlates for handicap (e.g., who are unemployed and socially isolated) are unhappy whether or not they also happen to be disabled. The factors that differentiate between people with high and low QOL can be seen as objective factors that are *only contingently associated* with impairment. Perhaps we can make epistemologically sound judgments about the QOL of disabled people after all! We need not rely on intuitive conceptual connections between disability and low QOL – we can study the patterns of correlation between impairments and the objective correlates of QOL.

If the factors that relate to high and low QOL are really the same for disabled and nondisabled people, then one way of making an objective assessment of the QOL of disabled people is to measure those correlates. Here we can actually find evidence of a lower QOL for disabled people. Consider QOL-lowering factors such as unemployment, isolation, and being a crime victim. Disabled people score significantly higher than nondisabled people on these factors. These are demographic facts, not philosophical intuitions or implications of "our concepts." Wouldn't these empirically measurable facts serve the biomedical ethicists better than conceptual analysis in proving the inherent superiority of the normal?

In fact, I believe they would not. When we get down to actual causes of disadvantage, and we study them in a way that allows unbiased empirical comparison between disabled and nondisabled people, the social causes become more apparent. Each of the demographic QOL-lowering factors that applies to disabled people at a higher rate than to nondisabled people *does so for social reasons*. The impact of the Social Model is much clearer when we attend to specifics than when we abstractly think of reified *abnormality* as a person-type. For example, consider crime victimization. Disabled people are no more responsible for the crimes committed against them than are the victims of rape; victimhood is no more *essentially* tied to disability than it is to womanhood. Consider unemployment and isolation. An important cause of unemployment and isolation is the lack of suitable transportation. This fact is true for disabled and nondisabled people alike. A wheelchair user in a town with wheelchair-inaccessible transportation is in a position very similar to that of a nondisabled person in a location that has no transportation. Neither can hold down a job, and each has limited social contacts.

Certain customary ways of talking disguise the fact that disabled and nondisabled people share the problem of transportation. Our bioethicists (and others) often label transportation that is accessible to disabled people as "special transportation." This label is merely one more way of stigmatizing disability, by falsely making it appear that "abnormal" people have different needs than "normal" people. Everyone needs transportation. No one needs *special* transportation! (Are racially integrated lunch counters *special* lunch counters?) When we look at the details, we see shared social problems. In order for these demographic facts to support the bioethical endorsement of normality, the bioethicists would have to *argue* that the Social Model is wrong and the Medical Model is right, that transportation is a different thing for disabled and nondisabled citizens. This is much harder to do when we attend to the actual causes of disadvantage in the world than when we assume it as an aspect of "our concept."

The Social Model of disability is not familiar to most disabled people who are not academics or activists. Nevertheless, their QOL reports indicate no correlation between low QOL and degree of impairment, and a positive correlation between low QOL and exactly those things that cause low QOL among nondisabled people. Life quality is best explained not by the disabled person's degree of "normality" but by environmental accessibility.

11. CONCLUSION

The Medical Model of disability and the Standard View of the low QOL of disabled people are shared by popular and academic culture. Biomedical discourse assumes that the disadvantages of disability are intrinsic to the disabled state itself, and that abnormality is penalized by nature itself. To the contrary, I have argued that

1. low QOL is less typical of disability than popularly perceived;
2. philosophical arguments to the contrary are uncompelling in the face of the Social Model;
3. the moderate lowering of QOL that is actually experienced by disabled people is more likely due to discriminatory treatment than to any intrinsic feature of disability;
4. the use of low QOL to discriminate against disabled people in health care prioritization is unjust unless nondisabled people are treated in the same way according to criteria that can apply to both, but that
5. the nondisabled public would never tolerate this treatment for themselves;
6. a truly objective and demographic study of low QOL among disabled people would show that it is caused by the same factors that cause low QOL among nondisabled people;
7. these factors are not essentially tied to impairment or abnormality but follow from social arrangements, and
8. the social arrangements that lower QOL are the same for disabled and nondisabled people alike.

Nevertheless, from one perspective I cannot quarrel with the philosophical analyses examined in this paper. They indeed represent "our concept of a good life," in the sense that they represent the dominant values and biases of popular and academic culture. The stigma of disability is embedded in those biases. Even a familiarity with the literature of the disability rights movement does not change that bias very much. The recent book *From Chance to Choice: Genetics and Justice* is coauthored by two of the bioethicists discussed here and two others – Allen Buchanan, Dan W. Brock, Norman Daniels, and Daniel Wikler (Buchanan et al., 2001). The book contains a great deal of discussion of disability activists' critiques of the uses of genetic technology. The authors give their liberal endorsement to the general goals of the disability rights movement, while rejecting almost every specific argument of its advocates. My interest is not in the authors' rejection of the disability rights arguments. It is rather in the fact that the authors show only a verbal understanding of the Social Model. Even after reporting, reasonably accurately, on the perspective itself, the authors immediately refer to the biomedical conditions of impairment and disability as the *direct causes* of disadvantage. Two examples:

We devalue disabilities because we value the opportunities and welfare of the people who have them. And it is because we value people, all people, that we care about limitations on their welfare and opportunities. We also know that disabilities as such diminish opportunities and welfare. . . . (Buchanan et al.: 278)

People with disabilities have more to gain from these [genetic] techniques than others do since their deficits, real and imagined, serve to marginalize and exclude them. (Buchanan et al.: 332)

Disabilities (all by themselves) limit welfare and opportunities. Deficits (all by themselves) marginalize and exclude people who have them. Elsewhere in the book, the authors acknowledge that social arrangements contribute to the disadvantage of people with impairments. But when they find themselves pledging their respect for people with impairments, the social causes of disadvantage are forgotten. This is the power of the Medical Model over biomedical ethics. No matter how sincere the authors' respect, the social causes of disadvantages are the first things to slip from their minds. From the perspective of the Social Model, the problem of disability has been whitewashed. The ethicists' explanation of exclusion as due to impairment makes no more sense than if they were to explain racial segregation as caused by *race itself*, as if the social phenomenon of racism played no part in the matter.

I confess that I have given the reader very little reason to actually *accept* the Social Model, to think of the range of impairments in much the same way that we now think of race and gender. That argument must be given elsewhere. But I will end with two observations that I consider relevant to the question. First, less than a century ago race and sex were themselves considered by the scientific community to be *literally* disabling. It was not a simple scientific discovery but a social change that gave rise to modern egalitarianism regarding sex and race. Disability activists envision a similar social change with respect to disability itself. It will require a change in "our concept of a good life," but a change no greater than those that have already happened regarding race and sex.

Finally, many bioethicists express a widespread but utopian hope that medical advances can wipe out or drastically reduce impairments ("...we are committed to the judgment that in the future the world should not include so many disabilities..." [Buchanan et al.: 278]). This vision is misplaced. Medical science does more than repair and prevent impairments. It also allows people to survive while living with impairments. A simple example is the fact that a person newly quadriplegic from a spinal cord injury had a life expectancy of less than a year prior to World War II. Today, the same person's life expectancy approaches that of an unimpaired person. The demographic consequence is that quadriplegics are a larger proportion of the population today than they were fifty years ago, and the same applies to many other impairments. Greater numbers of increasingly "abnormal" people are living among us, and the trend will continue. This spectacular achievement goes unnoticed by the biomedical advocates of normality. Despite the utopian rhetoric one sometimes hears from some enthusiasts of the Human Genome Project, tomorrow's world will contain a greater proportion of people with impairments than today's. The social movement for the civil rights of disabled people will certainly continue. It will not be rendered moot by idealistic dreams of biological perfection.[8]

NOTES

1. Here is a brief explanation of why I intend neither to defend the Social Model nor to work a compromise between the models. The Medical/Social contrast is a kind of nature/nurture debate. When a modest advocate of the

importance of nurture finds herself debating an extreme genetic determinist, her best tactic may be simply to try to prove that the genetic determinist has not taken social causes into account. She need not present an entire theory of the interplay of nature and nurture in order to demonstrate successfully that her adversary has failed to take account of nurture. I consider the Medical Model to be so dominant and so determinist that my only ambition is to convince the reader that an important perspective is being ignored. If it sounds as if I consider biology irrelevant to disability, that appearance is a by-product of my tactic.

2. Notice that I am already speaking as an activist. The Medical Model was given its name by advocates of the Social Model. Advocates of the Medical Model typically do not see it as a model at all, but rather as the simple truth.

3. The correlation between extremely wide opportunity range and QOL asserted by Daniels and Brock deserves further discussion. It does not seem to me to describe the expectations of average people. I consider it a kind of American cultural ideal that is satisfied only in a very few, very privileged people. Most people expect to make good lives within the limitations they encounter, and to make the best of what they have. Many things in life have very large effects on one's opportunity range. Few of these carry the stigma that disability carries.

4. Menzel suggests that QOL considerations used in rationing health care to disabled people should be "regarded as contrary to the ADA only if we would reject them as legitimate considerations if they were not sometimes to deny care to persons with disabilities" (Menzel, 1992, p. 24).

5. At least two stronger criteria for unfair discrimination exist. One would reject facially neutral practices that embody biased conceptions of the individuals under assessment, such as physical requirements for firefighters that are biased toward physical performances that are easier for men than for women. A second would require that practices be designed to redress past wrongs, such as affirmative action policies.

6. It has been pointed out that section 8 does not, while section 9 does, involve the Social Model in arguing against potentially discriminatory treatment of disabled people. This seems correct. The only relevance of the Social Model to section 8 is that *if* general social discrimination were ameliorated, as the Social Model implies it should be, then (according to the model) disabled people would not be grouped together with people of low QOL in the first place!

7. The 1980 document has been superceded by the International Classification of Functioning, Disability, and Health, from which the term "handicap" has been removed. See <www.who.int/icidh>.

8. This chapter has benefited from comments by the participants in the workshop. Anita Silvers, David Wasserman, and Jerome Bickenbach helped especially on points related to the ethical principles in sections 8 and 9. Thanks also to Shelley Tremain for discussion of *From Chance to Choice*, and to Larry Heintz for early wise advice.

REFERENCES

Albrecht, Gary, and Devlieger, Patrick. 1999. "The Disability Paradox: High Quality of Life Against All Odds." *Social Science and Medicine* 48: 977–88.

Amundson, Ron. 2000. "Against Normal Function." *Studies in the History and Philosophy of Biological and Biomedical Sciences* 31C: 33–53.

Bach, John R., and Tilton, Margaret C. 1994. "Life Satisfaction and Well-being Measures in Ventilator Assisted Individuals with Traumatic Tetraplegia." *Archives of Physical Medicine and Rehabilitation* 75: 626–34.

Boorse, Christopher. 1977. "Health as a Theoretical Concept." *Philosophy of Science* 44: 542–73.

Brock, Dan W. 1993. *Life and Death*. Cambridge: Cambridge University Press.

    1995. "Justice and the ADA: Does Prioritizing and Rationing Health Care Discriminate against the Disabled?" *Social Philosophy and Policy* 12: 159–85.

    2000. "Health Care Resource Prioritization and Discrimination against Persons with Disabilities." In Leslie Pickering Francis and Anita Silvers (eds.), *Americans with Disabilities: Exploring Implications of the Law for Individuals and Institutions*. New York: Routledge, pp. 223–35.

Buchanan, Allen E., et al. 2000. *From Chance to Choice: Genetics and Justice*. Cambridge: Cambridge University Press.

CBS *Morning Show*. Interview with Jerry Lewis. May 20, 2001.

Daniels, Norman. 1981. "Health-Care Needs and Distributive Justice." *Philosophy & Public Affairs* 10: 146–79.

    1985. *Just Health Care*. Cambridge: Cambridge University Press.

Fuhrer, Marcus J., Rintala, Diana H., Hart, Karen A., Clearman, Rebecca, and Young, Mary Ellen. 1992. "Relationship of Life Satisfaction to Impairment, Disability, and Handicap among Persons with Spinal Cord Injury Living in the Community." *Archives of Physical Medicine and Rehabilitation* 73: 552–7.

Longmore, Paul K., and Umanski, Lauri (eds.). 2001. *The New Disability History: American Perspectives*. New York: New York University Press.

Menzel, Paul T. 1992. "Oregon's Denial: Disabilities and Quality of Life." *Hastings Center Report* 22(6): 21–5.

Nosek, Margaret, Fuhrer, Marcus, and Potter, Carol. 1995. "Life Satisfaction of People with Physical Disabilities: Relationship to Personal Assistance, Disability Status, and Handicap." *Rehabilitation Psychology* 40: 191–202.

Silvers, Anita. 1998. "A Fatal Attraction to Normalizing." In Erik Parens (ed.), *Enhancing Human Traits: Ethical and Social Implications*. Washington, DC: Georgetown University Press, pp. 95–123.

Chapter 5

Values for Health States in QALYs and DALYs

Desirability versus Well-being and Worth

ERIK NORD

INTRODUCTION

In cost-utility analysis of health interventions, and in burden-of-disease measurement, health problems of different degrees of severity are assigned numerical scores on a scale from zero to unity. The scores are used to weight life years in calculations of quality-adjusted life years (QALYs) and disability-adjusted life years (DALYs). The scores are controversial for a number of reasons. One is that they may be seen as a devaluation of the lives of people with chronic illness or disability. While this is not necessarily the intention of the constructors and advocates of QALYs and DALYs, it is certainly the way in which people with chronic illness or disability tend to perceive these approaches (Dahl, 1992).

I believe some of the controversy over health state scores could be avoided if those who develop and use them could be both more clear and more restrictive about what the scores are supposed to mean. More specifically, I think there is a need to distinguish between the *worth* of a person with a given problem, the *well-being* associated with that problem, and the *desirability* of avoiding or getting rid of the problem. These are three separate issues. It is a serious mistake to think that they can be measured in the same way or expressed in one single index.

I discuss each of these concepts in the following. Then I explain a little more about QALYs and DALYs and show how the advocates of these measures have failed to clarify their meaning in the past. I proceed to argue that clarification of meaning helps to resolve the issue of "whom to ask" about health state values. Finally, I discuss the use of the term "quality of life" in relation to the concepts of subjective well-being and desirability.

DEFINITIONS

I define the *worth* of a person as the value attached by society to the enhancement of the interests and opportunities of that person relative to the interests and opportunities of other persons. One important form of enhancement of interest is the protection of the person's life. If society regards two persons as being of equal worth, it means, among other things, that it is willing to do equally much to protect their lives.

The worth of persons with specific traits may be judged differently by different people and different societies. Some judgments made by some people may be quite unacceptable to others. This is one of the themes of this paper, to which I will return.

I will use the expression *the value of a person's life* relative to another life as meaning much the same thing as the worth of a person. The value of a person's life is thus in my terminology different from the *quality* of it (see below).

I define *subjective well-being* as a personal emotional category, synonymous with the feeling of happiness, contentedness, satisfaction with life, having a good feeling inside, and so forth.

The *desirability* of a health state is perhaps most meaningfully defined through its counterpart, which is the *undesirability* of the health problems associated with the state. The undesirability of a health problem may be defined in two ways. Either it is the strength of the preference to be relieved of the problem, in terms of willingness to sacrifice, of a person with a given problem, or it is the strength of the preference to avoid getting the problem, in terms of willingness to sacrifice, of a person without the problem. I call the former desire for cure, and the latter desire to avoid.

Desire for cure is strongly related to expected gain in subjective well-being. But expected gain in subjective well-being is not the same as actual gain. A person who cannot walk may think that he would be much happier if he could walk. But it may not turn out to be so. The grass may seem greener on the other side of the fence, even when it isn't.

Similarly, desire to avoid a health problem is strongly related to the loss of subjective well-being believed to result from the problem. But expected loss in subjective well-being is not the same as actual loss. Viewed from the outside, a problem may look worse than it really is after one has learned to live with it.

In short, desirability has to do with cognitive assessment of objective symptoms and levels of functioning, while subjective well-being is the actual feeling of life as good as experienced by those who are in specific states.

As an aside, we may note that the separation of well-being from desirability runs counter to the conventional economic theory of welfare, in which the assumption is made that if A is preferred to B, then A in fact yields more well-being than B. The assumption is simplifying, inasmuch as it spares economists having to pass subjective, paternalist judgments on whether or not people's purchasing decisions actually give them utility gains. But the assumption has a weak empirical basis.

The term *quality of life* has come into widespread use in the last three decades. It is used in two different ways. Either it refers to subjective well-being and is thus synonymous with "happiness" and "utility" (Campbell et al., 1976), or it refers to an overall assessment of the goodness of a life when both subjective well-being and objective characteristics such as ablebodiedness, access to social activities, and standard of living are taken into account (Erikson and Åberg, 1987). In the latter case, the term "quality" (of life) takes on much the same meaning as "desirability." For reasons I will explain later, I shall use the term "quality of life" as synonymous with subjective well-being in the following.

QALYs AND DALYs

The use of health state scores in economic evaluation and decision analysis goes back more than forty years (Chiang, 1965). A scale running from zero (dead or as good as dead) to unity (full health) was adopted. The more burdensome a condition is to the individual concerned, the lower its score on the scale. Health state scores are used as weights for life years, so that, for instance, a year in a state with score 0.8 counts as 0.8 life years, and a given scenario of life years with chronic illness or disability comes out as equivalent to some lower number of life years in full health. The down-weighting of years with health problems is called "quality adjustment," and life years thus down-weighted are called quality-adjusted life years (QALYs). In cost-utility analysis, the benefit of a health intervention is expressed as the difference between the number of quality-adjusted life years the individual faces with and without intervention.

The idea of scoring health states and life years on a 0–1 scale was later adopted in burden-of-disease measurement (World Bank, 1993). Here the scale is turned around to become a severity scale, so that zero represents "no health problem" and unity represents being dead or some state equivalent to that. Life years adjusted for health problems are called disability-adjusted life years (DALYs). The DALY is used as a unit of measurement, meaning the value of a healthy life year or the equivalent of that. A life year in a state with a severity score of 0.2 counts as 0.8 healthy years. A gain of such a year thus yields 0.8 DALYs. The burden of disease associated with that year is 0.2 DALYs.

THE PROBLEM

The problem with QALYs and DALYs referred to in the previous section is that if health problem A is assigned a value of 0.8 (a severity weight of 0.2) in terms of *treatment desirability*, the following two interpretations are also possible:

a. Life-extending programs for people with problem A are deemed less valuable than similar programs for people in full health, all else being equal.
b. The quality of life of people with problem A is judged to be lower than than of people in full health.

The former proposition violates many people's ethical views. The latter proposition is inconsistent with the way many people with chronic conditions or disabilities actually feel about the quality of their own lives, and is therefore insulting.

THE WAY OUT

The obvious solution to the problem just described is to be more clear about the meaning of health state scores. Desirability, well-being, and worth are three different phenomena. Since they are different, we must be prepared to have three separate measures for them. It is only under very special circumstances – namely, when there is strong empirical covariation between them – that we can hope to use one single measure to cover them all.

Do we actually observe such covariation?

The answer is clearly no.

First, take desirability and well-being, and consider the case of wheelchair users. Is their condition as desirable as being in full health? Clearly it is not to people who are not dependent on a wheelchair themselves. They much prefer to be able to walk. And the wheelchair users can well understand them. In fact, were the wheelchair users offered a treatment that would restore their walking ability, most of them would probably accept it with joy (for notable exceptions, see Weinberg, 1984).

But are the wheelchair users unhappy? Well, some are, certainly, just as there are unhappy people among those who are able to walk. Also, some wheelchair users are certainly frustrated by their condition or "fate." But casual observation suggests that many accept their condition, focus on enjoyable things in life that do not require walking ability, and spend their lives in a reasonably good mood, often not much different from that of able people. For many of these people, it would clearly be wrong to say that their well-being is as poor as their condition is undesirable. Consequently, no one single number could appropriately express both the desirability of their condition and their well-being.

I present this as a casual observation that I feel certain most readers will recognize. For chronic illnesses and disabilities in general, such casual observation is supported by a host of empirical studies showing that in the long run well-being is often clearly less affected by health losses than one might expect at first glance (Pearlman and Uhlmann, 1989; Stewart et al., 1989).

If there is limited covariation between desirability and well-being, there is even less covariation between each of these, on the one hand, and the strength of claims on life-saving resources, on the other. In fact, the latter has very little do to with desirability and well-being. Within an extremely wide range of human functioning, all individuals are regarded as equally valuable (Universal Declaration of Human Rights, 1948) and hence equally worthy of continued life (Nord, 1993; Ubel et al., 2000). Admittedly, there are conditions that most people find undignified, conditions in which they would not wish to live or would not think it right to prolong other individuals' survival, particularly not at the expense of gaining good life years for other people. But such conditions are few and far between. The vast majority of people living with chronic illness or disability are perceived as living lives that are dignified and therefore fully worthy of protection, even if their lives are difficult and frustrating at times and not to be desired compared to a life in full health. Values assigned to health states on the basis of their desirability can therefore not serve as measures of the worth or value of life.

In summary, a single score for a health state, of the kind used in QALY and DALY calculations, cannot express the three types of value.

Providers of such scores need to choose *one* of the value concepts described here and make it clear that it is this, and only this, concept that the scores refer to. Inferences to be made from health state values – about welfare or health policy or whatever – will have to be restricted accordingly.

THE HISTORY OF QALYs

All this may seem trivial. But the history and current practice of health economics is quite problematic on these accounts.

First, desirability and subjective well-being have been conflated in the QALY literature. Early writers seem to have thought of utilities as measures of (ex post) subjective well-being. For instance, Weinstein and Stason (1977) propose the following question for eliciting preferences: "Taking into account your age, pain and suffering, immobility, and lost earnings, what fraction, P, of a year of life would you be willing to give up to be completely healthy for the remaining fraction of a year *instead of your present level of health status for the full year*?" (my italics). Clearly, this is asking for an ex post judgment. Presumably, many of those who refer to health state valuations as measurements of (health-related) *quality of life* have a similar focus on actual experience, given that in everyday language the term "quality of life" is often used synonymously with "subjective well-being." Moreover, while constructers of multiattribute utility instruments are in considerable disagreement about what their numbers precisely mean, they all claim that the numbers predict the sacrifices that patients would be willing to make to be relieved of their conditions (Nord and Wolfson, 1999). Such claims presuppose that the utilities reflect (ex post) well-being rather than ex ante desirability. On the other hand, multi-attribute utility instruments (MAU) are, in effect, based on questions to the general public about the (ex ante) *desirability* of different health states, and the U.S. Cost-effectiveness Panel (Gold et al., 1996) explicitly recommends that utilities be given this latter meaning. It is a confusing state of affairs.

Second, the distinction between the desirability of a condition and the worth of a person has generally been given little attention in the QALY literature. The *effect* of this has been to equate the two in QALY calculations. Since little has been written explicitly about the issue, it is not so easy to know exactly what values health economists actually hold regarding the worth of people with different levels of health. But one exchange in the literature gives us an idea. In a major critique of the whole QALY approach, Harris (1987: 121) wrote the following:

One of the prime functions of the State is to protect the lives and fundamental interests of its citizens and to treat each citizen as the equal of any other. . . . Society, through its public institutions, is not entitled to discriminate between individuals in ways that mean life or death for them on grounds which count the lives or fundamental interests of some as worth less than those of others. If for example some people were given life-saving treatment in preference to others because they had a better quality of life than those others, or more dependants and friends, or because they were considered more useful, this would amount to regarding such people as more valuable than others on that account. . . . Because my own life would be better and even of more value to me if I were healthier, fitter, had more money, more friends, more lovers, more children, more life expectancy, more everything I want, it does not follow that others are entitled to decide that because I lack some or all of these things I am less entitled to health care resources, or less worthy to receive those resources, than are others, or that those resources would somehow be wasted on me.

In response to this, Williams (1987) encapsulated his position in the following three propositions:

1. Health care priorities should be influenced by our capacity both to increase life expectation and to improve people's quality of life.
2. A particular improvement in health should be regarded as of equal value, no matter who gets it, and should be provided *unless it prevents a greater improvement being offered to someone else* [my italics].
3. It is the responsibility of everyone to discriminate wherever necessary to ensure that our limited resources go *where they will do the most good* [my italics].

Williams went on to express "very serious doubts . . . as to whether Harris realised the grave implications of the position he had adopted."

In the context of Harris's critique, Williams's response seems clearly to imply that if a heart transplant could be offered to either a blind person or a sighted person (all else being equal), Williams would at the time have given priority to the latter, since more QALYs would be gained. This would have meant equating desirability with worth. Whether Williams would make the same choice today is not clear. I have earlier proposed that for all health states that are preferred to death, all saved life years should count as one (Nord, 1999). This proposal and related ideas are further discussed elsewhere (Nord et al., 1999; Menzel et al., 1999; Ubel et al., 2000). Williams (2001) strongly disagrees with my proposal, which he interprets as follows: "Thus, whether people can be offered miserable extra years or healthy extra years would make no difference. . . . the benefits of each intervention should be regarded as equally valuable!" The exclamation mark is presumably there to suggest that the proposal is too unreasonable to deserve more careful consideration.

Williams goes on instead to recommend the application of the fair innings argument in economic evaluation, since "this does not require us to detach the value of a better quality of life from the value of additional life years." The fair innings approach centers initially on the feeling that everyone is entitled to some "normal" number of life years – say, seventy to seventy-five years in Western Europe. The implication is that anyone failing to achieve this life span has in some sense been cheated, while anyone getting more than this is "living on borrowed time" (Williams, 1997: 119). Williams proposes that gained life years in people facing less than a fair innings should be valued more highly (be assigned a larger weight) than life years gained in people expecting to have a fair innings or more. Williams furthermore argues that in order to

capture the full flavour of this kind of thinking, the concept of a 'fair innings' needs to be extended beyond simple life expectancy to embrace quality-adjusted life expectancy. Otherwise it will not be possible to reflect the view that a lifetime of poor quality health entitles people to special consideration in the current allocation of health care, even if their life expectancy is normal. (p. 121)

So, for instance, if quality-adjusted life expectancy (QALE) is 70 QALYs in a population as a whole, and this is considered to be a fair innings, and QALE is 73, 67, and 64 QALYs in subgroups A, B, and C respectively, then (according to Williams) QALYs gained in subgroup C should be weighted more than QALYs gained in subgroup B, which in turn should be weighted more than QALYs gained in subgroup A.

However, equity weights for QALYs based on the fair innings argument are, according to Williams, meant to encapsulate a *trade-off* between efficiency and equity. For instance, ten gained years for a disabled person with utility level 0.8 might be assigned an equity weight of 1.1. The ten gained years for the disabled person would then be as valuable as 8.8 gained years for a person in full health. But the gained years for the disabled person would still be less valuable than an equal number of years gained for a person in full health. The point is simply that weights that are meant to encapsulate *trade-offs* by definition do *not* encapsulate the principle of protecting the lives of the disabled and the nondisabled *equally strongly*. They do not do so because they are not meant to do so, and that is precisely the ethical problem.

THE HISTORY OF DALYs

With DALYs, practice regarding the valuing of life is internally inconsistent: in burden-of-disease measurements, each *lost* life year is counted as one, whatever the level of health of that year would have been. At the same time, in cost-effectiveness analysis, *gained* life years are discounted by their disability weight. The writing on this point by the developers of DALYs is equally inconsistent. On the one hand, Murray seems to think that all (or most) lives are equally valuable when he states that "I find this attribute of cost-effectiveness analysis (i.e. devaluing lives in less than perfect health [author's comment]), as currently practiced, a vexing moral problem" (1996: 31–2). On the other hand, Murray's 1996 DALY valuation protocol takes it for granted that respondents will value life-extending programs for disabled people less than life-extending programs for otherwise healthy people.

Let me explain the latter point in detail. Disability weights in DALYs used to be based on valuing health states on a rating scale from 0 to 1. In 1995, the rating scale approach was replaced by a variant of the person trade-off technique (PTO). This technique consists in asking subjects to state their preferences between projects with different health outcomes rather than to value health states as such (Nord, 1992). From these stated preferences, which are essentially resource allocation preferences, values for health states (or disability weights) to be used in burden-of-disease calculations or cost-effectiveness analysis may be inferred. An example is as follows. You are told that you can either save ten lives or cure X people with condition A. What must the number X be for you to be indifferent between the two options? If a sample of subjects on average answer $X = 50$, then the disability weight of condition A, according to these people, is $10/50 = 0.2$, and the value of condition A is $1 - 0.2 = 0.8$.

When subjects answer questions of this kind, they may take into account both the size of the health gain in each option and concerns for fairness, including perhaps concerns they might hold for giving priority to the worse off. Person trade-off questions are, in other words, *meant* to incorporate concerns for fairness in valuations of health states (or in the assessment of the severity of a disease).

In the Global Burden of Disease (GBD) Project, person trade-off questions have since 1995 been framed in two different ways. Take, for example, the state "blindness." First subjects are asked what is referred to as "PTO1" (although in other words): Project A can extend the life of 1,000 healthy people by one year, while project B can extend the life of X blind people by one year. What must X be for you to consider the two projects equally valuable? Then subjects are asked "PTO2": Project A can extend the life of 1,000 healthy people by one year, while project B can give Y people their eyesight back for one year. What must Y be for you to consider the two projects equally valuable?

Assume that the median answer to PTO1 is 2,000. That implies a value for blindness of 0.5 ($1,000 \times 1.0 = 2,000 \times 0.5$). Assume that the median answer to PTO2 is 4,000. That implies a value for "blindness" of 0.75 ($1,000 \times 1.0 = 4,000 \times (1 - 0.75)$).

Invariably (and unsurprisingly, given our general knowledge about framing effects in preference measurement), PTO1 and PTO2 produce different health state values. In the GBD project, it is assumed that in calculations of burden of disease or cost-effectiveness, a single value for each health state is required. In a second step of the valuation process, subjects are therefore instructed to adjust their initial responses to PTO1 and PTO2 so that they yield the same values.

When I say that the GBD project has taken it for granted that subjects will find it less valuable to extend the life of disabled people than to extend the life of healthy people, I first have in mind the start point of the excercise: 1,000 healthy against 2,000 blind people. Why doesn't it start with 1,000 versus 1,000? There is no mention of the ethical argument in favor of regarding all lives as equally valuable (at least, all lives above some minimum level of functioning and well-being). Altogether, the question seems to *invite* responses that run counter to this basic egalitarian argument (Arnesen and Nord, 1999).

The second problem is that it is very difficult for subjects doing valuations in the GBD project to stick to the egalitarian argument even if they should happen to think about it and agree with it, since they are forced to reach numerical consistency between PTO1 and PTO2. In practice, we must assume that this means reaching a compromise between the two initial valuations.

The odd thing is that there is no mathematical need for numerical consistency of this kind in measuring burden of disease. It is perfectly possible to have a valuation model that counts lost life years in disabled people as heavily as lost life years in healthy people, and which uses severity weights to quantify losses associated with living with illness relative to the loss of losing life itself. I therefore submit that DALYs have been operationalized differently not out of logical necessity, but rather because of a heritage from utilitarian thinking in the QALY approach, in which one single value for each health state seemed natural and in which the equal valuation of life for disabled people was not recognized as a salient societal concern.

Murray and Acharaya (1997: 726) explicitly defended the value assumption of PTO1 against criticism from Anand and Hanson (1997) when they claimed that "the results are quite consistent across groups that individuals prefer, after appropriate deliberation, to extend the life of healthy individuals rather than those in a health state worse than perfect health." It is unclear to me whether they would still defend this position. But it is a fact that the WHO now is exploring alternative ways of valuing health states, particularly ways that focus on the quantification of health only and avoid controversial ethical distributive issues (Murray, Salomon, and Mathers, 1999).

WHOM TO ASK

I concluded earlier that providers of health state scores need to choose *one* value concept and make it clear that it is this, and only this, concept that their scores refer to. Inferences to be made from health state values – about welfare or health policy or whatever – will have to be restricted accordingly.

An important benefit resulting from such conceptual clarification is that the thorny issue of "who should be asked to value health states" then partly resolves itself. If health state values are supposed to indicate subjective well-being, then obviously one must ask people with direct experience of the kinds of ill health in question – that is, current or former patients and disabled persons. Alternatively, if health state values are supposed to reflect the ex ante undesirability of different conditions (desire to avoid), then samples of people in normal health are the appropriate people to ask.

What kind of people in normal health one might ask is yet another question. Ex ante undesirability depends heavily on how informed people are. The U.S. Cost-effectiveness Panel (Gold et al., 1996) argued that health state values should be elicited from informed members of the public. Being informed must in this case include knowing how states of illness or disability are experienced by those who are actually in them.

This means that even if one wants health state values to reflect ex ante undesirability, one would need to elicit valuations from people with direct experience first and then feed this information to those people in normal health from whom one wanted judgments of undesirability. Those people would then not be representative of the general public. Given the difficulty of the valuation task, they would to some extent have to be selected on the basis of intelligence and education in the first place, and then they would have to be educated even further (about experiences with illness). The status to be assigned to judgments from these people in resource allocation decisions would have to depend on the intensity and degree of success of the latter education.

As noted earlier, the WHO now is exploring ways of valuing health states that focus on the quantification of health only, with a view to avoiding both controversial distributive judgments in resource allocation and the issue of the valuation of life itself in people with less-than-perfect health. It seems that in this endeavor, the WHO will focus on the ex ante undesirability of diseases rather than on the actual subjective well-being associated with them. It remains to be seen whether these ex ante judgments of undesirability will be based on satisfactory information about the actual well-being in the chronically ill and disabled.

QUALITY OF LIFE

As noted earlier, the term "quality of life" can be used with two different meanings. Either it refers to subjective well-being, or it refers to an overall assessment of the goodness of a life when both subjective well-being and objective characteristics such as ablebodiedness, access to social activities, and standard of living are taken into account.

The two different uses are in part due to differences in views on the measurability of inner feelings (Moum, 1993). Those who are skeptical about such measurements tend to have recourse to the measurement of observable traits that are commonly regarded as conducive to happiness, and then, for simplicity, to refer to these measurements as measurements of quality of life.

But this is not the whole explanation. Regardless of measurement problems, some feel that the desirability of a life is not determined by subjective well-being only (Brock, 2001). They are concerned about *opportunities*. They say that even if person A has the same subjective well-being as person B, all things considered person B's life may still be better and more desirable – for instance, because he objectively has access to a number of enjoyable activities and goods that are inaccessible to A. People who hold this position tend to use the term "quality of life" to designate the overall desirability of a condition rather than to indicate subjective well-being only.

Note that the issue here is not whether opportunities influence well-being. Surely they often do so in a positive way. An uneducated, unemployed, poor person is likely to feel a whole lot better if given the opportunity for free schooling and a paid job. The point, however, is that the same level of subjective well-being (happiness, contentedness) may be observed in people who differ enormously in opportunities. The question is whether these people may be said to have the same quality of life, or whether those with more opportunities have a higher one.

Note also that the issue is not whether reports of high well-being in people with fewer opportunities than others are false (i.e., exaggerated). I am referring to the fact that some people think that the life of person B in the earlier example is of higher quality than the life of person A, even if they accept that the well-being of the two is the same. The issue is thus not potential measurement error, but disagreement about what *constitutes* quality of life. Some say that subjective well-being is all that matters, while others claim that some opportunities are valuable per se.

One might argue that the issue is merely a matter of definition, and that it is immaterial which of the two definitions of "quality of life" is chosen as long as the definition is made explicit. But I don't think that is true. The term "quality of life" has a strong positive, normative loading. When analysts and decision makers use it to characterize a given life, it refers to how good or desirable they consider that life to be relative to other lives or kinds of life, and thus *to the strength of their preference for seeking or allowing or encouraging that kind of life relative to seeking or allowing or encouraging other kinds of life.* This is the way the term "quality of life" is understood and functions in everyday language and communication. Quality of life is right at the top of people's goal hierarchy – together with protection of life itself. Any attempt to define "quality of life" ad hoc as something less is bound to create confusion and misunderstanding.

To choose between the two definitions of quality of life is therefore to some extent also to make a material value judgment – namely, to decide which is the more important goal for policy making: (a) to maximize individuals' subjective well-being or (b) to maximize a combination of their well-being and their opportunities. In the latter case, opportunities are viewed as having intrinsic value. The possibility of sacrificing well-being in order to win opportunities then arises as a logical consequence.

I am personally wary of assigning value to opportunities per se. The reason is that when we value opportunities per se, we tend to value *specific* opportunities per se – namely, those opportunities that are important to ourselves. We tend to overestimate the importance of these specific opportunities to people different from ourselves and to underestimate the specific opportunities enjoyed by people living in circumstances different from our own.

To see how problematic it potentially can be to value specific opportunities per se, consider the valuation of opportunities that flow from money and intelligence. People strive for wealth way beyond necessity in order to obtain all sorts of opportunities – often with a sad loss of peace of mind and heart as a result. Similarly, many parents are extremely ambitious on behalf of their children with respect to intellectual achievement or to cultivating all sorts of capabilities in music, sports, and so on. The resulting opportunities for these children are, in a sense, impressive. But the downside may be the development of stress, competitiveness, and selfishness and the loss of empathy, kindness, and personal serenity – all of which are essential (negatively or positively) for human well-being.

It seems to me that the heart of the problem in these examples is precisely the valuation of certain goods and activities per se. Having a big house and a big car is turned into a goal in itself. Living with such items is deemed "better" per se than living in a small house without a car. Similarly, a person who enjoys Bach is automatically considered richer than a person who never heard of Bach and instead enjoys watching a game of football.

I call this "value absolutism." It is the belief that what is valuable to me is valuable to everybody. To me, it is cultural naivité and arrogance at the same time. It is related to the attitude that "what I personally am unfamiliar with and/or do not understand is probably of lesser value." It can, at worst, be a form of authoritarian attitude, an expression of lack of humility. But even if that is not the explanation or the intention, the effect of the attitude can easily be repressive to those on the receiving end.

The tendency to regard some of our own values as true in some absolute and objective sense is deeply imbedded in most of us, probably for historical, Darwinistic reasons. I believe that it is a continuing moral challenge for each of us to restrict this tendency in our daily lives.

So this is the reason why I dislike using the term "quality of life" to include specific objective traits of a person's situation. Those specific traits are selected on the basis of some outside judges' personal values and preferences. The more I think about it, the more I find such selections – often made by a very small, healthy, wealthy, highly educated, culturally biased part of the world's population – to be of quite limited interest.

I believe that the opportunities for human well-being are almost limitless. Under almost all imaginable sorts of conditions, people have found peace and happiness throughout the history of mankind. These widely different cultures and sets of values deserve our respect. One way of expressing such respect is not to place too much emphasis on objective characteristics per se in the valuation of a person's life.

For these reasons, I use the term "quality of life" to mean "subjective well-being." If a person reports high subjective well-being in a convincing way, then I think we should conclude that his or her quality of life is good. Full stop. I see no good reason why we should try to impose our personal values on others.

CONCLUSION

There is a need to distinguish between the *worth* of a person with a given problem, the *well-being* associated with that problem, and the *desirability* of avoiding or getting rid of the problem. These are three separate issues. It is a serious mistake to think that they can be measured in the same way or expressed in one single index of the kind used in QALY and DALY calculations.

The equal worth of persons with different levels of health must be respected. Values for health states must therefore be interpreted either in terms of well-being or in terms of the desirability of avoiding or getting rid of a problem. Providers of health state scores and/or disability weights need to choose *one* of these two value concepts and make it clear that it is this, and only this, concept that they are trying to operationalize and quantify. Being clear about this choice makes it easier to judge and reach agreement about the validity of different candidate quantification procedures. For instance, it resolves the issue of "whom to ask" about health state values. Inferences to be made from health state values – about welfare or health policy or whatever – will have to be restricted in accordance with their clearly defined meaning.

Additionally, I suggest that the term "quality of life" be used as synonymous with subjective well-being, as judgments based on a wider definition of the term that includes objective characteristics tend to imply some people's imposition of their own values on others.

REFERENCES

Anand, S., and Hanson, K. 1997. "Disability-Adjusted Life Years: A Critical Review." *Journal of Health Economics* 16: 685–702.

Arnesen, T., and Nord, E. 1999. "The Value of DALY Life: Problems with Ethics and Validity of Disability Adjusted Life Years." *British Medical Journal* 319: 1423–1425.

Brock, D. 2001. "Priority to the Worse Off in Health Care Resource Prioritization." In M. Battin, R. Rhodes, and A. Silvers (eds.), *Health Care and Social Justice.* New York: Oxford University Press.

Campbell, A., Converse, P. E., and Rodgers, W. L. 1976. *The Quality of American Life: Perceptions, Evaluations, Satisfactions.* New York: Russel Sage Foundation.

Chiang, C. L. 1965. *An Index of Health: Mathematical Models* (PHS publication no. 1000, series, no. 5). Washington, DC: U.S. Government Printing Office.

Dahl, G. 1992. "QALY: A System That Ultimately Assigns Different Values to Life." *Journal of the Norwegian Association of the Disabled* 1: 26 (text in Norwegian).

Erikson, R., and Åberg, R. 1987. *Welfare in Transition: A Survey of Living Conditions in Sweden 1968–81.* London: Clarendon Press.

EuroQol Group. 1990. "EuroQol – a New Facility for the Measurement of Health Related Quality of Life." *Health Policy* 16: 199–208.

Gold, M. R., Siegel, J. E., Russell, L. B., and Weinstein, M. C. 1996. *Cost-effectiveness in Health and Medicine.* New York: Oxford University Press.

Harris, J. "QALYfying the Value of Life." *Journal of Medical Ethics* 13 (1987): 117–23.

Menzel, P., Gold, M. R., Nord, E., Pinto-Prades, J. L., Richardson, J., and Ubel, P. 1999. "Toward a Broader View of Values in Cost-effectiveness Analysis of Health." *Hastings Center Report* 29: 7–15.

Moum, T. 1993. "Needs, Rights and Indicators in Quality of Life Research." In L. Nordenfelt (ed.), *Quality of Life: Concepts and Measurement in Health Care.* Dordrecht: Kluwer.

Murray, C. "Rethinking DALYs." In C. Murray and A. Lopez, *The Global Burden of Disease.* Cambridge, MA: WHO/Harvard University Press, 1996.

Murray, C., and Acharaya, A. K. 1997. "Understanding DALYs." *Journal of Health Economics* 16: 703–30.

Murray, C., Salomon, J. A., and Mathers, C. 1999. *A Critical Examination of Summary Measures of Population Health* (GPE Discussion Paper no. 2). Geneva: World Health Organization.

Nord, E. 1992. "Methods for Quality Adjustment of Life Years." *Social Science & Medicine* 34: 559–69.

Nord, E. 1993. "The Relevance of Health State after Treatment in Prioritising between Patients." *Journal of Medical Ethics* 19: 37–42.

Nord, E. 1999. *Cost-Value Analysis in Health Care: Making Sense out of QALYs.* Cambridge: Cambridge University Press.

Nord, E., Pinto, J. L., Richardson, J., Menzel, P., and Ubel, P. 1999. "Incorporating Societal Concerns for Fairness in Numerical Valuations of Health Programmes." *Journal of Health Economics* 8: 25–39.

Nord, E., and Wolfson, M. 1999. "Multi-attribute Health State Valuations: Ambiguities in Meaning." *Quality of Life Newsletter* 21.

Pearlman, R. A., and Uhlmann, R. F. "Quality of Life in Chronic Disease: Perceptions of Elderly Patients." *Journal of Gerontology* 43: m25–m30.

Sintonen, H. 1981. "An Approach to Measuring and Valuing Health States." *Social Science and Medicine* 15c: 55–65.

Stewart, A., et al. 1989. "Functional Status and Well-being of Patients with Chronic Conditions." *Journal of the American Medical Association* 262: 907–13.

Ubel, P., Nord, E., Gold, M., Menzel, P., Pinto Prades, J. L., and Richardson, J. 2000. "Improving Value Measurement in Cost-effectiveness Analysis." *Medical Care* 38: 892–901.

Ubel, P., Richardson, J., and Pinto Prades, J. L. 1999. "Life-saving Treatments and Disabilities. Are All QALYs Created Equal?" *International Journal of Technology Assessment in Health Care* 15: 738–48.

Universal Declaration of Human Rights. 1948. Resolution 217A III, United Nations General Assembly.

Weinberg, N. 1984. "Physically Disabled People Assess the Quality of Their Lives." *Rehabilitation Literature* 45: 12–15.

Weinstein, M. C., and Stason, W. B. 1997. "Foundations of Cost-effectiveness Analysis for Health Analysis and Medical Practices." *New England Journal of Medicine* 296: 716–21.

Williams, A. 1987. "Response: QALYfying the Value of Life." *Journal of Medical Ethics* 13: 123.

Williams, A. 1997. "Intergenerational Equity: An Exploration of the Fair Innings Argument." *Health Economics* 6: 117–32.

Williams, A. 2000. Book review. *Health Economics* 9: 739–42.

World Bank. *World Development Report 1993: Investing in Health.* New York: Oxford University Press, 1993.

Chapter 6

Preventing the Existence of People with Disabilities

JEFF McMAHAN

I. WHEN LIFE WOULD BE "WORTH NOT LIVING"

It is commonly held that there are both cases in which there is a strong moral reason not to cause the existence of a disabled person and cases in which, although it would be permissible to cause a disabled person to exist, it would be better not to. Yet many disabled people are affronted by the idea that it is sometimes better to prevent people like themselves from existing, precisely because these people would be disabled. One of their grounds for concern, which will be my particular focus in this chapter, is that claiming that there are reasons to prevent the existence of disabled people may be expressive of a demeaning and hurtful view of the status of existing disabled people, a view that may encourage discriminatory attitudes toward and treatment of the disabled.

I will contend that there can indeed be moral and prudential reasons for preventing the existence of a disabled person. But I will argue that it is less obvious than many people assume what, if anything, the recognition of these reasons expresses about disabled people. And I will contend that, even if the recognition of these reasons does express a perception of disabled people that is potentially hurtful, this effect could be offset by the social expression of a contrary view that I will claim is in fact compatible with, and just as valid as, the potentially hurtful view.

Whether it may be morally objectionable to cause a disabled person to exist depends, in part, on whether the person's life would be worth living. If it is ever objectionable to cause a disabled person to exist, the objections are surely strongest when the person's life would be "worth not living" – that is, would have aspects or features that would be bad for the person and that would decisively outweigh those, if any, that would be good. Such cases are, however, quite rare. Indeed, some people

142

question whether there are *any* disabilities so severe as to cause life to be worth not living. It can be argued that disability involves only the absence of certain abilities and that mere deficits cannot themselves make life too burdensome to be borne. Even if this is true, however, disabilities are often concomitants of *conditions* that not only deprive the victim of certain abilities but also inevitably cause great suffering. If, therefore, we assume that such "disabling conditions" come within the rubric of "disabilities," it seems clear that some disabilities can be so severe as to make life worth not living. If the bad effects of such a disability would be present at birth, or if they would appear early in life and euthanasia would not be an option after their appearance, it seems that there can be a strong moral reason not to cause an individual to exist if he would have the disability.[1]

The objection to causing such an individual to exist might be wholly impersonal in character. To cause such an individual to exist might be worse, not because it would be worse for that individual, but because (for example) it would increase the net amount of misery in the world. Alternatively, the objection might be that to cause such an individual to exist would be bad for that individual. To exist can be bad for that individual even though it would not be *worse* for him. For to say that a state of affairs would be worse for an individual implies that there is an alternative that would be better for that individual. But the only alternative to coming into existence is never to exist, and there is no one for whom never to exist is better than existence. So if one refrains from having a child in order to avoid doing what would be bad for that child, there will be no one whom one has prevented from having a bad life. There may never be any actual individual for whom what one has done is better.

Beyond these brief remarks, I will not be concerned in this chapter with cases in which a disabled person's life would be worth not living. I will focus instead on cases in which, although the disability would be sufficiently severe to make it probable that the disabled person's life would be less good *for the person himself* than an otherwise similar life without the disability, it would nevertheless not be so severe as to make the life worth not living. (It should be explicitly noted that such a claim about a certain type of disability is merely a generalization. At least in the case of most disabilities, and probably in the case of all merely physical disabilities, there is no reason to believe that they *necessarily* make a life go less well than it could have gone without the disability. Some disabled people, indeed, have lives that go conspicuously better than the lives of most people without disabilities. Thus the claim is only that some disabilities make it *likely* that the life will go less well.)

II. DISABLED-OR-NORMAL CHOICES

Once we restrict our attention to disabilities that in general allow for a life that is worth living, it becomes important to distinguish between two types of case. In describing these cases, I will focus on the most common way of causing a person to exist – namely, having a child. The first type of case involves a choice between having a disabled child and having a different child who would be "normal" – by which I mean nothing more than "not disabled" or "lacking a disability" – instead. Let us call this a *Disabled-or-Normal Choice*. The second type of case involves a choice between having a disabled child and having no child at all. Call this a *Disabled-or-None Choice*. I will focus primarily on cases of this second type. First, however, I will briefly discuss Disabled-or-Normal Choices. And I will return to these cases again in section VI.

Suppose that a couple discover that one of them has a condition that would cause any child they might conceive now to have a disability that, while allowing for a life that would be worth living, would nevertheless cause substantial suffering and restrict the range of goods accessible to the child. If, however, they delay conception for three months while the condition is treated, they will then be able to conceive a child without a disability. Because this normal child would be the product of the fusion of different gametes, it would be a different individual from the child they would have if they were to conceive now.[2]

Most people believe that, in these conditions, it would be better if they were to delay conception in order to have the normal child. But the reason why it would be better cannot be that to have a disabled child would be worse, or bad, for the child. For by hypothesis, the disabled child's life would be worth living, and it cannot be bad for an individual simply to be caused to exist with a life worth living.

Some have argued that to cause a person to exist with a certain disability can be wrong because it violates that person's rights, even if the person's life is worth living. I have argued elsewhere that this is implausible – for example, because it implies that it would violate an infant's rights, and therefore be wrong, to *save* its life if the only way to save it involved causing it to have this same kind of disability.[3] But I will not rehearse that argument here. My concern in this chapter is mainly with the expressive significance of certain views, and I suspect that most disabled people would be indignant to be told that their lives are such that their simply being caused or allowed to exist was a violation of their rights.

It seems, therefore, that the best explanation of why it would be better to have the normal child is *impersonal* in character. This explanation appeals to a principle advanced by Derek Parfit that I call the *Impersonal Comparative Principle*: "If in either of two possible outcomes the same number of people would ever live, it would be worse if those who live are worse off, or have a lower quality of life, than those who would have lived."[4] According to this principle, it is worse if the less good of two possible lives is lived. From an impersonal point of view, it does not matter whether these would be different possible lives of the same person or the possible lives of different possible people.

Two points should be noted about this principle. First, it is limited to the comparative evaluation of outcomes; it says nothing about what one ought to do. It therefore needs to be conjoined with some action-guiding principle – for example, the principle that one ought, if other things are equal, to do what would have the best outcome – in order to support the judgment that one ought, when faced with Disabled-or-Normal Choices, to have a normal rather than a disabled child.

Second, Parfit's formulation of the Impersonal Comparative Principle is explicitly restricted to *Same Number Choices* – that is, cases in which one's choice will affect which individuals will exist but not the *number* of individuals who ever exist. This principle is therefore silent about any choice involving whether or not to cause an individual to exist. Such a choice is what Parfit calls a *Different Number Choice* – that is, a choice that would affect the number of individuals who would ever exist.

The restriction of the Impersonal Comparative Principle to Same Number Choices is problematic because of certain indeterminacies about what counts as a Same Number Choice. Here is one example. Suppose that, as I believe, we do not begin to exist until sometime around the beginning of the third trimester of pregnancy.[5] In that case, a choice between having an early abortion and continuing the pregnancy may seem to be a Different Number Choice, since it will determine whether an additional person will exist. (A choice of whether to have a late term abortion is what Parfit calls a Same People Choice, as it does not affect either the identity or the number of the people who ever exist.) But suppose a woman in the early stages of pregnancy discovers that her fetus is damaged in a way that ensures that her child would be disabled.

She therefore considers whether to have an abortion *in order to* enable herself to conceive a different, normal child instead. Is this a Same Number Choice? Perhaps she may treat it as such and thus be guided by the Impersonal Comparative Principle, despite the fact that, after having the abortion, she may change her mind about conceiving another child, or may be unable to conceive another child. But what if she is considering aborting her defective fetus but is as yet undecided about whether to conceive another child? Here it seems unlikely that the Impersonal Comparative Principle can guide her choice.

This is not a significant problem. But there is a deeper worry about the restriction of the Impersonal Comparative Principle to Same Number Choices, which is that there may actually *be* no Same Number Choices – or, if there are, we cannot identify them. A Same Number Choice is defined by the fact that it does not affect the number of people who *ever* exist. But even a simple choice that causes one person to exist rather than another will almost certainly, given enough time, affect the number of people who will exist. If I cause A to exist rather than B, the number of A's progeny over time will almost certainly be different from the number that B would have had. And A and his progeny will very likely affect other people's procreative behavior differently from the way that B and his progeny would have. So any choice that affects *who* will exist will almost certainly affect how many will exist – that is, it will be a Different Number Choice. Therefore, if the Impersonal Comparative Principle is confined to Same Number Choices, its range of application may be restricted to the vanishing point.

Perhaps in applying the Impersonal Comparative Principle we can simply ignore unforeseeable effects on the number of people who ever live. Perhaps, moreover, the considerations underlying the Impersonal Comparative Principle can be applied relatively straightforwardly to certain very simple Different Number Choices, such as the choice between having and not having a child. Suppose, for example, that the reason why it is impersonally better to cause a normal child to exist rather than a disabled child is that the life of the normal child would be likely to contain a greater net amount of good. This suggests that the impersonal explanation of why it is better to cause a well-off person to exist *rather than a less-well-off person* also implies that it is better, if other things are equal, to cause a well-off person to exist *than not to cause anyone to exist.*[6] But if that is right, acceptance of the Impersonal Comparative Principle may commit us to accepting the idea that it is better, other things being equal, to cause more people to exist if their lives would be worth living. And this is a conclusion that most people would resist.

This is one reason for concern about the plausibility of the Impersonal Comparative Principle. Parfit, however, believes that Same Number Choices are sufficiently different from Different Number Choices that the considerations that apply in the former need not apply in the latter. If that is true, we may be able to accept the Impersonal Comparative Principle, applying it to cases in which our choice would not foreseeably affect the number of people who would exist, without being committed to accepting the idea that it would be better to cause more people to exist with lives worth living. But other doubts about the principle remain. It seems, for example, to favor a form of positive eugenics. If, for example, there is a positive correlation between the possession of high cognitive capacities and having a high capacity for well-being, the principle implies that it is better, other things being equal, to have an exceptionally intelligent child than a child of normal intelligence. If we further assume that there is a reason, other things being equal, to do what would have the best consequences, the implication will be that it is prima facie objectionable to have a child of normal intelligence if one could have an exceptionally intelligent child instead.

Although most people object to eugenics, it is not implausible to suppose that there is a moral reason to have a more rather than less intelligent child. But the eugenic implications of the Impersonal Comparative Principle become quite clearly implausible if we eliminate the principle's restriction to the human species. As Parfit states it, the Impersonal Comparative Principle refers to "people." But, particularly because the principle is explicitly impersonal in character, it seems arbitrary to restrict its scope to the human species. After all, if it makes no difference *who* an individual is, it should make no difference what species it belongs to. We should substitute "individuals" for "people" in the statement of the principle. But now suppose that one must choose between having a child and breeding one's horse. It seems that the revised principle must imply that it would be worse to breed one's horse, for the same reason that it would be worse to have a disabled child rather than a normal child: namely, that the horse's life would be less good than that of a human child. Yet it seems that one's reason to have a normal child rather than a disabled child must be different from the reason, if any, to have a child rather than to breed one's horse.

Suppose that, despite these objections, the Impersonal Comparative Principle grounds a plausible objection to having a disabled child rather than a normal child. Does the principle's preference for a normal child rather than a disabled child express a pernicious view of existing disabled people? It is often claimed that to prefer a normal child on the ground that her quality of life would be higher than that of a disabled child is to devalue the lives of the disabled. It is to imply that the lives of the disabled have less value.

I believe, however, that what is expressed or implied by this kind of preference is benign. We have to acknowledge that some people's lives go better than others'. This is a judgment about the *contents* of people's lives, not about the people themselves. To recognize that a person's life has gone less well than the lives of others is not to disparage that person or to suggest that he matters less or has lower worth or status than others. It is merely to recognize that he has suffered a misfortune, or that he has been less fortunate than others. Similarly, to anticipate that a person's life would be likely to go less well than the lives of others is not to imply that that person would be less worthy of life or that existing people who are relevantly like him matter less or have a lower status than others.

It may be easier to appreciate these points if we focus on cases in which the reason why a person's life would be less good is not that her quality of life would be lower because of a disability but simply that her life would be shorter. Suppose that one has a choice between having a child with a normal life expectancy and having a different child with a condition that does not cause disability but that inevitably causes death before the age of thirty. The Impersonal Comparative Principle implies, and most of us would agree, that because a longer life is ordinarily better than a shorter one, it would be better to have a child with a normal life expectancy rather than a different child condemned to die young. This judgment reflects no disparagement of the worth of those who are unfortunate in being doomed to an early death.

III. DISABLED-OR-NONE CHOICES

Consider now an instance of a Disabled-or-None Choice. Suppose that some people carry a gene that would cause any child they might have to have a certain disability. This disability would not be so severe as to cause the child's life to be worth not living but would nevertheless be likely to make the life significantly less good than the lives of most people who are similarly situated except that they lack the disability. Many people, if they were to discover that they were carriers of the gene, would seek to avoid having a child, even if they would want to have a child if they could have one without the disability. The expressive effect of this preference may seem pernicious. For this preference is for having no child at all rather than one with a disability, and it may therefore seem to express the view not just that a disabled child is less desirable than a normal child but that a disabled child is positively undesirable, or worse than no child at all. It might be thought to express the judgment that it would be better if disabled people did not exist at all.

It is, perhaps, unlikely that people would find this expressive effect so seriously objectionable that they would conclude that carriers of the gene *ought* to have children exactly as they would if the children could be expected not to have a disability. And even if some people believe that, in deciding whether to have a child, one ought not to be influenced by whether one's child would be disabled, few would conclude that carriers of the gene should or could legitimately be coerced to have children against their will.[7] But some do hold a closely related view: namely, that social efforts, such as programs that screen for genes associated with disability, that are intended to enable people to avoid having a disabled child ought to be prohibited.[8] For it can be argued that programs involving screening for disabling genes – especially programs with public financing – grant social recognition or validation to the implied view that the existence of people with disabilities is bad.

I noted earlier my belief that we – that is, individuals such as you and I – do not begin to exist until around the beginning of the third trimester of pregnancy, when the fetal brain develops the capacity to support consciousness. If that view is correct, a policy of screening fetuses for genetic abnormalities early in pregnancy, and permitting abortion in the event that an abnormality is discovered, would be a policy that prevents the existence of disabled people and allows different, normal people to be brought into existence instead. It would not be a policy that *kills* disabled individuals and replaces them with normal people. Nevertheless, many people's objections to prenatal genetic testing followed by abortion are inextricably connected to their intuitions about the moral status of fetuses and the morality of abortion. So, if our concern is with the expressive effects of genetic screening, it would be unwise to focus on prenatal screening programs, since what these programs might be thought to express depends on what those who approve of them believe about the nature and status of the fetus.

In order to separate our beliefs about the expressive significance of policies that prevent the existence of disabled people from our intuitions about abortion, let us focus on programs that screen for genes associated with disability prior to conception. And let us assume that, although some people would seek screening only to enable themselves to be better prepared to care for their child should it be disabled, many would have themselves screened in order to avoid having a child should they turn out to carry a gene that would cause their child to be disabled, or even to have a significant probability of being disabled. And let us assume further that it is entirely predictable that many people will seek preconception screening for this reason and that enabling people to avoid having disabled children is one reason why preconception screening programs exist.

In order to understand what kind of view preconception screening programs might be thought to express, we must first understand why people would prefer to remain childless than to have a disabled child. The reason cannot plausibly be that to have such a child would be bad for the child. As before, we are confining ourselves to cases in which the child's life can confidently be expected to be worth living. Nor is it plausible to suppose that to have such a child would be bad from an impersonal point of view. The considerations that make it worse impersonally to have a disabled child rather than a normal child do not seem to imply that it would be worse to have a disabled child rather than no child at all. Indeed, as I suggested earlier, it is arguable that these same considerations imply that it would be *better* to have a disabled child than to have no child. If it would be impersonally better, other things being equal, for an additional person to exist with a life worth living, the only difference it would make if the person were disabled might be to reduce the *degree* to which it would be better. (These claims may be false according to impersonal principles that require the maximization of the *average* level of the good. But these principles are notoriously implausible.)[9]

If it is not because of the effect on the child, and if having a disabled child would not be worse impersonally, then what is the basis of the view that it would be better not to have a disabled child? What would people's reason be for seeking preconception screening? It seems that their concern must be that to have a disabled child would be worse for preexisting people – for themselves, in particular. The most likely reason, in other words, that possible carriers of a gene associated with disability would have for seeking screening would be to avoid the distress and the burdens of responsibility that would be the likely concomitants of having a disabled child.

This reason for preferring not to have a disabled child does seem to express the judgment that, while a normal child would be welcome, a disabled child would not be worth the burden it would impose. If we socially sanction this judgment by providing preconception screening, that may seem to give emphatic social expression to the view that in general disabled people are not worth the cost, that they are on balance a burden to their parents. And to the extent that screening programs reduce, and are intended to reduce, the social costs of providing care and facilities for the disabled, they might also seem to express the view that the existence of disabled people is a burden to society. A disabled person might well be prompted to think: "These programs are intended to enable people to avoid having the kind of child that I was, and to prevent the existence of people like me, because they judge that our existence does not repay the effort required for our care."

It might be tempting to reject these claims by appealing to an analogy with the practice of contraception. Contraception is intended to enable people to avoid having an unwanted child. A policy that legitimizes contraception and makes it available thus caters to people's almost tautologous evaluation that an unwanted child would be a burden. Yet no one proposes that contraception should be prohibited because it expresses a hurtful view of those who were born unwanted. There is, however, a relevant difference between contraception, which enables people to avoid having a child, and preconception screening, which enables people to avoid having a disabled child. This is that those people who were born unwanted and whose existence might have been prevented by contraception were not unwanted because of any characteristic that distinguishes them from others. The reason they were unwanted would have applied to any other child their parents might have had – that is, to any other person. But disabled people whose existence might have been prevented if a policy of screening had been in effect when they were conceived might have been unwanted precisely because of their disability. And because the disability is likely to be important to their sense of identity, the suggestion that people are unwanted because of *that* can be profoundly wounding.

Can we make the same response in Disabled-or-None Choices that I made in the case of Disabled-or-Normal Choices – namely, that the preference for no child rather than a disabled child implies nothing about the worth of the disabled child and therefore expresses no view of the status of existing disabled people? It does seem true that, in Disabled-or-None Choices, as in Disabled-or-Normal Choices, the desire not to have the disabled child does not express or imply the judgment that the disabled child would have a lower status or be of lesser worth. But the idea that disabled people have lesser worth or status in themselves is not the only hurtful suggestion that might be conveyed by a policy, such as a policy of preconception screening for disability, designed to enable people to avoid having a disabled child. Such a policy might instead express the profoundly wounding suggestion that disabled people are burdensome to others, and that the world would be better without them.

I will argue, however, that we should be cautious about attributing expressive significance either to the preference that a person might have not to have a disabled child or to a policy of preconception screening for disabilities. I will contend that the desire to avoid having a disabled child is essentially perspectival and does not necessarily imply or suggest that those disabled people who actually exist are unwanted or regarded as burdensome.

IV. PROSPECTIVE AND RETROSPECTIVE EVALUATIONS

There is a striking asymmetry between the view that people typically have of the *possibility* of having a disabled child and the view that people typically have of *actually having* a disabled child. Very often, people who would otherwise want to have a child believe that it would be better for them not to have a child than to have a disabled child. I will call this the *prospective evaluation*. But when people actually have a disabled child, they typically do not regret that they had that particular child. When they discover, at birth or shortly after, that their child will be disabled, they may initially experience a certain rather unfocused regret, but this tends to dissipate rapidly as their love for the child increases. As they become increasingly attached and devoted to their actual child and discover the joys of parenthood, they soon find it impossible to wish that that child had never existed. They come to believe that their lives are actually better with their disabled child than they would have been without a child. I will call this view, which is very common among the parents of disabled children, the *retrospective evaluation*.

In a recent article in the *New York Times*, a woman is reported as saying: "I had a 14-year-old son who died suddenly.... Knowing he was going to die, would I have said, 'No, I don't want him?' Never."[10] We might interpret this remark as saying that if she had known before her child was conceived that he would die at fourteen, she would still have wanted to have the child. If that is her claim, it may involve self-deception based on reading her retrospective view into her hypothetical prospective view. A more plausible interpretation is that if she had known, earlier in her child's life, that he was fated to die at fourteen, she would still have been glad to have had him and would have believed her life was better for having had him. That is a characteristic and highly plausible retrospective evaluation of life with a child who was the victim of a tragic misfortune.

It might be thought that my characterization of the typical retrospective evaluation omits something important. For while the parents of a disabled child typically believe that it was better for them to have had their actual child than not to have had a child at all, they also believe that it would have been even better for them if they had had their actual child *without the disability*. The question, however, is whether this would have been possible.

There may be cases in which a gene that is responsible for a disability is a necessary condition of a particular individual's coming into existence. It might be, for example, that if the gene were removed from the gamete that contains it prior to conception, this would lead to the existence of a *different* person. (If, as I believe, we do not begin to exist until later in pregnancy, the removal of the gene from the *embryo* could have the same effect.) This is not to claim that a *disability* is ever essential to a person's existence. Even if a disabling gene is necessary for a particular person to come into existence, it may be possible for that person to survive the later deletion of the gene, and it is hard to think of a case in which a person could not in principle survive the *curing* of a disability.

Let us, however, put aside the difficult question of whether a particular gene or gene sequence might be necessary for a given individual's existence. For it remains true that the vast majority of children with a congenital or genetically based disability *would not* have existed if any of the recognized ways of preventing the disability had been employed prior to the child's coming into existence. Suppose, for example, that a child's congenital disability is the result of a preventable or treatable condition of one of the parents. In that case, if the parent had acted to prevent or treat the condition before conceiving a child, this would have affected the timing of the conception and would therefore have led to the fusing of different gametes, which in turn would have led to the existence of a different child. Or suppose that preconception screening would have detected a genetic defect in one of the parents. In that case, one option for avoiding having a disabled child would have been to avoid having a child altogether. Another might have been to correct the genetic defect. But any of the methods of correcting the defect prior to conception – for example, the removal or replacement of the defective gene in one of the gametes prior to fertilization *in vitro* – would also have led to the joining of different gametes and thus to the existence of a different child.

There is one possible method of correcting a genetic defect prior to the coming into existence of the individual that could, at least in some cases, be employed without affecting the identity of the individual who would exist. If we are distinct from our organisms and do not begin to exist until later in pregnancy, it is possible that genetic therapy performed on an embryo could prevent a disability without affecting the identity of the person who would subsequently develop from the embryo. But in virtually all actual cases, children with disabilities would not, and realistically could not, have come into existence if feasible action had been taken to prevent the disability. When people have a disabled child, therefore, the only realistic alternatives in most cases were for them not to have had a child at all and for them to have had a *different* child without a disability. If the parents of a disabled child realize that the only realistic alternative was for them to have no child at all, their retrospective evaluation is typically that, given these options, it was better for them to have had their actual child. If they realize that it was also possible for them to have had a different, normal child instead, they are typically glad nonetheless to have had their actual child.

It is true, however, that these two instances of retrospective gladness – at having had one's disabled child rather than no child at all, and at having had one's disabled child rather than a different, normal child – may reflect different forms of evaluation. I will explain this claim, and explore its significance, in section VI.

Return now to the typical prospective evaluation in Disabled-or-None Choices, the evaluation that prompts some people to seek preconception genetic screening: namely, that it is better to remain childless than to have a disabled child. Given the pervasiveness of the typical retrospective evaluation among the parents of disabled children, people can confidently anticipate, from their prospective point of view, that if they were to have a disabled child, they too would come to believe that their life with a disabled child was better than life without a child would have been. Yet the prospective evaluation remains stable even in the face of the uniformity of the retrospective evaluation among the parents of disabled children. Perhaps we should conclude that the prospective evaluation is simply the product of epistemic limitations and that if people confronted with a Disabled-or-None Choice had a full and vivid sense of what life with a disabled child would be like, they would prefer to have a disabled child, given their initial preference for having a child.

I believe, however, that this is false. The prospective evaluation is not the product solely of epistemic constraints. Consider, for the sake of comparison, the fact that some people who develop AIDS or a fatal form of cancer claim that they are actually glad to have contracted the disease because it roused them from a form of somnambulism, strengthened their relations with their loved ones, and caused them to value and appreciate their every remaining moment. Most of us, on hearing these claims, acknowledge that these people have experienced a special kind of transformative illumination; yet we continue to prefer not to get the disease ourselves, even if we could be confident that we would gain enlightenment along with it. From our point of view, a fatal disease is too high a cost to pay for the full epiphany. Yet we are reluctant to assert that those who are glad to have become fatally ill are deluded in thinking it has been better for them. Is our evaluation, then, the product of mere epistemic limitation? That seems implausible. We can, at one level at least, understand the illumination when it is explained to us; and many of us, at another level, have had direct glimpses of it. More importantly, if we concede that our preference is just the result of epistemic deficiency, we are conceding that it really would be better for us, if other things were equal, to get the disease if it would also bring us wisdom.

We can, I think, achieve a better understanding of this phenomenon if we consider another example. A friend of mine once told me, when I was considering whether to have a child, that if he had known before he had children how much time they would take from his philosophical work, he would probably have remained childless. But once he had children, he was glad that he had, despite their detrimental effect on his work. Again, it is not that when he had children he achieved a hitherto inaccessible insight into the rewards of parenthood, or that he came to understand that previously he had mistakenly overvalued his work in philosophy. It is, rather, that his values altered or evolved. He simply came to give more weight to the value of personal relations and a lower priority to the values of knowledge and achievement. Similarly, people who are glad, all things considered, to have contracted a fatal illness have come to attribute a higher value to the examined life, and a lower value to quantity of life, than most other people do.

I believe that the transition from the prospective evaluation to the retrospective evaluation also results from a shift of values rather than from an overcoming of epistemic limitations. *In general*, when people have their first child the priorities among their values tend to alter, often quite rapidly. The child becomes their primary focus of concern and their principal source of gratification. Their work, hobbies, and recreations, and even their relations with their spouse and friends, all begin to matter less. This process occurs in parents of disabled children in much the same way that it does in other parents.

In short, I claim that it is a change in values that explains why people who once preferred not to have a child than to have a disabled child nevertheless come to believe, after actually having a disabled child, that their lives have been better with the child than they would have been without a child. One objection to this claim appeals to a further evaluation that such people often make. Suppose that both members of a couple are carriers of a defective gene and that consequently any child they might have would be disabled. If they had known this earlier, they would never have had a child. But they discovered it only after the birth of their first child. They now endorse the typical retrospective evaluation: they believe their lives have been better for the presence of their disabled child. But they prefer not to have a second disabled child and believe that it would be worse for them were they to do so. Yet they would welcome a second child if it would not be disabled. If, however, the explanation of why they now accept the typical retrospective evaluation is that their values have altered in such a way that they now value life with a disabled child, it seems unaccountable that, looking forward, they continue to accept a variant of the typical prospective evaluation – that is, they would like to have a normal child but would prefer not to have another child than to have a second disabled child. This suggests that the explanation of why they are glad to have had their existing disabled child cannot be that their values have changed.[11]

Even if the pattern of preferences and evaluations described here is quite common, that does not show that the couple's retrospective evaluation does not reflect a shift in values. For there are good reasons why they might believe that a second disabled child would be worse for them that are compatible with their being highly receptive to the goods derivable from being the parents of a disabled child. It might be, for example, that while they are capable of meeting the demands of caring for a single disabled child, the further demands that a second disabled child would impose would take them over a critical threshold to a point at which the burdens of care would overwhelm their resources. Indeed, they might reasonably believe that satisfying the needs of a second disabled child would render them incapable of continuing to provide the level of care that their first child requires. This could be true even if having a second child who would not be disabled would not take them beyond the limits of their capacity to support a family.

There are other possible explanations as well. Although this is less likely, it is possible that, in addition to valuing life with a disabled child, the couple also value variety. Their evaluations might be similar to those of a couple who are in general indifferent between having a male child and having a female child but who, once they had a child, would want to have a second child only if it would be of a different sex from their first.

One might attempt to reinforce the objection by observing that if this couple were in fact to have a second disabled child (for example, through contraceptive failure), they would very likely *again* be glad that they had. If they could honestly express their gladness through the typical retrospective evaluation – that is, if they could sincerely believe that their lives were improved by their having had a second disabled child – that would suggest that my explanation of the shift from the prospective evaluation to the retrospective evaluation is mistaken. For in this case, there would be *two* such shifts: one after the birth of the first disabled child and another after the birth of the second. So unless we can distinguish two distinct patterns of values – one that supports the judgment that having one disabled child is better than either remaining childless or having two disabled children, and another that grounds the judgment that having a second disabled child is better than having only one – it seems that this couple's evolving series of evaluations cannot be explained by a series of shifts in their values.

This seems right. I therefore think that the best explanation of what happens in most instances of the kind of case I have described is that the couple undergo a change of values (or a change in the priorities among their values) after the birth of their first disabled child and then, after the birth of their second, experience what I will call *adaptation* and *attachment*. These are phenomena that some would claim account for the typical retrospective evaluation even in the case of a first or only disabled child. I will deny that but contend that they may plausibly explain why a couple who were initially averse to having a second disabled child might later be glad that they did. But before I explain what adaptation and attachment are, I will note another possible explanation of the retrospective evaluation that I think is clearly mistaken.

I have claimed that people who were averse to having a disabled child but have nevertheless become the parents of one are typically glad, in retrospect, to have had the child. Yet their retrospective gladness does not show that their having had the child was in fact better for them. There are various reasons why one might be retrospectively glad that one's life has gone the way it has even though it would have been better for one if it had gone differently. Putting aside explanations having to do with such obvious considerations as false beliefs about what one's life would otherwise have been like, I will discuss two types of case involving retrospective gladness that are relevantly different from the case in which people who initially accepted the typical prospective evaluation are nevertheless glad, in retrospect, to have had a disabled child.

In some cases, retrospective gladness that one's life has gone a certain way is the result of a shift of values that is recognizably a *corruption*. An idealistic person might, for example, take a job in politics and later be glad that he had, but the gladness might reflect the person's having been seduced into enjoying the exercise of power as an end in itself, a condition that would have been alien and repugnant to his former character and values. While he may believe that his life has gone better as a result of his entering politics, this evaluation is made relative to his present values, which are inferior to those he would have had had he not gone into politics. From a more objective perspective, his life has actually gone worse. If the gladness that people feel in having had a particular disabled child were analogous to this – that is, if it were the result of a deterioration of character or values – their retrospective evaluation would clearly have less significance than in fact it has. But I take it to be obvious that the values that lead people to believe that their lives are better with a disabled child than with no child at all are neither corrupt nor in any other way inferior to the values that support the typical prospective evaluation. The values that ground the typical retrospective evaluation are, in the main or perhaps entirely, just the familiar *parental* values that lead people to want to have children or to be glad they have them. (I will say a little more about comparisons among sets of values in section V.)

A person's retrospective gladness at having had a disabled child rather than remaining childless should also be distinguished from a second kind of retrospective preference, one based on *adaptation*. Looking back on their lives, people often realize that there were ways in which their lives could have gone better. In many cases, this is because a misfortune caused the life to veer away from a more promising course.

Consider, for example, cases of acquired (as opposed to congenital) disability. A person may suffer a disabling accident that precludes the fulfillment of her most important ambitions – for example, an athlete who aspires to compete in the Olympics may suffer a disabling injury that forces her to formulate new goals that are achievable in her disabled condition. Eventually, she may adapt to her new circumstances so completely that she may no longer regret that the accident occurred. Cases such as this, however, often involve a *narrowing* or *contraction* of the person's values. Although there is no corruption or lowering of values, the person may have to reduce her aspirations, abandoning the pursuit of certain values and concentrating her efforts on a narrower range of values to which she would otherwise have given a lower priority. Because adaptation to an acquired disability often involves this sort of forced retreat from a broader range of values and activities, people can seldom rationally claim to be glad to have become disabled, though they may adapt well enough to have no significant regrets.

There are, however, cases in which a person can *rationally* be glad that his life has gone the way it has, even when he recognizes that it would have been better for him if it had gone differently. Although these cases can include instances of adaptation to serious misfortune, such as a disabling accident or disease, more often they are simply cases in which one realizes that, although one's life has gone well enough, it could have gone better if some event or choice had been different. In these cases, one forms *attachments* to various *particulars* – most notably, particular persons – that are among the elements of one's actual life. One may therefore rationally prefer one's actual life to an alternative life that would have lacked the particulars to which one has become attached, even if that alternative life would have been better.[12]

Cases of this sort are more common that most of us realize. It is, for example, true of almost every married person that he or she could have had a better or more fulfilling life with a different spouse. For, in any particular case, it is exceedingly improbable that the person an individual married was the partner most ideally suited to that person of all the other people in the world. Many people could, in fact, have made a better marriage with someone with whom marriage was once a genuine possibility – for example, a person they dated in college. It might, for example, be true that my wife would have had a better life if she had married her boyfriend from high school rather than me. Suppose that an omniscient being were to assure my wife that this is in fact true: if she had married her high school boyfriend, she would have had a happier marriage and would have had children who would have given her even greater satisfaction than our children have. She could acknowledge that that would indeed have been a better life for her and yet rationally not regret that she has had her actual life instead. Given the attachments to me and her children that inform her actual life, she may rationally prefer this life even though she can concede that she is worse off than she would have been had she made that different marriage.

There is an interesting question about how this kind of case should be understood. I believe that it is implausible to claim that if the alternative life would actually have been better for my wife, her preference for her actual life cannot be rational. We need, therefore, to explain how her preference can be rational if the alternative life would have been better for her. One possibility is to see the alternative life as better *only* relative to the values that would have informed it, treating attachments themselves as values. For *within* that alternative life, my wife would have had different attachments and would certainly have preferred that life to her actual one. On this view, *each* life – her actual life with her marriage to me and the alternative possible life with a different marriage – would be better than the other relative to the values and attachments within it. Yet it seems that the alternative life would have been better in a more robust way than this. If we treat attachments as values, we can claim that the values that she would have had in the alternative life would have been better satisfied than her actual values are within her actual life. In short, the *degree* to which the alternative life would have been better than her actual life relative to the values that would have informed it is *greater* than the degree to which her actual life is better than the alternative life relative to her actual values. That explains the sense in which the alternative life would have been better for her, and leaves it intelligible how she could rationally prefer her actual life. For her actual values, including her attachments, which we may assume are not *lower*, are better satisfied in her actual life.

A different way of understanding this case may be to claim that my wife's basic prudential values – happiness, contentment, satisfaction in marriage, and so on – would have been the same, and would have been better satisfied, in the alternative life. And that is why that life would have been better for her. On this view, attachments do not count as values, perhaps because we seldom have generalizable reasons for being attached to one person rather than to another. Unless, therefore, there is some general, objective reason why it is better to be attached to one person rather than to another, one's attachments to particular people do not directly support judgments to the effect that one's life is better or worse than some alternative life, though they may support rational preferences for one life over another. On this view, my wife rationally prefers her actual life because of her attachments even though the alternative life would have been better for her even by reference to the values that inform her actual life.

I am uncertain how attachments are best understood. But the important point here is that the typical retrospective evaluation of the parents of a disabled child is relevantly different from my wife's preference for her actual life based on her attachments. For although my wife is glad in retrospect that she made the marriage she did, she is nevertheless obliged to concede that it would have been better for her to have made a different marriage – that is, that there is a robust sense in which her life would have gone better if she had married a different person. But the parents of a disabled child are not obliged to accept that their lives would have been better if they had remained childless. While they may have believed prospectively that they would have had better lives by remaining childless than by having a disabled child, they now believe that their lives have been *better* for having had a disabled child. Their retrospective evaluation is not merely a rational preference for what is in fact the worse of two possible lives.

V. PLURALISM

I have claimed that people who are as yet childless very often believe that it would be worse for them to have a disabled child than to remain childless. Yet if they in fact have a disabled child, they typically come to believe that it was better for them to have done so. What is curious about these evaluations is that, although they seem to conflict, neither seems mistaken. Such people's prospective evaluation seems plausible and, if they had in fact remained childless, they would no doubt have persisted in making that evaluation, even if they had had ample exposure to other people who were glad to have had disabled children. But their retrospective evaluation seems equally plausible. I suggested earlier that it would be overly simplistic to resolve the apparent conflict by treating the retrospective evaluation alone as correct by virtue of its being made in epistemically superior conditions. It is tempting, therefore, to conclude that *both* evaluations are correct. But is this even coherent?

Because these evaluations do not contain temporal indexicals such as "now," it seems that the time at which they are made cannot make a difference to their truth or falsity. Thus Derek Parfit notes that "we cannot consistently make a claim and deny this same claim later."[13] He contends that, if it *was* true earlier that it *would be* better if a certain individual were not to exist, it must be true *now* that it *would have been* better if this individual had not existed.[14] Applied to the case of the parents of the disabled child, this implies that their prospective and retrospective evaluations cannot both be true.

I believe, however, that the prospective and retrospective evaluations can both be true. They can both be true if a certain kind of pluralism about values is true.

The relevant form of pluralism is now commonly acknowledged. And it is recognized at both the individual and social levels. Most people now accept, for example, that different societies can have different *cultural values* and that, within a certain range, no one set of these values is better or worse than, or superior or inferior to, the others. And this supports the judgment that, again within a certain range, there are diverse ways of life, associated with different cultures, of which none is better or worse than the others. But neither are these different ways of life exactly equally good. If that were true, a slight improvement in one would make it better than all the others. Because each of these different ways of life is neither better nor worse than the others, and because it is implausible to suppose that they are all exactly equally good, it is often claimed that they must be incommensurable. And the same claim is often made of the different sets of cultural values that recommend the various different ways of life.

It may seem implausible, however, to suppose that various different ways of life cannot be comparatively evaluated at all. Obviously *some* ways of life can be comparatively evaluated – for example, certain ways of life extolled by Nazi culture are bad and therefore worse than other ways of life. And it is odd to suppose that this commensurability vanishes altogether among ways of life above a certain threshold of acceptability. But is there an alternative? Ruth Chang has argued that it can be true of a set of goods that (1) all are in principle commensurable, (2) none is better or worse than the others, and (3) all are not exactly equally good. She says of such goods that they are "on a par."[15] I will adopt this suggestion in claiming that different ways of life, inspired by different cultural values, may be on a par. (Nothing of significance hinges on the claim that goods that seem unrankable may be on a par rather than incommensurable. Those who doubt that the relation of parity is a coherent alternative to incommensurability may simply read "incommensurable" where I write "on a par.")

I believe that a parallel claim can apply to cultural values themselves: one value or set of values may be on a par with another in that neither is superior or inferior to the other and yet the two do not have exactly equivalent status. In some cases, though not in all, the explanation of why certain *goods* are on a par may be that the corresponding *values* that support or endorse the different goods are themselves on a par.

Just as certain cultural values may be on a par, so may the *personal* values of different people. Personal values are values specific to or embedded in various distinctive individual ways of life. They identify forms of experience and activity that may be good in some lives but not as good, or not good at all (perhaps even bad), in others. But, although personal values are not universal, they may be objective. It is just that whether a particular personal value applies to a given person depends on what that person's individual tastes, dispositions, talents, and so on are. Some people, for example, care enormously about their relations with their family members and friends, while others have a consuming concern for personal achievement. These different values may not be fully combinable in a single life: one may, as Yeats suggested, be "forced to choose perfection of the life, or of the work."[16] Yet these values, and the lives that successfully instantiate them, may be on a par. It is difficult to believe that a life of solitary achievement is, in general, either better or worse than a life of humble devotion and loyalty to those one loves. Yet it is also hard to believe that they could be exactly equally good.

If the different personal values of *different people* may be on a par, so may the different personal values that the *same person* may have at *different times*. The colleague whom I consulted about having children gave priority to the value of achievement at one point in his life but later came to care more about personal relations. This shift in priority among his values seems an instance of neither progress nor decline. For the values that informed his life at different times are on a par.

(There is an interesting question here as to why we resist changes in our values even when we acknowledge that the values that we might acquire, or to which we might give a different priority, are on a par with our existing values. The answer to this question is probably quite complex, but one element is presumably that our actual values seem to demand our continued adherence or allegiance even when they do not proclaim their superiority to the rival values. The rival values may seem perfectly acceptable but, because they are *personal* values and are not, at the time, one's *actual* values, they can assert no claim to guide one's action. One's preferences will rationally be dictated by the defensible values that are operative within one's life at the time. Another factor is that changes in one's values can be disruptive of the overall psychological or narrative unity of one's life as a whole. While my colleague was able to accommodate the one change I have described without undue discontinuity, we have only to imagine this kind of change occurring at frequent intervals to appreciate the potential that shifts of value have to reduce one's life to a series of fragmentary episodes.)

Thus far, I have claimed that different and conflicting cultural values can be on a par and that different personal values, both those of different people and those held at different times within the life of the same person, can also be on a par. It is perhaps worth adding that the different personal values that the same person might have in different alternative possible lives could also be on a par. The idea that different personal values can be on a par enables us to see how the prospective evaluation and the retrospective evaluation can both be correct. For both these evaluations reflect the personal values of those who make them.

The typical prospective evaluation – made when people do not as yet have a disabled child – is that life with a disabled child would be *worse*. This evaluation, I suggest, is implicitly indexed to the personal values that the people have at the time. Relative to those values, the evaluation may be correct.

The typical retrospective evaluation – made after people have had a disabled child – is that life with a disabled child is *better*. This evaluation is implicitly indexed to the reordered set of personal values the people have come to have as a result of their experience with a disabled child. Relative to those values, the retrospective evaluation may be correct.

The relevant difference between the prospective and retrospective evaluations, in short, is not that they are made at different times but that each is made with implicit reference to a different set of evaluative standards. Of course, if the personal values that inform the retrospective evaluation were inferior to or less defensible than those that inform the prospective evaluation, or if the couple's life with a disabled child were less successful relative to the values that inform it than the life they would have had with no child would have been relative to their earlier values, then it would be highly problematic to claim that the retrospective evaluation is just as defensible as the prospective evaluation. But if both sets of personal values are on a par, and the couple's life with a disabled child is no less successful relative to the values that inform it, then there is a clear sense in which both the prospective evaluation and the retrospective evaluation can be correct: each is correct relative to a set of personal values that is on a par with the values to which the other evaluation is implicitly indexed.

Because, moreover, each evaluation is relativized to a different set of values, the two are not in fact contrary to one another. In their role as parents, for example, these people can claim that, relative to the values they have now, their life with a disabled child is better and therefore that the life they might have had without a child would have been worse. But they can and should also accept, as fully compatible with this, that their life with a disabled child is worse, and that the life they might have had without a child would have been better, *relative to* the values they had before they had a child.

(It is perhaps worth noting that we tend to evaluate *other* people's lives in a way that abstracts from the personal values that inform them, which we may not share. We tend to appeal, not to values that are individual or perspectival, but to those that we take to be to the greatest extent universal, including the value of the successful realization of defensible personal values, whatever they may happen to be. Taking up this external evaluative perspective, we might judge that the life a person would have without a disabled child and the life that person would have with a disabled child would be more or less equally good provided, first, that each would be more or less equally successful relative to the personal values that would inform it and, second, that neither set of personal values would be inferior to the other. Or we might judge that the two possible lives would be on a par. This would be compatible with recognizing that each would be *better* relative to the personal values that would inform it.)

The important point here is that the retrospective evaluation that life with a disabled child is *better* than life with no child is *no less authoritative* than the prospective evaluation that life with a disabled child would be worse. And it is also significant that while the prospective evaluation is of a merely possible life with a hypothetical disabled child, the retrospective evaluation is of life with an actual disabled child. If, therefore, the retrospective evaluation expresses a view about disability, it is the view that those disabled people *who actually exist* are not burdensome but enrich the lives of their parents and others.

Of course, programs for preconception screening cater to those who accept the prospective evaluation, not the retrospective evaluation. But rather than respond to this by seeking to discourage or prohibit screening for disabilities, perhaps we could seek to offset any expressive effect that screening programs might have by publicly acknowledging or giving social expression to the retrospective evaluation and to the values that support it. How this might be done is a question I will not address, for it is a question of policy, not philosophy. It is enough here to note that any expressive effect that screening programs might have can in principle be countered by giving social expression to the view of disability implicit in the retrospective evaluation, which is no less firmly grounded than the evaluation that prompts people to screen for disabilities.

VI. LIMITATIONS OF THE ARGUMENT

I will conclude by confessing the limits of my argument. One limit may seem obvious: nothing I have said undermines or eliminates the negative judgment signaled by the prospective evaluation. It might be suggested that my focusing attention on the retrospective evaluation is rather like saying some nice things at the end of a book review to mitigate the harshness of the negative judgments expressed earlier.[17]

It is important to see, however, that my claim is not that the prospective evaluation is counterbalanced by the retrospective evaluation in the way that a nasty criticism in a review might be counterbalanced by a bit of praise for a *different* aspect of the book. My claim is rather that the prospective and retrospective evaluations are both valid evaluations *of the same thing*: namely, life with a disabled child. Suppose I tell you that you are ugly. This might be counterbalanced, though not very consolingly, by my adding that you also dress remarkably well. It would be different if I added, perhaps paradoxically, that the claim that you are beautiful is no less true and no less authoritative than the claim that you are ugly.

Still, the core of this objection is sound: nothing in my argument challenges the rationality of the prospective evaluation that life with a disabled child would be worse. But this is unavoidable, for it is in fact rational to believe that life with a disabled child would be worse, even if one recognizes that if one *were* to have a disabled child, one would *then* rationally believe that one's life was better. Given that the prospective evaluation is rational and defensible, it seems that to note that the retrospective evaluation is no less rational is a better response than to attempt to prohibit screening for disabilities. My argument does not eliminate or impugn the rationality of the prospective evaluation; but neither would a prohibition of screening programs.

I turn now to a second and more disturbing limitation of the foregoing argument. Although I have focused in the previous three sections on Disabled-or-None Choices, the more *common* kind of choice is actually that between having a disabled child and having a different, normal child. In my earlier discussion of these more common Disabled-or-Normal Choices, I considered the *moral* reason for preferring a normal child, claiming that it is impersonal and implies nothing about the moral status of people with disabilities. But I failed to note that the reason for preferring a normal child that is more likely to *motivate* people to screen for disabling genes is not moral but prudential. In general, people prefer to have a normal child rather than a disabled child not because they are concerned with the impersonal value of the outcome but because they believe that a disabled child would be more burdensome to them. Thus to have a disabled child when it would have been possible to have a different, normal child instead is commonly regarded as a misfortune for the parents.[18] It seems, therefore, that people often seek screening in order to avoid the burden of having a disabled child *rather than a normal child*. Thus the expressive objection to screening arises in Disabled-or-Normal Choices as well as in Disabled-or-None Choices. For these choices seem to give social expression to the view that disabled children are more burdensome than normal children and that to have a disabled child rather than a normal child is a misfortune. To accord social recognition to this view may be hurtful to existing disabled people.

Before discussing the expressive objection in the context of Disabled-or-Normal Choices, let me digress briefly to consider a different objection to programs that screen for disabilities, which is that they are *discriminatory*. This charge is sometimes supported by appealing to a comparison with screening intended to facilitate sex selection. People typically seek screening for disabilities because they believe that having a disabled child would be burdensome in a way that having a normal child would not be. But people in certain societies who want to screen for the sex of the fetus have the same reason: they believe that having a female child would be burdensome without promising many of the rewards they seek, such as perpetuation of the family name, having someone capable of providing for them in their old age, and so on. In societies in which women must take their husband's name and are excluded from remunerative employment, these are not unreasonable concerns. Nevertheless, the solution in this case is to eliminate the social discrimination, not to eliminate the victims of it. Sex selection merely affirms and perpetuates the pernicious social discrimination.

Some advocates for disabled people make a parallel claim – that is, that to the extent that a disabled child imposes a burden on the parents, this is a consequence of social discrimination. They contend that disability is relative to the environment, so that if we were to change the environment, what we now regard as disabilities would cease to be disabilities. There is some truth to this; it is true in the case of some disabilities. But it is not wholly true. It is not true in the case of disabilities that involve serious cognitive deficits, nor in the case of disabling conditions that involve suffering or premature death. And many such disabilities that cannot be wholly neutralized by adjustments to the environment are also correlated with burdens to the parents. So the burdens to the parents of having a disabled child could not be wholly eliminated by eliminating social discrimination in the way that the burdens of having a female child could; therefore, screening for disability is not necessarily discriminatory in the way that screening for sex in fact is.

Return now to the expressive objection. The strategy I developed in the discussion of Disabled-or-None Choices cannot, it seems, be extended to Disabled-or-Normal Choices. It is true that, even in Disabled-or-Normal Choices, the parents are very likely to have a retrospective preference for their life with their actual disabled child over the life they might have had with a normal child. But this is unlikely to be relevantly like the parents' retrospective evaluation in a Disabled-or-None Choice. The retrospective evaluation in a Disabled-or-None Choice is typically, as I suggested, that life with a disabled child has been better for the parents relative to the personal values they have developed as parents. But in the case of people who have had a disabled child but could have had a different, normal child instead, it is not true, in general, that their lives have gone better, relative to their personal values, than they would have if they had had a normal child. In fact, it is probably true that their lives have gone worse, even relative to their actual personal values, than they would have gone with a normal child. (It is conceivable that life with a disabled child may be better relative to certain slightly deviant or eccentric personal values – for example, those of parents who especially cherish their child's lasting dependency. Whether such personal values could be on a par with more familiar parental values is a question I will not pursue here.)

This is not to deny that, if the parents of a disabled child prefer their actual life to the life they might have had with a normal child, their preference is rational. The rationality of their preference may be grounded in their attachment to their actual child. Their preference is, in other words, analogous to my wife's preference for her actual marriage over a different marriage that would have been better for her. Just as it can be rational for my wife to be glad she made the marriage she did, so the parents of a disabled child can rationally prefer the life they have with their actual child; but they should be willing to concede that the lives they would have had with a different, normal child would probably have been better.

Is there any way to mitigate the hurtful expressive effect of screening in Disabled-or-Normal Choices? We might observe that the claim that a disabled child is more burdensome to care for than a normal child is true only as a broad generalization. In some instances, raising a disabled child is *more rewarding*, relative to almost *any* set of personal values, than raising a normal child. And there are numerous traits that are compatible with normalcy that can make a nondisabled person more difficult to live with or to care for than a disabled person typically is.

More importantly, what seems to be true as a generalization about disabled people is also true, to a greater or lesser degree, of most or even *all* of us individually. Who can honestly claim that he is the best child that his parents could possibly have had, even given their present values? In this respect, disabled people are picked out quite fortuitously: the characteristics that may cause difficulties for their parents are often associated with genes that can be identified prior to conception. By contrast, there are no prenatal tests for the features of my endowment that have been particularly burdensome to my parents.[19]

NOTES

1. For a description of a disabling condition – dystrophic epidermolysis bullosa – with effects that cause life to be worth not living and that are present at birth, see Jonathan Glover, "Future People, Disability, and Screening," in Peter Laslett and James S. Fishkin (eds.), *Justice between Age Groups and Generations* (New Haven, CT: Yale University Press, 1992), pp. 129–30. For a clinical description of the condition, with photographs that give some indication of its grisly nature, see Robin M. Winter et al., *The Malformed Fetus and Stillbirth: A Diagnostic Approach* (Chichester: Wiley, 1988), pp. 205–6.

2. See Derek Parfit, *Reasons and Persons* (Oxford: Oxford University Press, 1984), Chapter 16.

3. See my "Wrongful Life: Paradoxes in the Morality of Causing People to Exist," in Jules Coleman and Christopher Morris (eds.), *Rational Commitment and Social Justice: Essays for Gregory Kavka* (Cambridge: Cambridge University Press, 1998), pp. 208–47; the relevant discussion is on pp. 223–5. A revised and abridged version of this paper appears in John Harris (ed.), *Bioethics* (Oxford: Oxford University Press, 2001), pp. 445–75.

4. Parfit, *Reasons and Persons*, p. 360. I discuss this principle at length in "Wrongful Life," section IV of the original version.

5. See Jeff McMahan, *The Ethics of Killing: Problems at the Margins of Life* (New York: Oxford University Press, 2002), Chapter 1, section 5, and Chapter 4, section 1.

6. See McMahan, "Wrongful Life," pp. 234–9 of the original version, and McMahan, *The Ethics of Killing*, Chapter 4, section 8.2.

7. People do sometimes claim that a good parent should be just as happy to have a disabled child as to have a normal child. I suspect that people think that this claim is somehow implied by the plausible view that it is right and admirable to want to be, and to try to be, the kind of person who would love his or her child equally whether it was disabled or not. But in fact, it does not follow from this plausible view that it is also admirable to be indifferent about whether one has a normal or a disabled child. It is also admirable to want to be the kind of person who would love his or her child equally even if the child were to become a criminal, but it does not follow from this that it is admirable to be indifferent about whether one's child will grow up to be a criminal. (This is not, of course, to suggest that disability is analogous to criminality. The point is only that, if there is no implication in the case of criminality, there should be none in the case of disability either.)

8. An important question for those who hold this view is whether it commits them also to opposing social efforts to discourage people from *causing* themselves to have a disabled child rather than a normal child. There are two possibilities: (1) causing a child to be disabled when he or she would otherwise have been normal (for example, through the ingestion of drugs late in pregnancy) and (2) causing the existence of a disabled child rather than a different child who would have been normal (for example, through the ingestion of drugs prior to conception). I am indebted to discussions with Robin Jeshion for encouraging me to address the question of the relation between our views about screening for disability and our views about causing disability – for example, through prenatal injury. I discuss this and related questions in another paper provisionally called "On the Morality of Preventing, Allowing, and Causing the Existence of People with Disabilities."

9. See Parfit, *Reasons and Persons*, pp. 420–2; and Jeff McMahan, "Problems of Population Theory," *Ethics* 92 (1981): section VI.

10. "Genes, Embryos, and Ethics," *New York Times*, March 3, 2002.

11. I owe this objection to Tad Brennan, though I have added to his example the stipulation that the couple would like to have a second child if it would not be disabled, so that their ranking of the outcomes is: normal child, no child, disabled child. This addition strengthens the objection because it rules out as explanations of the parents' preference those considerations that often lead people who are glad to have had one normal child not to want a second.

12. Here I follow Robert M. Adams in his seminal and important paper, "Existence, Self-Interest, and the Problem of Evil," *Nous* 13 (1979): 53–65.

13. Parfit, *Reasons and Persons*, p. 360.

14. Ibid.
15. Ruth Chang, "The Possibility of Parity," *Ethics* 112 (2002): 659–88.
16. W. B. Yeats, "The Choice," in M. L. Rosenthal (ed.), *Selected Poems and Two Plays of William Butler Yeats* (New York: Collier, 1966), p. 131.
17. I owe this objection to Shelly Kagan.
18. It might be objected that, if life with a normal child is better than life with a disabled child, and life with a disabled child is not worse than life without a child, it follows that life with a normal child is better than life with no child. And that seems a false generalization. In general, being a parent does not seem even presumptively to offer a better life than remaining childless. There are, however, various reasons why the conclusion does not follow. I will note only one. The three comparative evaluations I have cited seem to be made from a point of view that abstracts from personal values. Understood in this way, the second claim – that life with a disabled child is not worse than life without a child – does not imply either that life with a disabled child is better or that such a life is exactly equally as good as life without a child. It must be understood, instead, as asserting that life with a disabled child is on a par with, or perhaps incommensurate with, life without a child. But if A is better than B, and B is on a par or incommensurate with C, it cannot be inferred that A is better than C.
19. I am greatly indebted for comments on an earlier draft to Tad Brennan, David Wasserman, Robert Wachbroit, and audiences at Yale University, Ohio State University, and the University of Pennsylvania School of Law.

Chapter 7

Where Is the Sin in Synecdoche?

Prenatal Testing and the Parent-Child Relationship

ADRIENNE ASCH AND DAVID WASSERMAN

The principal targets of what has become known as the disability critique of prenatal testing (PNT) have been health professionals and the policies they establish, not individual parents and the decisions they make. Indeed, one of the strongest complaints about professional practices and policies is that they infringe upon rather than enhance the reproductive freedom of individual parents, by pressuring them to abort fetuses that are likely to develop substantial impairments (e.g., Clarke, 1991; Wachbroit and Wasserman, 1995; Shakespeare, Chapter 8, this volume). Moreover, the "expressivist" objection to prenatal testing – that it reflects or embodies a conviction that children with impairments are a burden to themselves, their parents, and society – is more appropriately directed to the practices and policies adopted by professional groups than to the often confused and ambivalent decisions made by individuals in the face of those practices and policies.

Nevertheless, we believe that it is critical to examine the attitudes and beliefs with which individuals respond to the testing technology that is offered to them, however coercively. To some extent, that technology is made available in the belief that it serves the preferences and values of those who employ it. If the routinization of prenatal testing is in part an attempt to introduce eugenic policies through the "back door" (Duster, 1990), it is also in part a response to perceived consumer demand. Even more important, the individuals to whom prenatal testing is offered are in the process of forming families, and the attitudes and beliefs with which they respond to the technology both reflect and inform the attitudes and beliefs with which they create families. We will argue that some of those attitudes and beliefs are inconsistent with the moral posture that parents should adopt toward their future children and their families-in-the-making.

In this chapter, we will focus on what one of us has called "synecdoche"[1] – not the literary device, in which the part stands for the whole, but the characteristic response to a stigmatized trait, in which the part obscures or effaces the whole. We will distinguish this attitude from others that may also play a significant role in the use of prenatal testing. We recognize, of course, that a melange of attitudes and beliefs shapes reproductive choices, and that it is difficult or impossible to determine their comparative contribution to those decisions. We will not attempt to do so. But we believe that it is important to distinguish among these attitudes and beliefs, because they may be subject to different moral appraisal and different policy prescriptions.

In this chapter, we concentrate on moral appraisal, arguing that synecdoche involves a distinct failing, to which certain individuals not directly affected by the decisions it shapes may reasonably take offense – those who share the stigmatized characteristic. We maintain that synecdoche differs in this respect from consumerist and perfectionist attitudes associated with the use of prenatal testing – that it underwrites the objections of existing people with impairments in a way that these other attitudes do not. At the same time, we suggest that *all* of these attitudes reflect, and contribute to, a morally impoverished conception of parenthood and family.

SYNECDOCHE, STEREOTYPING, AND STIGMA

One of us began her most recent account of the wrong involved in prenatal testing for disability with a classroom analogy:

You are a professor at a philosophy department of a large urban university. In your class of fifty students, you notice that five students have pierced tongues and lips and that a few others have dyed their hair in unnatural colors. You have difficulty even looking at these students because of their style, and you ignore their raised hands when they want to participate in class discussion. Midway through the semester, a man with dyed hair comes to your office to raise questions about the work in the course, and you realize that he actually has some interesting observations to make about the class and find yourself chagrined at your avoidance of his raised hand, of which you were only half aware until he appears at your door. (Asch, 2000: 235)

This analogy is intended to suggest that the prospective mother who aborts after a finding of Down syndrome or cystic fibrosis (CF) is, in an important respect, like the teacher who ignores a student on the basis of his dyed hair. Prenatal testing yields only a first impression, and aborting on the basis of that impression is unreasonable.

In the case of the teacher, it is fairly easy to identify the false assumption on which he acted – that someone with outrageously colored hair couldn't have anything to contribute to the class – and the wrong he committed – to exclude someone from taking part in a class on the basis of a false assumption about the value of his contribution. The wrong of writing off a student on the basis of a superficial characteristic may involve a number of distinct errors. First, the generalization that students who dye their hair have nothing to contribute to class does not hold true of all such students: at least one student with dyed hair clearly had a lot to contribute. (The generalization might also be mistaken as a rule of thumb: it might be that students with dyed hair are, on average, among the most helpful participants in class discussion.) Second, it might be unreasonable or unfair to rely on that generalization, even if it were statistically valid, or even if it were in fact true of this individual. It might be unreasonable for two reasons. It might be wrong to rely on that generalization unless it were supported by a particular kind of evidence: it would be wrong to exclude students from class participation based on their reputations, or even based on their behavior in other classes, however good a predictor that was, rather than giving them a chance to do better in this class, however unlikely they were to do so. Or it might be that the generalization, even if well grounded, simply didn't provide an adequate basis for exclusion: even if a student had repeatedly given sincere but mistaken answers, the reasonable expectation that he would continue to do so would still not justify excluding him from class discussion.

Turning to prenatal testing, we need to ask analogous questions: what are the assumptions being made, are they adequately grounded, and do they provide a reasonable basis for the act of abortion? We are not concerned with the accuracy of the prenatal test, and are willing to agree for the sake of argument that a medical diagnosis of Down syndrome or CF could be completely accurate. The questionable assumptions concern the quality of life enjoyed by a child with Down syndrome or CF, and by the parents of such a child. The error lies in the belief "that this one piece of information suffices to predict whether the experience of raising that child will meet parental expectations" (Asch, 2000: 236).

This claim of error rests on three propositions. First, many parents rely on this belief in testing and terminating for impairment. Second, that reliance is misplaced, because "this one piece of information" does *not* suffice to predict the satisfaction of (ordinary or modest) parental expectations; rather, it triggers a false or exaggerated generalization. Third, reliance on this generalization is morally problematic, even if it is explained and mitigated by social and institutional pressures. We will briefly defend the correctness of the first two propositions and then turn to the third, which is our main concern. The first seems clearly correct, and it is supported by a great deal of empirical research and informal observation. Many people believe that raising children with Down syndrome, CF, deafness, or blindness would fail to meet even very modest parental expectations, because the lives of those children and their parents would be extremely painful and burdensome. It is also clear that this belief is false, or greatly exaggerated. As research on families with disabilities consistently indicates, many or most children with a very wide range of impairments, and many or most parents of those children, lead rich and rewarding lives (e.g., Gallimore et al., 1989; Krauss, 1993; Baxter et al., 1995; Cahill and Glidden, 1996; Ferguson, Gartner, and Lipsky, 2000; Ferguson, 2001). The most that can plausibly be claimed is that being or having a child with a disability is at times different and more difficult than being or having a "normal" child, and that specific impairments are very unlikely to meet specific parental expectations (e.g., a child with Down syndrome is not likely to become a great mathematician like her mother).

The classroom analogy also suggests that parents who seek prenatal testing based on this false belief display a distinct kind of moral weakness. In making out this claim, it will be helpful to compare attitudes and beliefs associated with prenatal testing that do not appear mistaken in the same way: the "consumerist" desire for a child compatible with the parents' projects, ambitions, or lifestyle, and the perfectionist desire for "the perfect baby." We will argue that these attitudes are distinct from synecdoche and less disability-specific, although they are also subject to moral criticism. We are more skeptical of the distinctiveness of two other sets of attitudes and beliefs. The first concerns the expected burdens of raising a child with an impairment, from the financial costs of obtaining quality care to the emotional strain of confronting the prejudices of the larger society. These concerns are certainly not groundless, but we suspect that they are typically inflated by the parents' preoccupation with the stigmatized trait – that they are, in part, expressions of synecdoche. We believe that most of the costs and strains of raising even a severely impaired child are bearable by parents of ordinary means and resolution, and that they are not significantly greater than those borne by many parents of unimpaired children.

We are even more skeptical about concerns for the child's suffering than about concerns for the parents' capacities. Except in those extremely rare cases where a child's suffering is expected to be so intense, pervasive, and protracted that it can be said to make his very existence harmful to him overall, the failure or refusal to see the child's suffering in the context of his worthwhile existence appears to epitomize synecdoche.

DIFFERENT REASONS FOR PRENATAL TESTING

Consider, then, several types of reasons for which parents seek prenatal testing. Parents may act for any or all of these reasons, and they may be uncertain or mistaken about the reasons for which they act. Our interest is in distinguishing and assessing the reasons that parents might have, even if it will be difficult for the parents themselves to know the reasons for which they seek testing in actual cases.

The first type of reason is the one we have called synecdochal. Prospective parents with ordinary, often inchoate expectations (perhaps shaped by their own upbringings) about the rewards and burdens of raising children, may assume – falsely, we believe – that these expectations cannot be met by a child with a significant impairment. They – and, far too often, their doctors and counselors – take this as self-evident, requiring no inquiry or research. The only constraint on their decision to test and terminate for impairment may lie in moral reservations about abortion, and even those may be a good deal weaker when the fetus to be aborted is thought to be defective.

The second type of reason parents may have for seeking PNT is that raising a child with a severe impairment would not serve their objectives or satisfy their constraints in having children – to raise a child to share or promote their pleasures, passions, commitments, aspirations, or vocations, or less ambitiously, to raise a child who would not require the sacrifice of their pleasures, passions, commitments, ambitions, or vocations. This second type of reason may be "projectivist," in William Ruddick's sense of raising a child as a project, with specific goals or expectations (Ruddick, 2000: 99–100). But reasons of the second type cover only a subclass of Ruddick's projects, because they are concerned with goals and expectations arising from the parents' own interests and projects. For this reason, we will, perhaps uncharitably, call such reasons "consumerist." (Reasons of this second type may also be "familialist" in Ruddick's sense, if they concern the interests or projects of the family as a whole, or of existing members of the family [102–4]). For Ruddick, by contrast, a project may be as narrow as having a child lacking "the specific illness or disability that, in [the parent's] view, had ruined the life of her natal family" (Ruddick, 2000: 99) – a reason we would regard as synecdochal because it treats the impairment as the sole cause of the natal family's "ruination," ignoring the discrimination and lack of resources that probably contributed to the family's burdens, as well as the social and environmental reforms that may well alleviate any burden on the family now being created. Or the project may be as ambitious as raising a prodigy or messiah – a reason we would regard as perfectionist.

Consumerist reasons are neither so narrow nor so ambitious; they are the modestly selfish reasons that most parents have in raising children to become partners, companions, collaborators, or successors. We do not wish to suggest that having such aspirations is incompatible with the moral basis of family life; what concerns us is the refusal to raise a child who will not fulfill those aspirations. Moreover, we will suggest later that the most modest reasons of this sort are difficult to distinguish from the mere desire to establish an intimate parent-child relationship, a desire that might possibly be incompatible with some especially severe impairments. For example, it may be uncertain or debatable whether a prospective parent who declines to have a child almost certain to lack the cognitive or affective requisites for a sustained, loving relationship is acting on the belief that such a child will frustrate her projects and ambitions, or on the arguably more defensible belief that she cannot achieve the central goods of parenthood with such a child. We will turn to this issue toward the end of the chapter.

A third type of reason, closely related to the second, may be called "perfectionist." Parents may seek to have children who embody their ideals, lack their own deficiencies, or improve on their own virtues. Perfectionism is more exacting and ambitious than consumerism. Although it may also be more child-oriented, in the sense of focusing on the child's strengths rather than the parents' or families' needs, it treats the child herself as a project, and her enhancement as an impersonal goal. A prospective parent unwilling to have a child who cannot embody her ideals appears to have a distorted view of the nature of the parent-child relationship, and of the goods of parenthood. Again, we will turn to this issue at the end of the chapter.

We can charitably assume that parents who seek testing for either of these reasons intend to nurture, and hope to cherish, the child once it is born, whether or not it fulfills their expectations or promotes their projects. Yet we may still criticize these reasons, as we do later in the chapter, because they are not appropriate for a relationship as intimate and unconditional as that between parent and child.

The first reason for seeking PNT, however, seems different from the other two in resting on false or exaggerated beliefs about impairment. Moreover, the beliefs on which it rests are no innocent falsehoods. The impairment dominates and distorts the parents' judgment of the future child's life, and of their lives with him. Impairments, unlike a mere lack of physical strength or musical talent, are stigmatized, pervading the personal and social interactions of those who bear them and relegating them to inferior status as "damaged goods" (Goffman, 1963: 3–5). Many parents find it difficult or impossible to see through the dark glass of prejudice to the fullness of life as, or with, a child who is blind, deaf, or unable to walk.

Taken at face value, consumerist and perfectionist reasons for seeking PNT appear to rest on valid beliefs – that the child's impairment is likely to preclude a specific objective for which he was conceived, or that the child will be born with substantial physical, affective, or cognitive imperfections. Parents who act on these beliefs may have a fuller or less distorted view of the future; they just don't like what they see, because the child's future life, however rich, will lack something critical to their specific project or to the ideals they wish him to embody. Any wrong arising from a reliance on these reasons would not seem to involve an error of perception or judgment; parents who rely on those reasons may act wrongly, but they appear to see clearly. Moreover, their reasons seem less specific to disability. There are many characteristics besides impairments that may threaten parental projects or family welfare, or that may be regarded as significant imperfections. Both consumerist and perfectionist reasons can be understood as universalist about disability, in the sense that they treat impairments merely as some among the many attributes that may interfere with parental projects or frustrate the quest for the ideal child. But few of these other attributes can be revealed or predicted by PNT.

Indeed, it might be argued that the preoccupation with impairment that we have characterized as synecdochal is less a product of stigma than an artifact of existing testing technology. Jeff McMahan (Chapter 6, this volume) suggests something along these lines in his contribution to this volume: "Disabled people are picked out quite fortuitously: the fact about them that may cause difficulties for their parents is one that our technology enables us to detect prenatally. By contrast, there are no prenatal tests for the features of my endowment that have been particularly burdensome or irksome to my parents." It is, however, doubtful that the selection of disabled people really has been fortuitous – though many more complex traits cannot be tested for genetically, others as "burdensome or irksome" are less likely to be tested for just because they are not stigmatized, or are less likely to lead to abortion if detected.

Consider the ease with which doctors have long been able to detect the presence of multiple fetuses. Though being a multiple may not be "a feature of [the future child's] endowment," there is surely some increased financial and psychological burden involved in having more than one child at the same time. Yet because multiples are not regarded – perhaps mistakenly, from a biological perspective – as impaired (although they may have a higher-than-average incidence of impairment), they are rarely "thinned" by abortion, except in cases where the doctor advises that the presence of so many fetuses threatens the survival of all. The revelation that a small percentage of healthy multiples has been aborted in the UK merely to reduce parental burden was met with indignation, as an abuse of health care resources (Raymer, 2003). Contrast this with the 92 percent termination rate for fetuses diagnosed with Down syndrome during the years 1989 to 1995, as reported by the British National Health Service (NDAN, 1996), and the complacent or approving reaction that such statistics evoke. Because multiples are not stigmatized, their parents, and the larger society, can more readily apprehend the joys as well as burdens of raising them – the birth of sextuplets or septuplets, let alone of twins or triplets, is generally regarded as cause for celebration, not grieving. Similarly, as one of us has noted elsewhere, the discovery that one's child is a mathematical or musical prodigy (a discovery that, so far, can only be made postnatally) is usually greeted with celebration, not grief, despite the enormous demands that the cultivation of her talents may place on her parents (Asch, 1999). The child with an impairment is seen merely as a drain on her parents and society, with little or nothing to contribute; the child prodigy is seen as having the potential for great contributions, and the burdens assumed by her parents and society are seen as a reasonable sacrifice or a wise investment.

If, as we suspect, the stigma associated with certain traits affects virtually all parental decisions to detect those traits prenatally, perhaps we shouldn't take the other reasons for seeking PNT at face value. Perhaps stigmatized traits are so frightening to prospective parents that synecdoche lies behind consumerist and perfectionist reasons as well. It might well be that if parents didn't have an exaggerated view of the burdens of impairment, or a visceral aversion to raising a child with a severe or visible impairment, they would realize that their personal and parental projects could be adapted to conform to their children's abilities and interests, or that their ideals of perfection needed to be modified or abandoned. As we suggested earlier in discussing Ruddick, the "project" of avoiding the ruinous effects of an impairment is likely to be an expression of synecdoche. So it may be that, as a matter of psychological reality, the two other reasons we have described are really forms of synecdoche, rather than alternative explanations for the decision to test and abort.

This suspicion seems even more firmly grounded when we examine two other reasons commonly offered for seeking PNT: to avoid the suffering of the impaired child, and to avoid the heavy burden that would be imposed on the parents in raising him. Except in those rare cases where the child would be born with an impairment that would truly make his life not worth living – Lesch Nyans syndrome may be the only clear case – the invocation of the child's suffering as a reason for not having him seems quintessentially synecdochal: it focuses on the child's suffering to the exclusion of the joy and good in his life that the prospective parents have equally strong reason to expect. Laura Purdy displays this highly selective concern in defending selective abortion:

The thought that I might bring into existence a child with serious physical or mental problems when I could, by doing something different, bring forth one without them, is utterly incomprehensible to me. (1996: 58)

But these "serious physical or mental problems" are not free-floating evils that any sane person would wish to avoid; they are an unavoidable part of a particular future life that is likely, on balance, to be rich and rewarding. Like many prospective parents, Purdy cannot even glimpse that worthwhile whole because of her fixation on a painful part.

A final type of reason concerns the parents' capacities rather than the child's suffering. Prospective parents may be especially anxious or ambivalent about having a child, or another child, and fear that they would simply not be up to the task, financially or psychologically, of providing adequate care for a child with a severe impairment. They may believe that they would be willing and able to raise such a child if they possessed greater resources or resilience, but not in their present condition.

The contrast we drew earlier with multiples calls into question the extent to which doubts about parental capacity do function as independent reasons for PNT. One hardly needs to read the literature on families with disabled children to recognize that raising three or four, let alone seven or eight, concurrently born children demands at least as much time, effort, and money as raising one severely impaired child. And yet many or most parents faced with the former prospect rise cheerfully to the occasion, with the moral and often the financial support of their communities. They are not seen as coping bravely with a tragic situation, or as engaging in adaptive self-deception, but as taking on a bracing and rewarding challenge. If the prospective parents of a single child with a severe impairment are not seen, or do not see themselves, in this way, this suggests that it is not the costs – in time, effort, and money – that make it seem overwhelming to raise such a child. Raising a child with an impairment is seen as a burden rather than a challenge precisely because the impairment is a stigmatized trait. Doubts about parental capacity, then, are less likely to provide an alternative explanation for the use of PNT than to reflect the distorting effects of stigma.

Despite our suspicions about the pervasive role of stigma in the decision to test and abort, we will assume for the sake of argument that some parents *do* act, at least in part, for consumerist or perfectionist reasons, because that assumption will permit us to tease out the distinct moral concerns raised by synecdoche. Moreover, it keeps open the possibility of debating the legitimacy of reasons for PNT based on parental or family interests, a debate that is obscured if we assume that the desire for PNT always arises from the stigma-driven generalizations we have described as synecdochal. We will return to this debate in the last section.

The classroom analogy with which we started suggests that the moral concerns raised by synecdoche are distinct. Acting for consumerist or perfectionist reasons may display inflexibility or insufficient commitment. Parents who are unwilling to adapt their interests, projects, and goals may take an overly narrow view of parenthood, one that either treats the child's value as instrumental or ignores many sources of intrinsic value in its existence and development. And parents who strive for perfection may treat their child entirely as an object, however lofty their aspirations for it. These attitudes may reflect an impoverished or distorted view of parenting and families, but they do not involve the distinctive "sin" of synecdoche: the uncritical reliance on a stigma-driven inference from a single feature to a whole future life.

That sin, we will argue, is to allow a single known characteristic of the future child to so overwhelm and negate all other hoped-for attributes that the prospective parents no longer desire the coming-into-being of that child. The sway exercised by that single characteristic is not accidental or idiosyncratic – it is the sadly predictable effect of stigma, "spoiling the identity" (Goffman, 1963) of the future child in the most radical possible way, by precluding him from ever forming an identity in which the impairment might play only a slight or negligible role. In responding to that characteristic as they do, parents who test and abort for an impairment ratify and perpetuate its stigmatization, however unwittingly or reluctantly. Synecoche is thus a sin about which other people – people stigmatized by possession of the same impairment – have special standing to complain. In acting for consumerist or perfectionist reasons, by contrast, prospective parents display problematic attitudes toward parenthood in general, but they do not give any particular individual or group a basis for complaint.

JUDGING A BOOK BY ITS COVER: WHAT'S WRONG AND WHO'S WRONGED?

Let us return, then, to the classroom analogy. Dismissing a student on the basis of a first impression or superficial characteristic is obviously unfair to that student, even, or especially, if that judgment is unreflective. But that is because the student has a right to fair consideration, which such a judgmental shortcut denies him. It would be even worse if the characteristic in question were not a transient, voluntary one like dyed hair, but a permanent, involuntary one, like being tall, large, or "naturally" athletic. And it would be worse still if an "immutable" characteristic, like dark skin or impairment, were stigmatized. In that case (and possibly in the second one as well), the student might not be the only one with a grievance. Others with the same characteristic might also complain about the teacher's unwarranted inference from that characteristic to the student's potential contribution to class discussion. Those others would have suffered, or would be at risk of suffering, the same kind of stereotyping.

But a first- or second-trimester fetus judged on an equally mistaken first impression has no right to fair consideration – no right, at least, that a liberal or feminist critic of PNT would wish to assert. We agree with such authors as Gillam (1999) and Satz (1999), who – in discussing the disability critique of PNT – assert that the early fetus lacks the moral status of a person and cannot be a target of wrongful discrimination. The early fetus itself lacks, or can be presumed to lack, the moral standing to complain if aborted for any reason or for no reason. However unwise it may be to judge a book by its cover, the book cannot complain.

But what about adults who share the characteristic on the basis of which the fetus was aborted? If that characteristic is an impairment, it is almost certainly stigmatized, dominating and adversely affecting the social interactions of those who possess it. If they have standing to complain about actions toward an impaired student based on a stigma-driven generalization, why can't they complain about actions toward an impaired fetus based on a stigma-driven generalization? We suspect that those who dismiss the disability critique as originating with unacknowledged discomfort with abortion in general, as opposed to concerns about stigma and stereotyping, fail to appreciate the harm done to people with impairments when their opportunities in life are constrained by prejudicial attitudes and actions; it is these people with impairments – indisputably moral persons – who are harmed by the social attitudes underlying the uncritical use of PNT and selective abortion.

The defender of PNT might answer that in the classroom hypothetical, but not in the case of PNT, there is a rights violation, and that third parties have standing to complain only when there is such a violation and they stand in a certain kind of relationship with its victim – for example, as guardians, or, as in the case of the student, as people vulnerable to the same kind of rights violation. In the case of PNT, we may judge the parent to be weak or unreasonable in her uncritical reliance on stereotypes of impairment, but that is a judgment any of us can make, not a complaint limited to people with impairments. We can fault the parent for a flawed character, and condemn the social practices that exploit that flaw. But the parent herself does not wrong or offend anyone in manifesting that flaw, and her flaw is, in that sense, her own business.

It is, however, implausible to limit complaints to rights violations. There may be wrongs that do not violate anybody's rights, but that still give certain people standing to complain. Critics of PNT could argue that selective abortion for impairment is such a wrong. They might take either of two approaches: they could identify an independent wrong in selective abortion – the unwarranted destruction of a valuable object – and argue that people with impairments have special standing to complain about that wrong; or they could argue that even without such an independent wrong, selective abortion wrongs or gives offense to people with impairments, by treating them as moral inferiors. We will consider these approaches in order.

DESTROYING A VALUABLE OBJECT FOR A BAD REASON

There is some conduct that wrongs people even if it does not materially harm them, giving them special standing to complain. Say, for example, that someone destroys a great painting. That is surely a wrong to the owners, to potential viewers, and to all of us, because it reduces the world's stock of beautiful objects. (The looting of objects of antiquity in Iraq provides a disturbing contemporary example.) But if it turns out that the painting has been destroyed because the painter was Jewish or Muslim, that would give Jews or Muslims a special ground for complaint, distinct from that of the owners and viewers. The more beautiful and rare the painting, the greater the wrong to the owners and viewers, and also, arguably, to Jews or Muslims – "You must really hate us to destroy something so lovely just because one of us created it!" The wrong to Jews might also compound the wrong to the others – if it is a great wrong to owners and viewers to destroy a beautiful painting out of spite or revenge, it might be an even greater wrong to them to destroy it because of the ethnicity or religion of the painter.

In 1986, one of us argued "that fetuses were more than ideas" (Asch, 1986) in order to justify her contention that the act of terminating a pregnancy because of a diagnosed impairment was perhaps different from the act of delaying conception for a brief period in order to avert the same impairment. Ronald Dworkin (1993) has suggested that the fetus can be seen as an object with intrinsic value – something like an unfinished painting or symphony, an object of considerable intrinsic value – without claiming that it has the moral status of a person, or is any sort of rights holder.

If this view is plausible, it could be argued, first, that the fetus's impairment rarely provides an adequate reason to destroy it, because it rarely detracts substantially from its present intrinsic value (a point on which Dworkin himself chooses to remain agnostic), and second, that people with that impairment will have special standing to complain about the fetus's destruction. Destroying something of great intrinsic value because it has a characteristic they share may be a wrong to all of us, but it is particularly offensive to them.

Even if this provided a satisfactory account of the wrong of selective abortion, however, and of the special grievance it gives to those with the characteristics selected against, it would be difficult to extend to pre-implantation selection, let alone to gamete screening. Few people who regard developing fetuses as objects of great intrinsic value regard *in vitro* embryos as having similar value, and far fewer people regard gametes as having significant intrinsic value. So if pre-implantation or gamete screening is wrong, it must be wrong for a different reason. If it gives people with the impairments selected against grounds to complain, their complaints cannot be predicated on the intrinsic value of the object destroyed because of a characteristic they also possess.

BUT WOULD YOU WANT YOUR SISTER TO CARRY ONE?

To tease out an objection that does not rest on the value of the entity destroyed, it will be helpful to return again to the classroom analogy. Unlike the student with a right to fair consideration, a gamete or early fetus lacks, or so we have stipulated, a right to gestation, or even a right against being denied gestation for a bad reason. Nor do these entities have a right to equal treatment, or to be treated as equals. Adults who share their impairments, however, do have rights of this sort. But it would be implausible to claim that a couple or individual who aborts a fetus on the basis of its impairment violated those rights, in part because a rights violation is generally thought to require some setback to the interests of the rights holder, and the rights holders in question – actual people with impairments – do not appear to have suffered such a setback as a result of any individual decision about PNT. (The routinization and professsional endorsement of PNT may adversely affect them, but we are concerned here only with the harm done or the offense given by a single parental decision.) Moreover, it might be argued that even if they were adversely affected, as they would be if they were rejected as romantic prospects on the basis of their impairments, they would suffer no violation of their rights to equal treatment, or to treatment as equals, because those rights apply only in certain domains – in assigning a grade, for example, but not in filling out a dance card. It is instructive to recall that Dworkin imputes an obligation to display "equal concern and respect" only to states and to those acting as their agents, not to private individuals (Dworkin, 1977).

Critics of PNT might claim that a parent who declines to have a child with an impairment is like Joel Feinberg's "honorable bigot" (Feinberg, 1982), who scrupulously respects the rights of the group he is bigoted against but treats them as moral inferiors in every domain where they have no right to equal treatment. Unless we insist that legal and moral rights violations exhaust the domain of morally censurable conduct, the honorable bigot is still subject to censure for the bigotry he displays, and the subjects of his bigoted attitudes have special standing to censure him. His conduct reveals that he regards them all as morally inferior, even if it is directed at only one of them, or even, as in the case of selective abortion, if it is directed at an entity lacking the moral status to complain.

The defenders of PNT, then, must argue not merely that those who select against impairment do not violate the rights of existing people with impairments, but that they do not treat them as moral inferiors. They must claim that one can treat people with a given characteristic as moral equals without being willing, actually or hypothetically, to enter into certain sorts of intimate relationships with them. Someone can respect people with certain characteristics or traits as friends, colleagues, or fellow citizens without wanting to become the parent of a child with those characteristics or traits, or to marry a person with those characteristics or traits. (Obviously, giving birth to a person is a lot different than marrying one, but the contrast cuts both ways: the burden of commitment is greater for the mother, but the consequences of a refusal to commit are more dire for the fetus.)

The exception for intimate relationships has become suspect in American racial discourse: "But I wouldn't want my sister to marry one" is now regarded as a racist sentiment (although Martin Luther King once declared that black people sought to be the brothers of white people, not their brothers-in-law). The legitimacy of the exception may depend on the reason for excluding intimate relationships. We recognize some moral difference between a Jew who would date or marry only another Jew, and a Jew who would date or marry a white Christian but not a black of any faith; between those who restrict themselves to "their own kind" and those who exclude only certain other "kinds" (although the line between the two is sometimes very hard to draw; Alexander, 1992). The former attitude may be insular or clannish, but it need not offend in the same way as the latter, because it need not convey disrespect. In marriage, and perhaps in parenting, one may believe that equals can and should be separate.

Critics of PNT would deny that biostatistical normality is the sort of affinity that makes restrictions on intimate relationships more acceptable or innocuous. Being biostatistically normal (BSN) hardly establishes a deep cultural or spiritual kinship, even if certain departures from BSN, such as deafness, may help to establish membership in a second linguistic culture (e.g., Lane and Grodin, 1997). (Nor does the mere possession of a given impairment define a social or cultural "kind," or confer membership in a "disability culture" or "community," although the experience of being disabled by social attitudes and practices may confer minority status in some contexts, such as political action.) So it would be hard for a parent who tests and aborts for impairment to claim that she is merely displaying a strong positive preference for her own kind.

But this doesn't settle the issue. The defender of PNT might argue that even if one didn't have a good reason for declining to establish an intimate relationship with someone possessing a given characteristic, one needn't convey disrespect to people with that characteristic by declining. We can be close colleagues and good friends to people who would not have dated us for what we would regard as a bad reason – for example, because we are "hyper" or intense. More broadly, a defender of PNT would maintain that one can treat people as moral equals even if one would be unwilling, for reasons others would consider inadequate, to enter into certain intimate relationships with them or with people "like them." These reasons may be personally important in making such momentous decisions, and in acting on these reasons one would not treat those with whom one declined intimate relationships as moral inferiors – however painful one's decisions might be to those people.

Critics might respond to this defense by arguing that the actual or hypothetical refusal to enter into an intimate relationship with someone is not consistent with regarding that person, or people like him in relevant respects, as an equal if the characteristic on which the refusal is based is integral to the person's identity, or if it has been subject to a history of persecution and stigmatization. The various idiosyncrasies that make a person "hyper" or intense are neither integral, nor perhaps even valued, parts of a person's social identity, as deafness may often be, nor attributes long subject to stigmatization, as many impairments still are. It is harder to imagine being friends with individuals who dislike people who are of Jewish origin, regardless of their current state of religious observance or communal affiliation. We wouldn't be friends with someone who would have refused to date one of us because he or she disliked Jews (of course, such an individual probably wouldn't be friends with us either). It may be less disrespectful to decline to enter into an intimate relationship based on an overreaction to characteristics that are less important or historically freighted than race or religion, such as poor career choices or off-putting idiosyncracies.

A defender of PNT might, in turn, respond by insisting that the (counterfactual) refusal to enter into an intimate relationship with someone who possessed a stigmatized trait need not be synecdochal, even if the refusal were in some sense based on that trait. If a woman's aversion to pudgy or short partners reflected the shallow, conventional sexual aesthetic that consigns short or pudgy people to very narrow romantic and marital options, the latter might well take offense. But their offense would not, or should not, be as great if the woman were a physical perfectionist, attracted to and involved with only the most beautiful and athletic partners. Short and pudgy people might well find the woman's perfectionism noxious, but they would take their own exclusion less personally. They would be less offended still if the woman had highly idiosyncratic cravings, choosing as lovers only people conventionally regarded as ungainly, ugly, or grotesque and rejecting the beautiful and athletic as well as the short and pudgy. But in the latter two cases, the woman would be displaying different forms of inflexibility in her sexual choices, and not, arguably, synecdoche.

Thus, the critic's response would be to agree that respecting a person as an equal does not require even a hypothetical willingness to enter into an intimate relationship with that person. Such respect would be inconsistent only with *certain* reasons for refusing to do so. While a person can't truly respect someone with whom she would refuse to enter into an intimate relationship on the basis of invidious stereotypes, that need not be her reason. If she would refuse to marry a couch potato as well as a paraplegic, because neither would provide the kind of active companionship she required, her decision would arguably not be disrespectful to the latter. More broadly, if one's decision is based on inflexible or unrealistic requirements for an intimate relationship, the person denied intimacy can accept his consignment to friendship without a loss of self-respect. Being deprived of intimacy because of a friend's delusional quest for the perfect mate may be frustrating and painful, but it need not be demeaning. After all, the would-be partner may not regard his friend as the perfect mate, either; he may just have more realistic expectations. He may regard his friend's rejection as a sign of immaturity, selfishness, or inflexibility, but not as an insult. If, however, his friend declined because of a false belief that anyone with an impairment like his lacked the more general desiderata for such a relationship, the decision would indeed be based on stigma and stereotype, and he could indeed take offense. It would be more difficult to stay friends under those circumstances without a loss of self-respect.

In assessing the partially analogous slight implied in declining to become a parent, the individual's reasons have a similar relevance. A potential parent may have demanding projects or exacting expectations that she sees as precluding not only impairments, but a range of other characteristics as well. Although she might be wrong in her assessment of her resources, or inflexible in her unwillingness to adapt her projects or adjust her expectations, her reasons would be neither disability-specific nor stigma-driven. If parents want their child to be a musician, they will abort tone-deaf as well as deaf fetuses; if they want an heir (in some places), they will abort a female.[2] Parents who seek to promote their own projects or pursue their ideals may have a distorted conception of the parent-child relationship. But however serious, the moral faults revealed by such parents need not involve negative attitudes or adverse judgments about impairment, and they may not give people with impairments special standing to complain.

By contrast, parents who uncritically assume that a child with a severe impairment cannot fulfill even their modest expectations about raising a child and forming a family act on a false, harmful assumption about impairment. In effect, they let the impairment define the identity of its bearers and make them "not quite human," in Erving Goffman's words (1963: 5). Acting on this assumption when making reproductive decisions expresses disrespect for people with impairment by deeming them ineligible, without good reason, for one of the most intimate of all relationships.

To the extent that the use of PNT is informed by this view of impairment, people with impairments have a basis for complaint, not only because they are harmed by that same view in pursuing their own ambitions and desires, but also because that view suppresses their distinct identities, lumping them together with "defective" fetuses, embryos, and gametes as bearers of a common taint. They have standing to complain about a defect of judgment that, in other contexts, harms and offends existing people with impairments, and their complaints apply to actions that may not involve the destruction of intrinsically valuable objects – such as the refusal to implant a preserved embryo, the use of gamete screening, or the simple timing of conception to avoid creating a child with a stigmatized characteristic.

IS SYNECDOCHE A VENIAL SIN?

The defender of PNT might offer two partial defenses of the individual decision to utilize that technology on the basis of synecdochal attitudes. The first would claim that it is unfair to condemn overgeneralizations from a single characteristic only when that characteristic is subject to widespread social prejudice beyond the individual's control. The second would claim that unless we were to endow gametes and fetuses with rights against discrimination, synecdoche involving them is at most a minor offense, hardly worth the effort to condemn.

First, the defender might argue that the critic's emphasis on stigma makes the offense depend on the social meaning or expressive significance of the (counterfactual) refusal to enter into an intimate relationship, rather than on the individual's own attitudes. This defense may be easiest to present in the context of marital relationships. The meaning of a rejection based on Nordic ancestry may be different than the meaning of a rejection based on race; Norwegians have not been stigmatized or lynched in the United States, while African Americans continue to face institutional discrimination, social prejudice, and physical danger just because of their race. Similarly, people with impairments, especially ones readily discerned on first meeting, continue to face discrimination and shunning. Even if a person's reason for declining to marry a Nordic, black, or impaired suitor were the same – that she wasn't sexually attracted to Nordic, black, or impaired men – her refusal would convey greater disrespect in the latter two cases than in the former.

But it seems unfair to condemn a refusal to enter into a relationship as intimate as marriage entirely on the basis of social context and social meaning. Those factors seem far more relevant to state actions and policies than to personal choices, and while they may be adduced to condemn the development and promotion of PNT, it could be argued that they should not be invoked to condemn an individual decision to utilize it. Why should it be objectionable to reject a suitor based on his deafness or his African ancestry, but not on his Nordic ancestry? The historical accident that Nordic ancestry is not stigmatized does not change the fact that the rejection rests on an attitude toward one characteristic, which – without more explanation of its meaning to the person who is rejecting intimacy – seems to reduce the rejected person to one trait and to negate all other attributes.

A critic of prenatal testing might respond that it is not, or not principally, the social meaning of the decision to test and terminate that subjects the prospective mother to reproach – as opposed to providing a basis for condemning the social practices – but rather her own attitudes and judgments. A woman who rejects a Nordic suitor based solely on an idiosyncratic aversion to Scandinavians *does* display synecdoche, even if the offense is not as great as it would be in the case of a deaf or African American suitor, because it does not reflect, and perpetuate, an oppressive, widely held aversion.

The defender might also seek to excuse, if not justify, the individual decision to use PNT as a trivial wrong. He might concede that synecdoche often plays a role in PNT, but deny that it is a significant moral failing, or that it gives serious offense. He would argue that synecdoche in reproductive decisions is at most a minor or superficial flaw: the beliefs underlying synecdoche are thin presumptions, overcome by a firsthand exposure that is regrettably not possible in the case of an early fetus. Someone who would abort a fetus for impairments is like someone who is initially wary, rude, or hostile to clerks and bureaucrats, but who readily sets aside his stereotypes as soon as he has the opportunity for extended contact. Of course, he doesn't always have that opportunity, so he ends up on unpleasant terms with a fair number of clerks and bureaucrats. But this hardly disqualifies him from becoming friends with a clerk or bureaucrat once he gets to know him. His initial reaction can be dismissed or set aside, even if it is sure to be repeated with other clerks and bureaucrats.

A critic might reject this comparison for two reasons. First, he might insist that aborting a fetus is a more serious piece of misconduct than barking at a clerk. But that would be so only if the fetus were an object of considerable intrinsic value, and it would not explain the objection to preimplantation genetic diagnosis, since it is hard to see how destroying a gamete could be regarded as a more serious offense than barking at a clerk. The other, stronger reason is that being a clerk is a comparatively superficial, transient, and voluntary aspect of one's social identity. People who are Jewish would find it hard to be friends with someone who typically greeted their coreligionists with anti-Semitic slurs, however quickly he overcame his initial aversion. They would find it offensive to force a person to run a gauntlet of abuse, even a very short one, because of a stigmatized characteristic that they shared.

Many loving couples tell humorous stories of disastrous or inauspicious first encounters, but these encounters are typically fueled by idiosyncratic aversions or less invidious stereotypes (e.g., about single professional women, or about divorced forty-year-old men). Couples' accounts of overcoming more invidious stereotypes are less humorous, typically involving serious self-examination or self-reproach on the part of one or both partners.

SOME OF MY MOST SIGNIFICANT OTHERS HAVE IMPAIRMENTS: DOES EXPOSURE PRECLUDE SYNECDOCHE?

Some critics of prenatal testing would agree that an anxious first-time parent may display synecdoche in aborting because of a positive test result. But they would also argue that those who are already spouses or parents of people with the impairments tested for have earned themselves an exemption from that charge. After all, they have seen through the part to the whole; they love their spouse or child in his infinite particularity. If they choose not to have another child with an impairment, it must be for other, presumably better, reasons. Although we are not eager to criticize individuals who make such choices, we respectfully disagree.

Surely, the denial of synecdoche in these choices cannot rest on the claim that having resisted the distorting effects of stigma in one relationship, an individual is somehow immune to them everywhere else. Literature on prenatal testing includes both fictional and nonfictional accounts of people who are comfortable with being partners of, but unwilling to become parents of, people with impairments, even if the children would have conditions identical to those of the mate. Is such a refusal synecdochal? It might not seem to be, since the partner who does not want a child with blindness or achondroplasia has chosen a person with that characteristic as a life partner and presumably knows a fair amount about how that characteristic affects intimacy and daily life.[3] But there may be synecdoche in the inference or generalization from the experience of marrying one person with a given impairment to the experience of parenting another, or from the experience of parenting one child to the experience of parenting another. Why should the prospective parent assume that her experience with a person having a given impairment is a reliable guide to her future experience with another person sharing (only) that impairment? That assumption makes the part the preponderant element in shaping her expectations of the whole, and it treats the future child as an instance of a type defined by the impairment. And that, we suggest, is a form of synecdoche.

We are all familiar with a similar, if less destructive, form of synecdoche in the desire of many parents of multiple offspring for "sex balance." The mother of two boys may wish fervently for a girl and experience transient disappointment when she has a third boy. Yet that third boy may be as different from the other two as any girl she might have had. Her desire for sex balance is comparatively benign, both because it does not, or need not, favor one gender over another, and because she typically does not act on it: she will welcome a boy or a girl, and she expects any slight disappointment to be quickly overwhelmed by the joy of intimate involvement. Her desire would be less benign if she sought to fulfill it through PNT – a use already approved by some professional groups. And the wish for "impairment balance" is even less benign, both because parents almost always seek to avoid an "imbalance" of impaired children, and because they can and do avoid it by selective abortion.

Although the preferences for sex- and impairment-balance may have different practical expressions, the error underlying the two is much the same: the assumption that a single known characteristic will dominate a myriad of unknown characteristics in the parent-child relationship. That assumption is as erroneous for impairment balance as for sex balance. Even with the same impairment, Child 2 may be easier to raise simply because the parent already has experience with Child 1, just as many parents and children report that second children generally have an easier time of it because their parents are better prepared.

More important, Child 2 might be very different from Child 1 despite their shared impairment, as different as many a second child with no impairment. Even if the parents of one child with muscular dystrophy can accurately list the ways the child's condition has affected their lives – from the expenses of physical therapy, architectural access, and adapted toys to the sorrows of social rejection and the frustrations of not being able to share certain activities – these are only the known or expected challenges, as opposed to the unknown joys and tribulations, of raising Child 2. The parent who says "I am already stretched to my limits with one disabled child and need one without a disability" has no idea what challenges she would face from a second child without a disability: they may be greater or lesser, similar or different. The parent who makes a decision about additional children in terms of their impairment status still makes a synecdochal judgment, even if it is not a judgment based solely on invidious stereotyping or reflex repulsion.

We are not claiming that synecdoche always lies behind the refusal to have another child with a given impairment. Perhaps the parent had deferred her desire to have a child who could match her at chess, or follow her into an academic career, a desire that she now seeks, to the extent possible, to satisfy. In employing PNT to avoid the birth of a second child with Down syndrome, she would appear to be acting on consumerist rather than synecdochal reasons. But as we will argue in the final section, that would not place her beyond reproach.

HOW STRONG A PREFERENCE AGAINST HAVING AN IMPAIRED CHILD? SELECTING *IN VITRO*, AVOIDING BY DELAY, AND EMPLOYING RISKY CORRECTIVE MEASURES

Thus far, we have not considered the strength of the preference against raising a child with an impairment expressed by the use of PNT, preimplantation genetic diagnosis (PGD), or gamete screening. It is important to note at the outset that prospective parents who utilize any of these technologies almost always intend to have a child. Their choice, to adopt a distinction one of us has previously made, is not whether to have *any* child but whether to have a child with a *particular* characteristic – an impairment (Asch, 1989). Given the nature of their choice, their use of any of these technologies expresses some preference against having such a child.

That preference at first seems strongest in the case of selective abortion, as compared to the other procedures, for two reasons. First, the woman is willing to destroy a partially developed fetus in order to avoid having the impaired child it would become. Even if one does not regard that fetus as a valuable entity, one may find a stronger resolve manifested by its destruction than by the failure to implant a conceptus or the attempt to screen out a gamete. Second, the woman who selectively aborts is unambiguously rejecting a single entity and not, as in PGD, picking one entity over another. Even if she intends to have a "replacement" child after she aborts, there is only one present candidate for gestation, and she declines to gestate it. (Even in the case of selective abortion, though, the degree of resolution may vary. A woman may be willing to abort after eighteen weeks but not after twenty two; she may be willing to abort, but not to put an impaired newborn up for adoption.) We will focus on this second factor, the extent to which the preference against having an impaired child is comparative or absolute. We will then suggest a third factor: the salience of the entity rejected.

Gamete screening, or avoiding impairment by delaying conception, appears to manifest the weakest preference against parenting a child with an impairment, since these actions do not involve the rejection of any identifiable entity that could become a child; at least for the foreseeable future, they merely reduce the odds of conceiving an impairment-bearing fetus. But the longer the delay required, and the greater its impact on the parents' own plans and lives, the stronger the preference against an impaired child appears to be. PGD might seem to be an intermediate case, since it involves the rejection of embryos with diagnosed impairments in favor of embryos without diagnosed impairments.

But PGD may be ambiguous, expressing either a blanket refusal to have such a child, or a mere preference for a child who will not have the impairment. In either case, it is a form of selection, and we might prefer that parents refrain from embryo diagnosis and simply implant any one (or more) of the viable embryos. Preferring a musical child to a nonmusical one, even in the abstract, still involves letting one characteristic dominate all others; while nonmusical people are not typically a stigmatized "group," the prospective parent should recognize that she may share more rewarding interactions with her outgoing but tone-deaf child than with an introverted composer. Rejecting an embryo suspected of tone-deafness *or* deafness still appears to rest on the doubtful assumption that any child possessing the rejected trait will be less rewarding and more difficult to raise, or will have a more difficult and less rewarding life, than the equally unknown child without that trait or impairment.

To illustrate the differences in the strength of preference that could be manifested by PGD, we can contrast two cases – one involving the opportunistic use of PGD by a couple who require *in vitro* fertilization (IVF) in order to conceive at all; the other involving the use of IVF by a couple who are able to procreate without assistance, in order to use PGD to screen out "impaired" embryos. The latter appears no less exclusionary, if less invasive and disruptive, than selective abortion. The former appears to express a milder attitude, akin to that of the deaf lesbian couple who sought a deaf child through IVF, but would have welcomed a hearing child: "A hearing baby would be a blessing. A deaf baby would be a special blessing" (Mundy, 2002: 24). This seems to express a preference *for* a deaf child rather than *against* a hearing one, although that line can obviously be hard to draw, and we do not endorse selecting for deafness any more than we endorse selecting against it. Selecting for deafness is just as synecdochal as selecting against it, in our view, because it assumes that intimacy and community can be achieved only through one shared characteristic. It defines "being like" the parent as achievable simply by sharing one attribute – when in fact the deaf child may reject many deeply cherished parental values and preferences and be quite unlike his deaf parents in other significant respects.

In general, a person appears to reject a parental relationship with an impaired child more emphatically if she sees herself as choosing between an impaired child and no child than if she sees herself as choosing between an impaired and an unimpaired child. In the latter case, she may be expressing a preference that is less hurtful than the categorical rejection involved in the former case. We suspect that most parents using PNT do see themselves as choosing between an impaired and an unimpaired child, since they typically intend to "try again" if the test results are positive. But the expressive significance of the procedure also appears to vary with the salience or immanence of the entity excluded. As one of us suggested in an earlier article, selective abortion (or selective implantation after PGD) may seem more exclusionary than avoidance by delayed conception even if both are seen by the parents as choices between an impaired and an unimpaired child, just because an identifiable, existing entity is excluded in the former case but not in the latter (Asch, 1986).

Preferences of varying strength against having an impaired child may also be revealed in measures taken to prevent or correct impairment in an existing fetus. To the extent that those measures (are known to) risk the death of the fetus, or the alteration of its identity, they express an aversion to having an impaired child. The decision to undertake a risk-free or negligibly risky procedure may certainly express concern for the child. But the higher the risk of death or identity loss, the more difficult it is to attribute the corrective procedure to such concern. No one who cared for an existing child would subject it to a 50 percent or even 10 percent chance of death in order to correct its clubfoot or its hearing, and to subject a fetus to comparable risk is to express some preference against having a child with that impairment, though perhaps a weaker preference than is expressed in the use of PNT, PGD, or gamete screening.

Preventative measures that do not directly affect the survival or identity of the future child may express an even weaker preference against having a child with a given impairment. For example, taking folic acid before conception may express concern for the capacities of any potential child, but need not express a refusal or even a strong reluctance to have a child with the impairment that folic acid is intended to prevent. A prospective parent who tries to preserve her child's capacity for unimpeded mobility by taking folic acid in order to prevent spina bifida may be willing, or committed, to having the child even if the preventative regiment fails.[4]

It remains to be seen if there is any moral significance to the strength of the preference against having an impaired child. It is clearly more insulting to be excluded from an intimate relationship on the basis of an absolute than a comparative preference. The latter may still be insulting, however, particularly if the routine use of PGD or gamete screening turns a comparative preference into what is, for practical purposes, an absolute one, resulting in the choice of an unimpaired child for each successive pregnancy.

But there is another, perhaps more powerful, consideration. In choosing to abort a fetus with an impairment, a woman is not merely rejecting the only available candidate for gestation, she is aborting a *process* in which she may have already made a substantial physical and psychological investment. At the same time, she may well have made a substantial investment even before becoming pregnant. We believe that the process of becoming a parent should be seen as beginning before the existence of the child or even the fetus, with the decision to undertake the steps involved in having a child of one's own, by whatever means. A woman who utilizes PGD, like one who utilizes PNT, has, except in unusual cases, already made a commitment to becoming a parent. We will argue in the next section that she may be compromising the commitment that she has made, or should have made, if she terminates a pregnancy on the basis of a fetal characteristic, or refuses to become pregnant with a particular embryo on the basis of that characteristic.

IS SELECTION ON THE BASIS OF A SINGLE TRAIT ALWAYS SYNECDOCHAL? IS IT ALWAYS WRONG?

The analogy to other intimate relationships we drew earlier may be helpful in addressing possible justifications for declining to have a child with certain impairments. After all, there are some single facts about an individual (as well as some uncertainty about what would count as a single fact) that would justify one in declining to enter into an intimate relationship. The fact that one's prospective mate was a mass murderer would certainly be one. But that would also be a reason for declining to be friends in the first place, not an explanation owed a friend with whom one declines further intimacy. What is needed is a reason that would be good enough to decline intimacy but not friendship. Moreover, it must actually be the reason for declining – the existence of a good reason hardly justifies a refusal that is really based on stigma and stereotype.

The defender of PNT might insist that the reason for refusing to enter into an intimate relationship may not be a bad one, let alone an offensive one, even if it is based in some sense on impairment. Suppose, for example, that one's favorite leisure time activity is hiking, which might be difficult to enjoy with a partner who could not walk, or who could walk only slowly on smooth, paved surfaces. People often seek a level of companionship from their partners that they needn't seek with every friend; if a prospective partner cannot provide that kind of companionship, his rejection is based not on synecdoche but on one's particular requirements for intimate relationships, desires that might be compromised even if the potential partner had other valued traits. Surely, one can be a friend to a person one does not consider, and would not have considered, as a romantic prospect for such a reason. Moreover, such reasons do not seem perfectionist or consumerist – what one seeks are qualities that are necessary for a certain kind of intimate relationship, not for an ideal or exceptionally rewarding relationship of that kind.

In more general terms, there may be goods central to intimate relationships that are not central to friendship. The honest belief that one cannot achieve such goods in a more intimate relationship with someone who is currently a friend appears, at least in theory, to provide a good reason to decline intimacy, a reason fully consistent with respect for one's friend. But this belief, even if honest, may be mistaken in two ways: the characteristics of the friend may not preclude those goods, or the goods may not really be central to the kind of intimate relationship sought. The first mistake may arise from the stereotyping and over-generalization we have described as synecdochal; the second, from the narrow or impoverished view of the relationship and its central goods reflected in consumerist and perfectionist attitudes.

Before illustrating these mistakes, we think it is important to acknowledge some tension inherent in assessing the legitimacy of selectivity in intimate relationships. On the one hand, the more intimate the relationship, the more selectivity may seem warranted – disqualifications that would be considered petty or inappropriate for more arms-length relationships, such as student or employee, seem perfectly reasonable for a lover or spouse. At the same time, more intimate relationships are morally privileged – on any plausible moral theory, we are permitted or even required to display partiality toward our lovers, spouses, children, and parents. To categorically disqualify a person from access to this "inner circle" seems a mark of presumptive disrespect, requiring a very good reason.

One type of good reason is that some characteristic of the person precludes one's attaining a central good of the relationship – for example, participation in a shared activity important to, or defining of, the relationship. It is conventionally held that some minimum of sexual attraction is an essential feature of a romantic relationship, and that a legitimate reason to decline to enter into such a relationship with someone is that one isn't attracted to him or her. (Defining "attraction" is complex and, fortunately, unnecessary for our purposes here.) And it is conventionally held that a central, but not essential, good of a marital relationship is procreation. So on the conventional view, a heterosexual individual could categorically decline to consider a sexual or marital relationship with a member of the same sex (if the latter were even legally recognized) without disrespect, because she could not achieve central goods of that relationship with that person.

Of course, one could have a narrow or impoverished view of the goods of an intimate relationship – perhaps sexual attraction should not be regarded as a necessary condition for romantic love or marriage, but merely as facilitating the expression of love or commitment; perhaps procreation is merely one of many long-term projects that one can appropriately undertake with one's life partner, from adoption to sailing around the world. Or one could be mistaken in one's belief that a given characteristic precluded a central good of the relationship – maybe sexual preferences in general, or one's own preferences in particular, are far more plastic than one has assumed.[5]

This suggests that we cannot decide if particular reasons for declining to enter into an intimate relationship are good or appropriate ones without some understanding about the goods of that relationship, and that debates about whether a reason is good or appropriate often reflect disagreement about the character of the relationship. Someone who held an Aristotelian conception of friendship, which understood the good of that relationship to be the mutual recognition, celebration, and promotion of shared virtues, would accept a far wider set of reasons for declining to become friends than someone who held a less elitist notion of that relationship, as based on spontaneous affection, shared history or interests, or any number of other affinities. For someone holding the latter notion of friendship, a person who would never become friends with anyone who lacked his formidable skills or achievements would display a noxious consumerism or perfectionism. In the next, final section, we will make somewhat analogous claims about parenthood: that the debate about what constitutes a good or appropriate reason for declining to become a parent is best understood as a debate about the moral character and central goods of parenting, and that many common reasons for declining to have children with impairments reflect a narrow and impoverished view of that relationship. We will argue that the central goods of parental and family relationships are different in important respects from the central goods of other intimate relationships, and that they are rarely precluded by impairment.

SYNECDOCHE, SELECTIVITY, AND THE PARENT-CHILD RELATIONSHIP

In the first part of this chapter, we attempted to distinguish synecdoche from other attitudes and beliefs that may lie behind the decision of individual parents to seek PNT. Here, we want to stress what those attitudes and beliefs have in common. Although we believe that synecdoche involves a distinctive moral weakness, we think it is reinforced by a conception of the roles of parents and families that make the fears of raising a child with an impairment seem more reasonable than they really are. This vague but powerful conception, reflected to varying extents in the consumerist and perfectionist attitudes we have described, suggests the distorting effects of a single model of human affiliation, as the voluntary association of self-interested individuals. If privilege and hierarchy were once justified by an analogy from the patriarchal family to society, selectivity and limited commitment within the family are now justified by analogy to liberal society. Without denying that the recognition of the moral and legal rights of individual family members, particularly women and children, has been terribly important, we think that parenthood and families are sui generis, a form of association significantly different from other social groups. And although we lack a fully developed account of the moral role of parents or the moral function of families, we think that some of the elements of such an account can be found in a critique of the selectivity involved in most reasons for seeking PNT.

In order to make out these claims, we first need to draw a contrast to the other form of intimate association to which we have up to now been drawing an analogy. We will argue that the kind of selectivity that may be appropriate in choosing a mate is not appropriate in choosing a child, that it may be more acceptable to be selective in the former case than in the latter. Because parental and family relationships are even less conditional than romantic and marital relationships, refusing to establish or maintain a parental relationship on the basis of incompatible characteristics conflicts more sharply with the moral character of parenthood than rejecting a marital relationship does with the moral character of marriage.[6]

We believe that becoming a parent should involve a stronger and less conditional commitment than becoming a marital partner. The traditional marital vows represent a commitment – in sickness and in health, for richer or poorer – increasingly observed in the breach. But while we regret the high rate of divorce, we do not think the divorce of a couple necessarily represents a moral failing. People recognize that marriages can turn out to be unsatisfactory to one or both partners, and divorce and break-up are common in marriage and same-sex relationships. We may regret the trend and seek to fortify the institution of marriage, but we do not condemn the act of divorce. We are far more disapproving of parents who sever a relationship with a child once that relationship has begun, even if the child suffers little material or psychological harm. If people can comfortably become ex-partners but not ex-parents, then perhaps we expect more of parents than of partners.[7]

Consider, for example, how we would react to popular advice about whether to stay in a parental relationship, akin to the advice that now proliferates about whether to stay in a marital relationship. There have been times and places where such advice to new parents was accepted, and perhaps common. Sherry Floyd and David Pomerantz (1999) note that the Romans wrote essays with titles such as "How to Recognize the Newborn Who Is Worth Rearing." Most of us would regard contemporary versions of such essays with distaste or indignation. We may be very sympathetic to the teenage girl who makes adoption plans for her child in order to give it better prospects, because we regard this decision as what one of us has called an "any" choice – the teenager does not believe she is ready to give *any* child the care and support it needs (Asch, 1989). We would be less sympathetic to parents who, having decided to start or enlarge a family, make adoption plans for a child with an impairment because they believe that raising that child is likely to be hard, unrewarding, and incompatible with valued projects. We regard "incompatibility" as a much poorer excuse for giving up a child than for giving up a mate.

It might be argued, however, that the greater strength of the parental commitment cuts the other way, or is at least double-edged. If we expect more of parents in terms of their commitment to and acceptance of children than we expect of adults toward their partners, perhaps we should allow and even encourage selection for and against offspring characteristics in order to reduce the possibility of postnatal rejection. While the harm of refusing to marry someone is frequently as great or greater than the harm of divorcing him if the marriage fails, the harm done by declining to implant or bear a child is typically quite small relative to the harm of giving up a child.

To a critic of PNT, however, this contrast merely suggests that the opposition to parental selectivity is fundamentally nonconsequentialist. What is wrong about such selectivity is not, or not principally, that it may have harmful consequences, but that it reflects, and expresses, an impoverished conception of parenthood and families. One of the features that makes families a morally significant form of association is precisely their lack of selectivity: the family enjoys elevated moral status and special legal protection just because it is not, in Leo Kittay's words, an exclusive club (Kittay, 2000).

Families begin with one or more adults "pledging" to love, nurture, and protect a person they have never met – a person to whom they will be bound not by compatible interests or tastes (though these may emerge), but by the profound dependency of that person at the onset of their relationship, and by their resolve to sustain and nurture that person when he is at his most vulnerable. One of us has previously argued that people should become parents out of a longing, and a commitment, to "give ourselves to a new being who starts out with the best we can give, and who will enrich us, gladden others, contribute to the world, and make us proud" (Asch, 1989).To those who insist that relationships and associations rest on expectations of mutual advantage, such a longing and commitment are anomalous, so anomalous that they must be explained by the exigencies of adaptation, by the figurative "selfishness" of the genes that parents pass on to their children (with the phenomena of adoption and step-parenting encompassed by the epicycles of a theory even more adaptable than its subject matter). For us, by contrast, the ideal of parenthood to which many parents aspire, and some may achieve, represents a kind of moral alchemy: the capacity of human beings to transmute biological impulses into moral ideals and practices.[8]

As inchoate as this understanding of parenthood and family may be, it suggests that what is wrong about PNT, and the selectivity that it serves and reinforces, is their affront to an ideal of unconditional devotion, as much as, if not more than, their harmful consequences. This understanding rejects the tolerant pluralism of William Ruddick, who argues that PNT is consistent with some, but not all, legitimate parental roles. Ruddick regards the ideal of unconditional devotion that we have articulated merely as characterizing one of three common and acceptable maternal postures, a posture he calls "maternalist." He finds equally legitimacy in the posture of parents who have children as a project, with specific expectations and goals, a posture he calls "projectivist," as well as in the posture of parents who have additional children in order to serve the interests of the family they already have, a posture he calls "familialist." While Ruddick's taxonomy may be good sociology, we regard it as misguided ethics. Most parents may be, to some extent, projectivist, but we believe it is a posture we should gently discourage, not legitimize and support with genetic technology. Parents do not have to be saints, but they should not have children unless they are willing to modify or forego the other projects in their lives.[9] And parents should certainly not ignore the interests of their existing children in having additional children, and so, in that sense, should be familialist. But they should expect their existing children to accommodate, if not embrace, the posture of unconditional welcome with which those children were themselves brought into the world, and they should want them to extend it to any new arrivals. Moreover, we see such adaptability on the part of parents and families not as a sacrifice demanded by a commitment even stronger than marriage, so much as an integral feature of the parenthood and families, fully consistent with the central goods of those relationships.

We contend that impairments, and other characteristics viewed as "burdensome and irksome," will rarely defeat reasonable hopes and dreams for rearing a child or preclude rewarding relationships with the child. And we then suggest that abandoning a parental project in the face of such characteristics, or making that project contingent on the absence of such characteristics, is inconsistent with the commitment to welcome and nurture any child the parents have, a commitment we regard as the moral foundation of the family. All children depart in some way from parental preferences. What adult can say that she has not displayed tastes, values, or temperamental traits that did not disappoint or frustrate her parents? What parent does not notice attributes of even an adored child that she wishes were different? If prospective parents refuse to have a child because of a characteristic that threatens disappointment or frustration, why should they commit themselves to appreciating, enjoying, and valuing children who will inevitably manifest other departures from their expectations and dreams?

Perhaps the strongest response to questions to this kind has been offered by Mary Ann Baily, in defense of her own decision to undergo PNT. As one of us has paraphrased the metaphor she employs:

Why climb the Mount Everest of parenthood with problems I can predict when I have the chance to climb Mount Ranier? Mount Ranier will have its own surprises and twists. (Parens and Asch, 2000: 22)

Even if the prospective parent does not make the (synecdochal) mistake of assuming that impairments pose a uniquely Himalayan challenge, the contrast itself is misconceived in two ways. First, it is wrong to suggest that virtually *any* knowable characteristic of a child will produce a differential in hardship comparable to that between climbing Ranier and Everest. Like climbing mountains, raising children contains an irreducible element of uncertainty, and one should come as ready as possible for all contingencies – even when scaling smaller mountains in temperate climates, climbers should be prepared for blizzards or avalanches. Second, the challenge of climbing with such uncertainty is something that mountaineers embrace, not avoid. People who love climbing may start with Ranier, but they aspire to Everest. While we would hardly encourage parents to seek the most challenging children possible (and would find the effort mildly perverse), we do think they should view having children and raising families as a great adventure, one whose spirit is dampened by too many anxious, and arguably futile, precautions.

At the same time, our understanding of parenthood and family suggests that there *could* be some reasons to decline to establish a parental relationship that arise from, or are associated with, impairment. Having argued that welcoming a child with a serious impairment is fully consistent with our conception of parenthood and families, we may still wonder whether there may be characteristics or circumstances associated with some impairments so extreme as to preclude the central goods of parenthood and family. We do not think an answer can be found in a catalogue of biomedical conditions that can be diagnosed by PNT.[10] If for no other reason than the variable expression or "penetrance" of the chromosomal and genetic variations associated with those conditions, such a catalogue cold never provide us with lists of conditions that are "appropriate" and "inappropriate" for PNT. We have steadfastly opposed, and continue to oppose, such attempts at line drawing as the basis for public policy on PNT (Asch, 2003; Wasserman, 2003). Rather, we ask whether we can imagine situations in which the presence of an impairment would preclude the enjoyment of goods central to parenthood and families, which would justify individual parents in seeking PNT. The claim that there are such situations is certainly a controversial one, about which people generally wary of PNT will disagree. But raising the question forces us to think hard about the nature and limits of parenthood and families.

We will discuss three situations about which such a claim could be made: severe, comprehensive cognitive impairments; very early death; and virulently oppressive social environments. The last illustrates, in a particularly dramatic way, the interactive model of disability, which emphasizes the interplay of impairment and social context in creating disability. Our suggestion is that extraordinarily hostile social environments may be inimical to the goods of a parental relationship with an impaired child. The first two raise what is for us the more difficult question of whether there are any impairments that may impose such formidable barriers to a parent-child relationship even in a welcoming social environment – in particular, cognitive impairments that prevent the development of mental faculties arguably required for intimate relationships, and physical impairments that radically shorten life span or involve a continuing loss of function from an early age.

It might be argued that a prospective parent could reasonably decline to have a child who is likely to be so impaired cognitively as to lack the mental requisites for an intimate relationship, such as self-consciousness or the capacity to identify significant others. Such incapacity could be seen as precluding the central goods of a parent-child relationship, which include some form of continuing recognition and sustained affection. An adult could hardly have what we understand as an intimate relationship with a child would could not distinguish her parents from a friendly grocery clerk. But very few conditions that can be detected prenatally involve such profound cognitive incapacity – Down syndrome and fragile X syndrome, among the most commonly diagnosed conditions, rarely, if ever, do. Moreover, it is terribly easy to exaggerate the limitations of a child with a cognitive impairment, as we can see from the literature about families that include members with significant cognitive and emotional impairments (e.g., Ferguson, 2001).

It could also be argued that the prospect of a radically shorter life span would deny a parent one of the central goods of parenting – that of seeing her child through most of her major life stages. The claim that impairment compromises the goods of parenthood in this situation is certainly controversial. This claim is typically expressed in terms of the emotional burden on parents of the premature death of a child. Conventional wisdom holds that the worst possible tragedy is to outlive one's child. Of course, some unimpaired children die in car accidents or drinking marathons or from aggressive childhood cancers. But raising a child knowing that there is a very slight risk of her never reaching her twenty-first birthday is qualitatively different from raising a child knowing that there is a very high probability that she will die well before reaching that milestone.

For our purposes, what matters more than the claimed emotional burden on parents of the predictable death of a child before her majority – though we take that claim seriously – is the argument that such early death precludes a central good of parenthood. A predictably early death need not deny the child a life worth living, but it may arrest the development of the parent-child relationship, and the progress toward independence and autonomy possible even for children with profound multiple impairments. A parent might decline to have a child almost certain to die young for much the same reason he would decline to have a child in his old age – because he would not be able to see that child grow up, and the truncated relationship possible under that constraint would preclude a central good of parenthood – the good of fostering and celebrating the growth of the child to adulthood. (The parent who chooses to have a child in old age, however, may shirk a parental responsibility in a way that the parent who has a short-lived child does not. The former, unlike the latter, is likely to "abandon" the child when she is still in her formative years; the latter is very likely to "be there" for the child as long as she lives.)

It is certainly possible, however, to deny that this is a central good of parenthood, rewarding as it may be. Perhaps the parents of a child with a shorter life span are even better situated than the parents of a child with an ordinary life span to fulfill the critical parental role of making their child's life rich and fulfilling, structuring her upbringing so as to achieve as much as possible in the limited time available. They can protect her from the innocent but often oppressive expectation that she will live a normal life span.

Yet some conditions involving short life spans also involve recurrent pain and increasing, but often unpredictable, loss of function. If we assume, as we have been doing, that the child's own life is worth living despite the pain, loss of function, and uncertainty, the question remains of whether, in extreme cases, those features deprive parenthood of its central goods. Consider a description of Juvenile Batten's Disease (from a disability support website), a genetic condition that manifests its first symptoms when the child is six to nine years old, causing the loss of sensory, muscular, and neurological function, progressing to severe dementia and almost complete immobility, and ending in death in one to fifteen years:

The speed of the inevitable degeneration . . . is variable and uneven. There can be periods of stability, periods of rapid degeneration, periods of recovery (although not to the previous level) and periods of gradual degeneration. All this, when coupled with the continued physical and psychological development of the child and the deteriorating mental and bodily functions, can be confusing and frightening at least, and often leads to severe emotional disturbance. (SeeAbility, 2004).

Perhaps a child with Juvenile Batten's Disease has a life that is not, on balance, worth living. But we can hardly be confident of that in all cases – it might well be worth living a life consisting of eight years of flourishing followed by a year or two of painful deterioration. Yet caring for a child with such a life may not only be "confusing and frightening," it may also be difficult even to see as a parental undertaking. It may be that one unique and valuable, if not essential, feature of parenthood is guiding the growth of one's child, however slow, limited, fitful, or atypical it may be. That good can be realized as fully, if differently, by the parents of children with most cognitive impairments as by the parents of an unimpaired or precocious child. But if the child's life is, from very early on, more of a process of decline than of growth, the parent may have little or no rearing or nurturing to do. While providing comfort and mitigating pain are valuable activities, with their own rewards, they arguably are not the central goods of parenting, even on a fairly expansive understanding of that role.[11]

We are, however, hesitant to endorse the claim that any impairment automatically precludes the central rewards of parenthood. The literature on raising children with CF and sickle cell, and even trisomy 18 and Tay-Sachs, reveals that many parents of children with conditions that impair cognition and shorten life span can, without denying the sadness of early death, find great satisfaction in raising a child even for such a brief life span, and win often maintain that they would not prevent the birth of another child with the same condition. Arguably, these parents are not exceptional. It may be possible for most parents to reap great rewards from the life of a child they create and raise, however long the child may live, as long as they can discern that their love and care make a positive difference to that child. In fact, if parents know at the beginning of a child's life, or before its birth, that its life is likely be shorter than average for the culture and society in which it will be raised, they can emotionally and intellectually prepare themselves to nurture their child for however long the child will live. Fostering and delighting in a child's development over ten, fifteen, twenty, or thirty years need not be an unreasonable parental project. There are too many families living rich lives even though one child has CF, sickle-cell anemia, muscular dystrophy, or juvenile diabetes to confidently assert that a parent who raises a child with one of these impairments is deprived of a central good of parenthood.

Thus, we believe that raising a child for however many years the child lives can be profoundly gratifying. Nevertheless, we acknowledge that the expected loss of a beloved child at the age of five, ten, or twenty may be almost unimaginably crushing. Although we are not of one mind on how to evaluate this situation, we wish to acknowledge its difficulty. We recognize that witnessing the inevitable, inexorable decline in capacity, enjoyment, and awareness of a child who develops typically until age seven or eight and then slowly fades away over five or ten years may be so difficult that many might claim that the goods of parenthood could be precluded by impairments of this sort. But at the same time, we recognize that other parents would find great reward in making the life of such a child as rich and full as possible. Both responses strike us as understandable, and as morally and psychologically compatible with the conception of the parent-child relationship we have been sketching. This suggests, to borrow John Rawls's phrase, that there is an "irreducible plurality" of reasonable conceptions of the goods of parenthood, all of which deserve our respect.

The final situation arises from a characteristic not of the child, but of the community into which he would be born. Few, we think, would disagree that parents would have reason to abort a fetus diagnosed with an impairment in an brutally eugenic society that euthanized impaired children. The decision to abort in such circumstances would be quite similar to the decision of parents to abort a fetus with a stigmatized characteristic such as Jewish or Romani ancestry in a society bent on the elimination of all children born with that characteristic. It would surely be difficult, if not impossible, to achieve the goods of parenthood and family with the near-certainty of leading a fugitive existence with one's child, under the constant threat of discovery or betrayal.

Our present society, however, for all its imperfections, does not attempt to kill or even quarantine children with impairments. It offers more options and greater support than it did a generation ago, at least for the middle- and upper-class people who are the main consumers of PNT, and it does not demand heroic self-reliance to raise a child with an impairment. The refusal to do so may reflect the parents' own stigmatization of that characteristic as much as the society's hostility and lack of support. As PNT becomes increasingly routine, however, we fear that this may no longer be the case. The somewhat greater acceptance and opportunity afforded to people with impairments of this generation may be in jeopardy if the next generation of people with prenatally diagnosable impairments is seen as the avoidable result of parental irresponsibility, as a failure of prevention rather than an expression of human diversity (Davidio, Major, and Crocker, 2000; Neuberg, Smith, and Ascher, 2000).

CONCLUSION

Although we remain uncertain at the margins, we believe that most decisions to abort for, or select against, impairment are misguided – based on harmful stereotypes, unreasonable expectations, or relentless institutional pressures. For this reason, we feel that a prospective parent should begin with a suspicion of, and a presumption against, the impulse to abort an impaired child. It may be possible for a prospective parent to allay that suspicion, and to overcome that presumption, with enough soul-searching and investigation. But the decision to abort even the most severely impaired child should be made with some degree of ambivalence, discomfort, or uncertainty.

We return, in closing, to the virtues we believe are central for parenting. We know that many people will not accept our characterization of the parental role, and we also know that no parent can fully succeed in that role, even if she or he shares our view. Building on Sara Ruddick's characterization of "maternal" (sic) parental practice (1989), we believe that parents must go beyond physical protection, nurturance, and the education and socialization required for acceptance into the community. We maintain that parents must appreciate, and convey their appreciation of, the uniqueness of their children. If they cannot communicate social expectations to their children, while at the same time rejecting expectations that stigmatize their children's differences, they cannot give their children the foundation of security and love they need for their growth and development.

To parents who have used or expect to use PNT (a group that includes the second author), our message or tone may sometimes seem moralistic or sanctimonious, despite our frequent qualifications and our desire to avoid such preaching. A parent who has anxiously sought PNT, and who has either felt intense relief at "negative" results or made a painful decision to abort in the face of "positive" ones, is not likely to welcome our opinion that he or she may have displayed moral weakness, or may have acted on an "impoverished" or "morally problematic" conception of parenthood and family. We have three parting thoughts that may not fully satisfy such parents, but that should go some way toward dispelling the impression that we are hectoring them from a self-assigned pulpit.

The first is that we are putting forth an ideal, an aspiration, that deserves more reflection and discussion than it has thus far received by those who enthusiastically endorse the selection or exclusion of offspring characteristics. Individual parents, or the larger society in which they live, may reject this ideal, but if so, that rejection deserves more recognition and discussion than has taken place to date. Second, even those who might praise this ideal of parenthood may conclude that neither they nor their social milieu are ready for whatever work they imagine is entailed in meeting the ideal. To claim that prospective parents act in a problematic way, or fail to live up to a moral ideal, is not at all to say that they act badly or shamefully. It is to condemn them, if at all, for the kind or degree of moral failing of which we are all guilty countless times in our lives.

Philosophers debate how demanding morality should be; for some, the mere fact that a moral principle prohibits the actions of a vast majority of people in a difficult situation makes it excessively demanding. We are reluctant to enter this debate. The most we want to claim is that prospective parents who select against impaired children do not act as well as they might; that they may be mistaken in their assessment of themselves, their strengths and their needs, or about the prospects and value of lives with impairments; and that by acting on their misapprehensions, they undoubtedly perpetuate the fears and stereotypes that mar the lives of existing people with disabilities and their families. If there is a "wrong" in their course of action, it is in participating in a system that encourages intolerance and exclusion of people based on one characteristic. But the blame falls mainly on the institutions, policies, and professional practices that make it almost impossible to opt out – that dismiss, scold, or condemn those who would willingly invite children with diagnosable impairments into their families.

Fifteen years ago, one of us wrote: "In order to imagine bringing a disabled child into the world when abortion is possible, one must be able to imagine saying to the child: 'I wanted you enough and believed enough in who you could be that I felt you could have a life you would appreciate even with the difficulties your disability causes.'" Most of the medical and bioethics professionals who are society's representatives vis-à-vis prospective parents work daily to make that message harder to convey. It is hardly surprising that almost no would-be parents can imagine a satisfying life raising any child born with an impairment. It is the routinization of, and standard justifications for, impairment screening that we find offensive, not the use of screening technology by anxious and vulnerable parents. We do not want to make such parents feel guilty about the screening they have done; we merely want to make them skeptical about the justifications they are offered for such screening, and to sharpen their discomfort about taking part in the enterprise. We hope to promote second thoughts, and perhaps a certain queasiness, about a practice that has become all too familiar.

If we were to offer a comparison to explain our objectives, it would be to the impact that Peter Singer's case against killing animals for food has had on the ranks of previously untroubled carnivores. Few have become vegetarians, but many, like us, now think twice (or more) about the habit of eating meat daily, and attempt to reduce their consumption for moral as well as for prudential reasons. This would not be good enough for Singer, and our comparison itself would doubtless strike him as inapt if not perverse, since the impact we seek would, by his reckoning, reduce rather than increase net utility; indeed, he would even find it justifiable to kill some of the infants whose prenatal exclusion we have argued against. Nevertheless, we feel that we will have achieved a great deal if we can sensitize people to the moral problems of impairment screening to the extent that Singer has sensitized them to the moral problems of eating meat.

NOTES

1. The term was first used in this context by Erik Parens to characterize Adrienne Asch's position, in Parens and Asch (2000), pp. 12–13, but although Asch adopted it, it never made its way into the text of that essay.

2. To the extent that it is bona fide, a concern about parental capacities raises no categorical objection to having a child with an impairment. Parents might claim that if they were rich, resilient, and resourceful, they could handle the demands of a child with a severe impairment and would willingly enter into a parental relationship with such a child. As we noted earlier, we are suspicious of such claims, because we think they may reflect an implicit cost-benefit analysis in which the costs of raising a child with an impairment are inflated by stigma, and the benefits ignored. Parents who seek to avoid excessive costs may simply display an insufficiently robust commitment to parenthood, but they are more likely to be driven, we suggest, by a preoccupation with the impairment to the exclusion of all that is likely to be rewarding in raising the child with that impairment.

3. See Kent (2000) for a personal account, and see Mawer (1998) for a fictional account of this situation.

4. And yet, taking folic acid, like almost any other action taken by the prospective parents before conception, may affect the identity of the future child merely by affecting the timing of conception. For this reason, it may be construed as expressing at least a mild preference for an impaired over an unimpaired child, even for parents who would not abort an impaired child, or even decline to implant an embryo diagnosed with an impairment.

5. Even if one were correct that a given characteristic precluded a central good of the relationship, it could do so for reasons that subjected one to reproach. One's failure to find a wide range of prospective lovers sexually attractive might reflect a deeply ingrained narcissism that demands a sexual partner who is as beautiful as one considers oneself.

6. Michael Sandel (2004) draws a similar contrast: "Parental love is not contingent on the talents and attributes a child happens to have. We choose our friends and spouses at least in part on the basis of qualities we find attractive. But we do not choose our children." Sandel draws this contrast in order to express misgivings about genetic enhancement of children, a distinct if related issue. We do not think that enhancement, at least identity-preserving enhancement, conflicts with the ideal of unconditional parental welcome as sharply as prenatal selectivity does. But we appreciate Sandel's concern that genetic enhancement may both express and encourage a conditional or contingent commitment to one's children.

7. It may also be that people are more inclined to synecdoche in selecting children than in selecting spouses or other partners. Because people typically identify more strongly with their children than with their spouses or partners, the sway of stigma may be greater in choices about the former. As we suggested earlier, someone who tells a spouse or other intimate with an impairment that she should never be the parent of someone like him may be displaying a form of synecdoche. See also Weiss (1996).

8. We do not wish to deny that this ideal is often observed in the breach. For disturbing and poignant evidence of how limited and contingent parental commitment to impaired children can be, see Weiss (1996).

9. Ruddick elsewhere (1999) acknowledges this in his Life Prospects Principle, which recognizes the need for parents to modify their projects in raising

children, but sets limits on the compromises that parents are required to make in their most important projects. We suspect that a projectivist parent would have trouble complying even with this modest principle.

10. As we have argued, there are only a *very* small number – perhaps no more than one or two – conditions that are so bad for those who have them that they make their lives as a whole not worth living. Creating a child with such a condition is a wrong to that *child* – the issue of whether it precludes a central good of parenthood or families is never reached.

11. It is instructive at this point to revisit the comparison with romantic relationships, to assess how these three reasons would fare as grounds for declining intimacy. Even more clearly than in the case of parenthood, the inability of another person to recognize one as a significant other would preclude a central good of a romantic relationship. While the loss of that ability due to illness, accident, or age might not warrant abandoning a relationship long enriched by mutual recognition, it would surely justify not establishing a relationship where such mutual recognition is impossible. On the other hand, a hostile or threatening social environment seems to provide a less compelling reason to avoid a romantic than to avoid a parental relationship. To provide support and succor for an existing individual persecuted or ostracized by his society is to realize the goods of a friendship or a romance in a particularly intense way. Finally, the likelihood of early death may seem less threatening to the goods of friendship than to the goods of parenthood. However fulfilling it is to grow old with one's partner, sharing a significant part of the other's life may not appear to be as important for a romantic as for a parental relationship. These are, of course, merely our preliminary thoughts; we need a great deal of further reflection on the character and goods of different types of intimate relationship.

REFERENCES

Alexander, L. 1992. "What Makes Wrongful Discrimination Wrong? Biases, Preferences, Stereotypes, and Proxies." *University of Pennsylvania Law Review* 141: 149–219.

Asch, A. 1989. Reproductive Technology and Disability. In S. Cohen and N. Taub (eds.), *Reproductive Laws for the 1990s*. Clifton, NJ: Humana Press, pp. 69–124.

Asch, A. 1999. "Prenatal Diagnosis and Selective Abortion: A Challenge to Practice and Policy." *American Journal of Public Health* 89(11): 1649–57.

Asch, A. 2000. "Why I Haven't Changed My Mind about Prenatal Diagnosis: Reflections and Refinements. In E. Parens and A. Asch (eds.), *Prenatal Testing and Disability Rights*. Washington, DC: Georgetown University Press, pp. 234–50.

Asch, A. 2003. "Disability Equality and Prenatal Testing: Contradictory or Compatible?" (Symposium, Genes and Disability: Defining Health and the Goals of Medicine) *Florida State University Law Review* 30: 315–341.

Asch, A., and Geller, G. 1996. "Feminism, Bioethics, and Genetics." In Susan Wolf (ed.), *Feminism and Bioethics: Beyond Reproduction*. New York: Oxford University Press, pp. 318–50.

Baily, M. A. 2000. "Why I Had Amniocentesis." In E. Parens and A. Asch (eds.), *Prenatal Testing and Disability Rights*. Washington, DC: Georgetown University Press, pp. 64–7.

Baxter, C., Poonia, K., Ward, L., and Nadirshaw, Z. 1995. "A Longitudinal Study of Parental Stress and Support: From Diagnosis of Disability to Leaving School." *International Journal of Disability, Development, and Education* 42: 125–36.

Botkin, J. 2000. "Line Drawing: Developing Professional Standards for Prenatal Diagnostic Services." In E. Parens and A. Asch (eds.), *Prenatal Testing and Disability Rights*. Washington, DC: Georgetown University Press, pp. 288–307.

Botkin, J. 2003. "Prenatal Diagnosis and the Selection of Children." (Symposium, Genes and Disability: Defining Health and the Goals of Medicine) *Florida State University Law Review* 30: 265–293.

Cahill, B. M., and Gidden, L. M. 1996. "Influence of Child Diagnosis on Family and Parental Functioning: Down Syndrome versus Other Disabilities." *American Journal of Mental Retardation* 101: 149–60.

Clarke, A. 1991. "Is Non-directive Genetic Counseling Possible?" *Lancet* 338: 998–1001.

Davidio, J. F., Major, B., and Crocker, J. 2000. "Stigma: Introduction and Overview." In T. F., Heatherton, R. Kleck, M. R. Hebl, and J. Hull (eds.), *The Social Psychology of Stigma*. New York: Guilford Press.

Duster, T. 1990. *Backdoor to Eugenics*. New York: Routledge.

Dworkin, R. 1977. *Taking Rights Seriously*. London: Duckworth.

Dworkin, R. 1993. *Life's Dominion: An Argument about Abortion and Euthanasia*. London: HarperCollins.

Feinberg, J. 1982. "Wrongful Life and the Counterfactual Element in Harming." *Social Philosophy & Policy* 4(1): 145–78.

Ferguson, P. M. 2001. "Mapping the Family: Disability Studies and the Exploration of Parental Response to Disability." In G. L. Albrecht, K. D. Seelman, and M. Bury (eds.), *Handbook of Disability Studies*. Thousand Oaks, CA: Sage, pp. 373–95.

Ferguson, P. M., Gartner, A., and Lipsky, D. K. 2000. "The Experience of Disability in Families: A Synthesis of Research and Parent Narratives." In E. Parens and A. Asch (eds.), *Prenatal Testing and Disability Rights*. Washington, DC: Georgetown University Press, pp. 72–94.

Floyd, S. L., and Pomerantz, D. 1999. "Is There a Natural Right to Raise Children?" In L. D. Houlgate (eds.), *Morals, Marriage, and Parenthood: An Introduction to Family Ethics*. Belmont, CA: Wadsworth, pp. 198–205.

Gallimore, R., Weisner, T. S., Kaufman, S. Z., and Bernheimer, L. P. 1989. "The Social Construction of Ecocultural Niches: Family Accommodation of Developmentally Delayed Children." *American Journal of Mental Retardation* 94: 216–30.

Gillam, l. 1999. "Prenatal Diagnosis and Discrimination against the Disabled." *Journal of Medical Ethics* 25: 163–71.

Goffman, E. 1963. *Stigma: Notes on the Management of Spoiled Identity*. Englewood Cliffs, NJ: Prentice-Hall.

Kent, D. 2000. "Somewhere a Mockingbird." In E. Parens and A. Asch (eds.), *Prenatal Testing and Disability Rights*. Washington, DC: Georgetown University Press, pp. 57–63.

Kittay, E., and Kittay, L. 2000. "On the Expressivity and Ethics of Selective Abortion for Disability: Conversations with My Son." In E. Parens and A. Asch (eds.), *Prenatal Testing and Disability Rights*. Washington, DC: Georgetown University Press, pp. 165–95.

Krauss, M. W. 1993. "Child-Related and Parenting Stress: Similarities and Differences between Mothers and Fathers of Children with Disabilities." *American Journal of Mental Retardation* 97: 393–404.

Lane, H., and Grodin, M. 1997. "Ethical Issues in Cochlear Implant Surgery: An Exploration into Disease, Disability, and the Best Interests of the Child." *Kennedy Institute of Ethics Journal* 7: 231–51.

Mawer, S. 1998. *Mendel's Dwarf*. New York: Harmony Books.

Mundy, L. 2002. "A World of Their Own." *The Washington Post Magazine*, March 31, pp. W22, 24.

National Digitial Archives of Datasets (NDAD). 1996. Data for Health Authorities Boundaries at April 1996 (PHO-A4.1B). Down's Syndrome: Diagnoses and Outcomes in the Period 1994 to 1996." (Data from the National Down Syndrome Cytogenic Register.) <http://ndad.ulcc.ac.uk/>

Neuberg, S. L., Smith, D. M., and Ascher, T. 2000. "Why People Stigmatize: Toward a Biocultural Framework." In T. F. Heatherton, R. Kleck, M. R. Hebl, and J. Hull (eds.), *The Social Psychology of Stigma*. New York: Guilford Press, pp. 31–61.

Parens, E. and Asch, A. 2000. "The Disability Rights Critique of Prenatal Genetic Testing: Reflections and Recommendations." In E. Parens and A. Asch (eds.), *Prenatal Testing and Disability Rights*. Washington, DC: Georgetown University Press, pp. 3–43.

Press, N. 2000. "Assessing the Expressive Character of Prenatal Testing: The Choices Made or the Choices Made Available?" In E. Parens and A. Asch (eds.), *Prenatal Testing and Disability Rights*. Washington, DC: Georgetown University Press, pp. 214–33.

Purdy, L. M. 1996. "Loving Future People." In his *Reproducing Persons: Issues in Feminist Bioethics*. Ithaca, NY and London: Cornell University Press, pp. 50–74.

Raymer, G. 2003. "Multiple Birth Mothers Have Their 'Spare' Babies Aborted." *Daily Mail* (London), March 10, p. 19.

Ruddick, Sara. 1989. *Maternal Thinking: Towards a Politics of Peace*. Boston: Beacon Press.

Ruddick, W. 1999. "Parenthood: Three Concepts and a Principal." In L. D. Houlgate (ed.), *Morals, Marriage, and Parenthood: An Introduction to Family Ethics*. Belmont, CA: Wadsworth, pp. 242–251.

Ruddick, W. 2000. "Ways to Limit Prenatal Testing." In E. Parens and A. Asch (eds.), *Prenatal Testing and Disability Rights*. Washington, DC: Georgetown University Press, pp. 95–107.

Sandel, M. 2004. "The Case against Perfection: What's Wrong with Designer Children, Bionic Athletes, and Genetic Engineering." *Atlantic Monthly* 293(13).

Satz, A. 1999. "Prenatal Genetic Testing and Discrimination against the Disabled: A Conceptual Analysis." *Monash Bioethics Review* 18(14): 11–22.

SeeAbility (Seeing beyond Disability). 2004. "Overview. Juvenile Batten's Disease. Symptoms." <http://www.seeability.org/randd/jboverview.htm>.

Wachbroit, R., and Wasserman, D. 1995. "Patient Autonomy and Value-Neutrality in Nondirective Genetic Counseling." *Stanford Law & Policy Review* 6: 103–11.

Wasserman, D. 1998. "Response: Wasserman on Mahowald." In A. Silvers, D. Wasserman, and M. Mahowald, 1998. *Disability, Difference, Discrimination: Perspective on Justice in Bioethics and Public Policy*. Lanham, MD: Rowman and Littlefield, pp. 277–83.

Wasserman, D. 2003. "A Choice of Evils in Prenatal Testing." (Symposium, Genes and Disability: Defining Health and the Goals of Medicine) *Florida State University Law Review* 30: 295–313.

Weiss, M. 1996. "Conditional Love: Parents' Attitudes towards Handicapped Children." Westport, CT: Bergin and Garvey.

Chapter 8

The Social Context of Individual Choice

TOM SHAKESPEARE

INTRODUCTION

Philosophers and disability activists have concentrated much energy on the moral status of decisions about prenatal testing and selective termination on the grounds of fetal impairment. On the one foot, there is a range of arguments about wrongful birth and the immorality of choosing disability or of restricting the open future of a potential child. On the other foot, there is the expressivist argument about the messages that decisions to terminate pregnancies affected by disability send to disabled people and to the society in which they live. Disabled people have reacted with anger to technologies and programs that seek to avoid the birth of "people like us" or that might have meant that "we would never have been born."

I am not persuaded by either set of arguments. My suggestion in this chapter is that resolving this interesting philosophical debate is not the priority for political and policy resolution of the selective termination issue. I do not believe that there is a single rational solution to the moral quandry of whether to terminate a pregnancy affected by disability, nor should there be. Every impairment is different, and each can impact on lives to a greater or lesser extent. Equally, every family and every life is different, so it is dangerous to generalize about the experience of impairment. Moreover, there are widely varying views about both disability and abortion within societies as well as between societies. Given the difficulty of achieving a universal answer to the question of whether to terminate a pregnancy affected by impairment, the emphasis falls on the individual choices of potential parents. This is the dilemma brought about by the mixed blessings of genetic and reproductive technologies. Having made this information available, and societies having accepted in principle that termination of pregnancy is not immoral, I believe it is wrong to deny women and their partners the right to receive information about their pregnancy, and to terminate pregnancy if they decide that this is the best solution for them, within parameters laid down by the state. Principles such as autonomy and privacy conventionally demand that individuals are free to act on their conscience, unless their actions infringe upon the rights of others.

The approach I am taking in this chapter reflects my background in sociology rather than philosophy in a number of ways. First, I want to concentrate on the everyday context of moral choice, rather than on abstract principles. Rayna Rapp has argued that

this technology turns every user into a moral philosopher, as she engages her fears and fantasies of the limits of mothering a fetus with a disability. (Rapp 2000: 128)

But the sort of bioethics that is carried out by women and men is an engaged and practical bioethics, rather than the balancing of harms and benefits or arguments about principles. As Ann Maclean argues:

Moral questions and issues, however, are neither abstract nor intellectual; and it follows that habits of thought cultivated in ivory towers are not necessarily the ones most appropriate to the discussion of them. (Maclean 1993, 203)

Logic and consistency and resolution are required of academic bioethics. In practice, pragmatism, feelings, and lived experience may lead individuals to decide in ways that are not intellectually rigorous, and this is not always a bad thing, especially if the particular questions are not definitively resolvable anyway. Moreover, we live in societies containing groups and individuals who hold a range of religious, cultural, and ethical beliefs. It is not easy, and sometimes impossible, to reach a consensus about the morality of particular practices. Abortion is a classic example of such a practice.

The training sociologists receive makes it hard for them to pass judgments on individual actions anyway, because social science concentrates on the "is" rather than the "ought" of social behavior. The sociological moral stance tends toward tolerance of individual choices, verging on relativism. Moreover, sociological approaches look beyond individuals and the morality of their actions to the social context in which they make their decisions. This leads me to suggest that the important political and social questions in this case have little to do with such questions as whether there is a duty to terminate affected pregnancies, or whether individuals are expressing hatred or prejudice against disabled people if they have abortions on disability grounds. The relevant questions are about collective morality, justice, and discrimination. That is:

- Do prenatal screening programs offer informed choice to pregnant women and their partners?
- Are national screening programs and national welfare regimes supportive of those who wish to continue pregnancies affected by impairment?
- Are states and societies supportive of disabled children and adults?

My claim is that selective termination is not an issue to which morality or rationality demands a universal response, and that it is appropriate to espouse an ethic of individual choice. When Dan Brock asks (Chapter 3, this volume):

Is there anything morally problematic about a public policy that seeks to prevent and ultimately eliminate genetically transmitted disabilities?

I want to answer "yes": the role of health care is to provide technologies that enable individuals and families to make choices about their lives, not to impose particular duties on individuals in the very private area of reproduction. Public policy should restrict itself to enabling couples to exercise choices to continue or to terminate pregnancy in cases where significant genetic or developmental conditions are diagnosed. Infringing upon autonomy without due cause is always morally problematic. I want to suggest that all choices are situated in social contexts, and that we have a duty to ensure that those contexts are supportive of individual decisions in the widest possible sense. Political philosophy, rather than moral philosophy, is the relevant context for the discussion.

MORAL JUDGMENTS ABOUT PRENATAL GENETIC TESTING

In this section, I will briefly explore two types of argument in favor of selective termination of pregnancies affected by impairment, before undertaking an equally brief examination of the key argument against testing. I will come to the conclusion that in the vast majority of cases of fetal impairment, these arguments neither compel individuals to terminate on the basis of information about fetal impairment, nor deny them the right to receive this information and to terminate if they believe this is right in their circumstances.

I believe that the two arguments for the duty to terminate fall down because they implicitly construct an ideal type of disability, which is regarded as more salient than any other social characteristic, and more problematic than any other social or intrinsic restriction or suffering. One argument suggests that failure to prevent impairment constitutes moral harm. Thus Dan Brock suggests (Chapter 3, this volume):

Individuals are morally required not to let any child or other dependent person for whose welfare they are responsible experience serious suffering or limited opportunity or serious loss of happiness or good.

As a nonphilosopher, I will leave aside the debate about person-affecting and non-person-affecting harms. There is an intuitive sense in which we can understand the difference, in terms of the duty to the potential child, between choosing to continue a pregnancy resulting in a child with an impairment, and terminating it.

Versions of this approach can be found, argued with various degrees of sophistication, in the discourse of bioethicists, scientists, clinicians, and members of the public. There are two problems with this approach. First, it involves the a priori assumption that disability is inevitably a serious harm, qualitatively different from other problems or restrictions in life. There is a popular prejudice that disability makes life not worth living, or that it would be better to be dead than disabled. Yet disabled people often testify to having a good quality of life, and it is wrong to equate impairment with awfulness or harm. Second, it involves the related tendency to link all forms of impairment together, creating an "ideal type" (or rather, a "nonideal type"). Conflating the experience of people with cleft lip and people with sensory impairment and people with Down syndrome and people with Tay Sachs disease is unsustainable. Each condition has very different implications: while some impairment is tragic, it is wrong to take the extreme cases to represent the whole range of experiences.

These two cultural assumptions are displayed in James Watson's book *A Passion for DNA* (Oxford, 2000). Watson talks unreflectively about "the horrors of genetic disease," "genetically damaged existence," and the "random tragedies we should do everything in our power to prevent." In response to the disability rights argument, he suggests that "seeing the bright side of being handicapped is like praising the virtues of extreme poverty." The implication of his comparison is that we really ought to get rid of extreme poverty with the same dedication that we devote to genetic screening.

Leaving aside the fact that extreme poverty is seen as a virtue in certain contexts, such as Buddhist and Hindu and Catholic asceticism, there are problems with the core argument. First, everyone's genome carries genetic mutations; everyone is subject to disease; and everyone will ultimately die. Given that 1 percent of births are affected by congenital abnormality, while 12 percent of the population are disabled, prenatal screening should not be a high priority if we want to reduce the burden of disease. Second, as disabled people have argued and demonstrated (Barnes, 1991), social barriers, not the direct effects of impairment, are the major reason why disabled people enjoy a lower quality of life. Third, life involves all sorts of sufferings and restrictions, from disease to bereavement to poverty to unrequited love. In particular, frailty is a fact of life. There is no reason to think that most impairments are a greater tragedy or difficulty than any of these other problems, nor are we compelled to agree with Sophocles that "never to have been born counts highest of all."

Like scientists, bioethicists are not neutral or above society; rather, they reflect social knowledge and prejudices. Their work contains many a priori assumptions about normality and full human existence. So, as Vehmas argues, referring to comments by Peter Singer and John Harris about cognitive impairment,

These loose remarks reveal a priori notions in bioutilitarianism, which are chiefly composed of ideas of 'normal' and 'full human existence' which require some sort of intellectual competence. Since the life of a normal human being is more full, it is also more valuable than the life of a person with intellectual disabilities. (Vehmas, 1999: 40)

These judgments reflect prejudice, not rationality. Vehmas argues that bioutilitarianism is an "intelligist" enterprise, because it judges quality of life on the basis of intellectual capacity. It is a matter of opinion that intellect makes life more valuable. What empirical evidence that does exist suggests that people with learning difficulties can live happy and fulfilled lives.

A second argument for prenatal testing avoids the debate about suffering and talks instead about infringing on the autonomy of the future child. Following Joel Feinberg, Dena Davis (2001) argues that failure to prevent impairment constitutes an infringement of the future choices of the fetus. We have a moral duty not to constrain future choices, which rules out designing our babies, choosing their sex, or forgoing the opportunity to avoid their impairment. Thus in the case of deafness, to

Davis it does not matter whether this experience is best described as an ethnic minority status or as an impairment: either way, it limits the child. This argument goes further than the first version of the harms argument because it is not necessary to demonstrate that the impairment involves suffering, only that it restricts opportunity. Yet while losing an existing opportunity or capacity may be experienced as a harm, not having access to the same opportunities as others from birth should be regarded not as a harm but as a fact of life.

In response to the open future argument, I want to reiterate the claims I made with reference to the suffering argument. There is a comparability between the restrictions imposed by many impairments and the restrictions experienced by everyone because of their embodiment and the limitations of their social context. The concept of human potentiality, in which we are all polymaths able to choose whether to climb mountains, enjoy Bach, or look at great art, is a myth. Lives are inevitably restricted, due to social circumstances and individual aptitudes and tastes. There is no morally salient difference between the restrictions faced by those who cannot see, hear, or perform feats of athleticism and the rest of the population.

While I do not find these arguments compelling in terms of a duty to terminate pregnancy, or as grounds for the development of more and more programs to detect fetal abnormality, I do find persuasive the argument that impairment is a significant characteristic of the fetus that parents should be permitted to find out about, and that parents should be allowed to terminate pregnancy if they believe that this is the best option for the potential child and for their family. I believe that in many cases, pregnant women take upon themselves the suffering of abortion in order to avoid the suffering of a potential child, or the stress upon the family. I believe that selective termination should be socially supported: I disagree that it is morally mandatory, except perhaps in the most extreme cases.

Disabled philosophers have argued that the existence of prenatal testing and selective termination expresses discriminatory attitudes toward disabled people. Adrienne Asch has said:

Do not disparage the lives of existing and future disabled people by trying to screen for and prevent the birth of babies with their characteristics. (Parens and Asch 1999: 2)

As I have argued elsewhere (Shakespeare, 2000), I do not find this a compelling argument. I agree with Asch that there are dangerous tendencies toward synecdoche – seeing only the impairment, and seeing the impairment as the defining characteristic of the person – and I agree with her and all those other commentators who have criticized the tendency to see all impairment as a terrible problem that must be avoided at all costs. Neutral language and balanced counseling are vital, as I will discuss later. Yet I do believe that impairment makes a difference to people's lives, and I do not believe that impairment is a neutral characteristic. If potential parents believe that a particular impairment is relevant and serious, then terminating pregnancy in order to avoid those harms becomes more important than the potential disparagement of disabled people that may be an associated outcome. That termination of a pregnancy affected by a particular impairment may be upsetting to an individual with that impairment should not preclude others from exercising the right to this choice.

The fact that your actions may be distressing to others does not in itself make your actions immoral or blameworthy: I understand why vegetarians are repelled by my enjoyment of meat, but it is their arguments for vegetarianism, not their distaste for my diet, that are relevant to my personal choices. I may find it regretable and distressing if a couple terminate a pregnancy affected by achondroplasia, but they should not take my feelings into account when weighing their options. However, they should listen if I testify that the condition has not significantly limited my life or undermined my quality of life, because this is information that is relevant to their choice.

Some expressivists (although not Asch in recent publications) argue that the use of prenatal diagnosis expresses the belief that life with an impairment is not worth living or that disabled people's lives are not valuable. But here I want to agree with those who have argued that individual decisions to terminate pregnancies affected by disability do not necessarily imply a moral judgement on the value of disabled people. Clearly, some individuals and policies make such judgments. But I believe that most prenatal decisions do not reflect beliefs that disabled people are less morally important, that disabled people do not have the right to be in the world, that disabled people are a financial burden on society, that diversity is not important, or that disabled people should not be supported and respected. I believe that the usual grounds for selective termination are the beliefs that a particular impairment will cause suffering and/or restricted opportunities for the potential child, and/or that it will cause difficulties and restricted opportunities for other siblings or the potential parents. There is clinical and social evidence that in some cases those beliefs are justified. Later, I will show how this is often a consequence of social arrangements, not of the intrinsic features of impairments, but the empirical question is whether such consequences are likely. If they are likely, for whatever reason, then parents have a moral right to avoid the birth of a child who will suffer in this way, or will cause other family members to suffer in this way. Parents have an interest in the health, happiness, and well-being of their children, and a right to take steps to maximize those outcomes, as long as they do not thereby injure others. However, the belief that all impairments will lead to suffering and stress needs to be challenged and deconstructed, as I will argue later.

Against those who argue for the moral duty to terminate affected pregnancies, or the moral duty not to, I want to argue that disability is not a medical tragedy, in all but the most severe cases, but neither is it irrelevant, nor is it a unitary experience. There are upwards of 4,000 single-gene conditions, and many other developmental and polygenetic disorders, most of which have varying phenotypic expressions, and all of which are experienced only in particular social, cultural, and economic contexts. The creation of a disabled "ideal type" – either as a neutral or benign experience, or as a negative and tragic experience – does not do justice to the complexity and variability of the experience of disability.

I have contended that current arguments that prenatal testing and termination are morally required or morally forbidden are not conclusive. It is therefore morally permitted for prospective parents to take advantage of prenatal diagnosis, in all but trivial cases, or to decline to do so, in all but very serious cases. The choice is a profound and personal one, because it impinges on deeply held beliefs about abortion. The choice to take advantage of prenatal diagnosis is therefore bound up with freedom of conscience and personal belief. States and societies should not impose duties contrary to people's deeply held religious or secular principles, unless serious harms to third parties would otherwise result. Because the choice of testing and termination is so morally important, and because it has a major emotional and psychological and spiritual impact on many people, it is not a consumer choice like others in modern society, nor should be treated as such. Clearly, decisions about pregnancies are more important than consumer choices about products and lifestyles. But reproductive decisions are also more important than other health decisions, and oblige states and professionals to respect the right to choose. A health service can bombard members of the public with warnings about heart disease and diet, because no great moral questions are raised by the choice of whether to eat more saturated fat. But pressuring people in the area of reproductive choice is rightly seen as an infringement on privacy and the right to autonomy when it comes to such issues as testing and termination of pregnancy. Abortion is a highly intimate question; and because it involves control over your own body, it should be private.

Decisions about selective termination are not, in my view, important merely because many people think they are, although respect for other people's deeply held opinions is part of my argument here. Nor are they important only because they are about a private and intimate area of life. They are important because termination of pregnancy is morally very important. I find Ronald Dworkin's position on the question of abortion persuasive. While I reject arguments about the personhood of the fetus or the rights of the unborn child, I believe termination of pregnancy is a morally serious step resulting in the end of a life. The fetus is not born with full human rights, but its moral status increases during pregnancy until birth. While termination of pregnancy on social or even "trivial" grounds may be acceptable in the first trimester, these choices are less morally acceptable later in pregnancy. If the moral seriousness of termination is to be justified later in pregnancy, then a reason of comparable moral seriousness needs to be provided. I do not believe that intimacy or privacy in themselves are sufficient. For the reasons outlined earlier, I believe that individuals who believe that a significant impairment is an appropriate reason for termination have the right to abortion. I also believe that individuals who do not believe impairment is morally significant have the right to continue pregnancy.

Because termination of pregnancy is morally serious, and also because many people believe it to be morally serious, it is incumbent on health systems and governments to be scrupulous about the provision of services. This requires full access to diagnostic screening, and it also requires the provision of high-quality information and counseling, so that people are free, on the basis of a clear understanding of the relevant issues in their situation, to make the decision that their conscience dictates.

SOCIAL RESPONSES TO DISABILITY

If it is accepted that there is no persuasive moral argument that demands or forbids selective termination, and if abortion is seen as a private

225

decision that each individual has the right to make for him- or herself, then it is relevant and necessary to look at the broader social and cultural context, and at both the extent to which it respects and supports this autonomy, and the extent to which it undermines it. In this and the following sections, I will discuss the societal treatment of disability, the role of screening programs, and the immediate context of reproductive choice. I will conclude that there is a major moral problem, because all these domains are weighted against disabled people and weighted against potential parents who choose to continue with pregnancies affected by impairment. This represents injustice, discrimination, and infringement of reproductive autonomy, and should be the main target of a disability rights approach to prenatal testing.

As I have argued, society is full of negative messages about disability. There is a common and unexamined assumption that "disability" makes life not worth living, and that it would be better to be dead than disabled. Disability studies researchers have demonstrated the ubiquitous cultural representations of disabled people as pathetic, as medical tragedies, as dependent, and as unfulfilled. Scientists often reproduce this prejudice, which underpins their faith in genetic screening as the solution to the problem of disability (Shakespeare, 1999). As Steinberg argues:

Clearly the investment of genetic disease with the spectre of an inevitably terrible life and early death fuels the sense that genetic screening is not only necessary but the only possible response. In this context, the fact that actual experiences of these and other "inherited illnesses" vary considerably is eclipsed, as is the possibility that the problems of "disability" are not biologically determined but produced through oppressive social responses to illness and disability. (Steinberg 1997: 118)

A second area of concern is the extent of social support available to disabled people and their families. Many social policy commentators have criticized the lack of services and social inclusion in societies such as Britain and the United States (e.g., Barnes, 1991). While the advent of civil rights statutes has made some difference, the failure to provide sufficient welfare benefits or to meet moral obligations to support the weakest members of society means that disability is still associated with poverty and disadvantage. Families with disabled children lack the necessary economic and practical assistance to survive (Beresford, 1994).

Social model approaches argue that it is these twin burdens of prejudice and discrimination, not impairment, that constitute the real problem of disability. Even if this strong argument is not supported, the fact of disadvantage is undeniable. The effect of the oppression of disabled children and adults is to make it less feasible for prospective parents to continue pregnancies affected by impairment. It means that often decisions about selective termination are influenced by the nature of the society in which people live, not the nature of the impairment that the prospective child will experience. It also means that class and other forms of social privilege modify the experience of impairment in important ways, and this compounds the injustice by making it more difficult for people in lower socioeconomic groups to survive as disabled people or with disabled children, or to believe that it is possible to do so.

If it is conceded, as it should be, that there is a large social component to the experience of disability, then support for the supposed moral duty to terminate affected pregnancies can be seen to have wider implications. It could be said to follow that, given the fact of social deprivation and the suffering associated with it, people living in deprived areas should be counseled against having children, or should be prevented from reproducing. It could also be said to follow that the prevalence of racism should be a factor in the reproductive decisions of members of minority ethnic communities. If these ideas are unpalatable, or alarming, then, to a significant extent, so should be the idea of a policy of terminating fetuses with impairments. Moreover, to entertain ideas of termination based on problems seems more than a little hasty when they can all but be eliminated by social and economic change.

THE POLITICS OF SCREENING

I concluded earlier that prospective parents have a right to access relevant information about pregnancy and the fetus. But questions about screening programs do not end there. Within a public health service such as that of the United Kingdom, there are questions that can be raised about the priority of screening programs versus other forms of health maintenance and illness prevention. There are also questions about the aim of screening programs, and the most appropriate way to evaluate them.

A technological imperative seems to have driven the development and adoption of prenatal screening technologies such as ultrasound and genetic testing. Abby Lippman has referred to the "geneticization" that has reduced many complex diseases and social experiences to genetic changes that can and should be prevented. This reductionism ignores the role that social and economic factors play in the generation of disease and morbidity. Given that most impairment occurs postnatally, it would seem more of a priority to reduce poverty, deprivation, bad working conditions, stress, poor diet, and other factors that determine the majority of ill health. It may be a factor that it is difficult to make a profit from interventions in these latter areas, whereas there is major commodification in the area of genetics and other high-tech interventions.

It is rare for explicitly eugenic statements to emerge from those designing or advocating genetic screening programs. Yet the implicit purpose and role of these programs is to reduce the incidence of impairment, despite protestations to the contrary. The way that ritual disclaimers operate has been highlighted by the medical geneticist Angus Clarke, in reaction to a statement by his colleague Marcus Pembrey that reducing the incidence of genetic conditions is not the object of genetic services:

Sadly such statements from senior members of the profession are not enough: their wishing does not make it so. Those health professionals (often not clinical geneticists) who wish to adopt a public health perspective to justify our existence through a cost-benefit analysis will be quite capable of learning to preface their remarks by explicit, but purely cosmetic, disavowals of eugenic intent. It is often these cost-benefit considerations, with crude reckoning of cash saved per termination achieved, that speak loudest to health authorities. (Clarke, 1991: 1524)

Clarke goes on to castigate the Royal College of Physicians of London report on "Prenatal Diagnosis and Genetic Screening" for just this combination of an "anti-eugenic" preface followed by a clearly "genetic hygiene" approach to inherited disease.

Angus Clarke argues that there is a complex relationship between the stated goals of a screening program, the ethos of a screening program, and the outcome measures that are used. He suggests that there are three possible goals of screening: avoiding costly disorders, avoiding the suffering of affected children, and promoting informed reproductive decisions. Within the context of public health economics, any screening program is justified in terms of the benefits derived versus the costs incurred. Prenatal screening programs are introduced when an argument can be made that the total cost of screening the relevant population is less than the medical and welfare costs of the ill or impaired babies who would otherwise be born (Wald et al., 1992). Such equations are immoral when applied to reproductive decision making. They serve to increase prejudice against disabled or different people, and to increase pressure on women to terminate affected pregnancies. Why should prenatal screening be the only part of the UK health service that should have to make a profit?

As Clarke argues, and as I will demonstrate later, the ethos of screening and obstetric services – in particular, the trend toward routinization of testing and the assumption that termination of pregnancy is the inevitable response to any diagnosis of disorder – undermine the possibility of informed consent and just outcomes.

THE IMMEDIATE CONTEXT OF SCREENING

Genetics professionals and policy makers claim that current clinical antenatal services offer informed choice to pregnant women and their partners. In practice, three factors undermine choice: the information provided, the attitudes of medical staff, and the routinization of antenatal services.

As the Hastings Center summary of the disability rights objections to prenatal testing makes clear, a major part of this critique is the claim that prenatal testing depends on a misunderstanding of what life is like for children with disabilities and their families. I find this a compelling argument. However, the salience of the argument is not to the individuals making decisions, but to the society and the health care providers who are failing to make available to people full and balanced and accurate information about living with impairment.

I do not accept arguments that it is immoral to choose to test or terminate a pregnancy, up to the end of the second trimester, on the basis of disability. But because termination is a morally significant act resulting in the end of a fetal life, there is an obligation to consider the issues fully and to act carefully. Particularly, there is a duty to act on the basis of good information, not on the basis of ignorance, prejudice, or biased or incomplete information. Full information about the diagnosis and prognosis of a genetic or developmental condition is vital. But evidence suggests that this is sometimes lacking. One research project found that prospective parents were given an overly pessimistic explanation of the effects of cystic fibrosis. For example, they were offered estimates of life expectancy that were much lower than those being achieved (Britton and Knox, 1991). Also, different parents are given different information: research found that parents whose babies were found to be affected by Down syndrome were given a much more positive prognosis than those who were being offered a prenatal test and the possibility of selective termination (Lippman and Wilfond, 1992).

Moreover, clinical information is only part of the picture. In order to understand the implications of a prenatal diagnosis, prospective parents need to be informed about the social experience of disabled people. They might want to know whether people with a particular condition have a good quality of life, whether they can go to mainstream schools, and what employment options and options for independent living and welfare benefits are available. All these issues are important in understanding the impact of impairment on the lives of disabled people. It may be particularly important to listen to the testimony of disabled people themselves, the people directly affected. Yet the voice of disabled people is never heard in prenatal situations, which are dominated by doctors and nurses.

Second, most people are ignorant about disability. They may not know any disabled people. They may be deeply fearful about disability. They may think it must be the worst thing that could ever happen to someone. But, as we've argued, disabled people usually don't think this way, and many have developed a civil rights approach to the disability problem. Yet this social approach is not usually shared by members of the medical profession. They have been trained to think of illness and impairment as a problem that must be solved through medical intervention. If a condition cannot be cured, it is not illogical to think that it should be prevented. Yet in the case of congenital impairments, at the moment this means removing the person, not just removing the disease.

People facing difficult decisions want guidance from experts: the responsibility of deciding may be too heavy for them to bear on their own. Yet counseling and support may be unavailable or inadequate. Research has found that 45 percent of obstetricians say they have inadequate resources for counseling women about serum screening for Down syndrome (Green, 1994), which is the commonest form of prenatal testing; the finding suggests that for rarer and more complex conditions, appropriate information and advice is even more likely to be lacking. Green's research also found that women were confused about the new tests: 81 percent of obstetricians found that "women not understanding the test" was a problem. These problems have occurred in the past within a limited screening program; as screening becomes available to more women for more prenatal conditions, the shortfalls of the resources and services will become more acute.

However, even where advice is available, it may not be reliable. In particular, different medical professionals give parents different accounts of illness and impairment. The idea that doctors and nurses are nondirective is a myth. Nondirectiveness is a goal of counseling, but research has found that it is usually not achieved in practice. Genetic counselors and nurses are least directive. Obstetricians are most directive. Geneticists themselves fall somewhere in the middle. Unlike genetics professionals, obstetricians do not tend to work with disabled people directly. They are concerned with delivering the "perfect baby." They tend to believe that selective termination of pregnancy is a good idea in the case of many impairments. For example, in cases of Down syndrome, 94 percent of genetic nurses, 57 percent of geneticists, but only 32 percent of obstetricians reported counseling nondirectively. The majority favored termination of fetuses with open spina bifida, anencephaly, Huntingdon's disease, Down syndrome, and Duchenne muscular dystrophy, and a substantial minority favored termination of fetuses with cystic fibrosis, sickle-cell anemia, achondroplasia, phenylketonuria, and haemophilia (Marteau et al., 1993; Marteau et al., 1994). Research by Wendy Farrant in 1985 found evidence for eugenic beliefs among obstetricians – for example, believing that genetic testing is a good thing because it allows people to have healthy babies instead of unhealthy babies; placing a negative value on people with certain conditions; seeing it as desirable to prevent the birth of certain fetuses; and erroneously believing that a genetic predisposition to homosexuality can be identified and that it might be acceptable to terminate selectively on that basis. Follow-up research by Jo Green in 1995 found that these attitudes had changed. However, one-third of obstetricians still would not give a woman diagnostic testing unless she agreed to have a termination of pregnancy if the fetus were affected by impairment.

One disabled woman who participated in the Risk and the New Genetics research project said:

I don't think the test for disability in the unborn child is presented as a choice, when I said I didn't want tested the doctor was shocked and she tried to talk me into it because it's an easy test, everybody gets it done nowadays, it's simple. But I don't think there is a choice, I think that we're pressured into taking as many of these tests as are available. (Kerr et al., 1998: 56)

The views that professionals hold are important. The way in which clinicians present options encourages women to engage in particular behaviors. Doctors are not bad people. In fact, their views probably reflect those of many members of the public. The problem, therefore, is that doctors and nurses are ordinary people, whereas sometimes we expect them to be wise and enlightened. Nor are doctors brainwashing or coercing women. There is no evidence for such a crude process of influence. Yet the exercise of power may be complex and subtle. The sociologist Stephen Lukes talks about power being exercised in structural rather than individual ways. This may not involve overt conflict; it may be based instead on cultural processes and social patterns. The exercise of power may appear to be consensual:

A may exercise power over B by getting him to do what he does not want to do, but he also exercises power over him by influencing, shaping or determining his very wants. Indeed, is it not the supreme exercise of power to get another or others to have the desires you want them to have? (Lukes, 1974: 23)

Finally, the process of testing in pregnancy also undermines informed consent. Obstetric procedures are now like a conveyor belt, where testing may take place without the knowledge of the pregnant woman, or where testing is presented as a routine procedure. In Britain, thousands of women are going through antenatal and obstetric services in the National Health Service, and time and resources are not allocated to ensure that they are fully informed and consenting freely. Research has proved that women are not encouraged to exercise choice and control, and that they place considerable trust in the expertise of their advisors (Porter and Macintyre, 1984). Farrant found that a quarter of consultants said their policy was to give the serum screening test routinely without offering women any explanation of its purpose or any choice about whether they participated in the screening program (Farrant, 1985: 110). Another research project found that one-third of pregnant women who had been offered serum screening to detect spina bifida could not correctly recall whether they had undergone the test (Marteau et al., 1988).

Within modern medicine, many procedures have become so routine that specific consent is not explicitly sought. An example is the testing of newborns for phenylketonuria (PKU). Unless a patient is well informed, they will not know of the test. Because the policy is "opt out" rather than "opt in," most patients will undergo such tests and procedures by default. For the efficient administration of health care, the wisdom of such a course is clear. But a distinction should be drawn between tests or treatments that do not generate decisions of major moral magnitude, and decisions that create knowledge that may lead to patients' having to assume responsibilities that they would not have wanted. For example, if a PKU test is positive, parents are empowered to put their newborns on diets that will protect them from mental impairment: while laborious, this is scarcely controversial. But if a prenatal test is positive, then parents are confronted with the need to make a choice that they may not have anticipated, and that they may find psychologically and emotionally damaging. When I surveyed parents of children with restricted growth in 1999, a common response was that they were glad that prenatal diagnosis had not been an option for them. Reproductive services raise moral questions that are not present to the same degree in many other areas of medicine, and sensitivity to the need for informed consent is arguably even more important.

Technologies such as prenatal testing are not neutral. The possibility of obtaining prenatal genetic information inevitably creates new choices that in turn can present new problems and dilemmas, The very existence of a test for fetal abnormality can create pressures to use the technology. The implication of developing new screening programs is that testing and selection is a desirable outcome. In this context, creating space for service users to think carefully about their options, and to exercise their right of refusal, becomes even more important. I have argued that the context of screening in the United Kingdom, according to empirical evidence, does not support informed choice and reproductive autonomy:

Pregnant women do not necessarily make an informed decision to undergo screening and diagnostic tests. They may not see it as appropriate to make a decision, they may not be given information on which to make a decision, may not read or understand information they are given, or may not know they are having a test. (Green and Statham 1996: 143)

This could be said to be a form of discrimination, intentional or otherwise, against potential parents. It undermines the claim that contemporary genetics is not eugenic. The continuation of such a situation *is* morally suspect as well as politically unjust.

CONCLUSION

While this chapter puts the principle of autonomy above other principles (such as the purported duty to avoid impairment), it is necessary to retain an understanding of the social contexts of choices. These include the three domains discussed earlier. A fourth area, as Michael Parker has argued, is the social condition of choice, by which he means that:

To be genuinely autonomous requires one to take seriously the social conditions of one's choices. Very few facets of one's life, if any, can be determined by oneself alone in isolation from others. Whilst there may be occasions when we feel that our choices do not depend on others and cannot benefit from discussion with others, this is in fact very rarely the case. (Parker, 2001: 89)

Parker argues for discussion and deliberations involving a range of different family and community members in health care choices. This suggests that individuals considering prenatal testing have a responsibility to think carefully about their choices, and to make them on the basis of an accurate understanding of the nature of disability, as revealed by personal testimonies and social research. It also suggests that it is important for young people, prior to reaching the age of reproduction, to be taught about both disability and genetics, and to have the opportunity to think through some of the moral dilemmas that they may face in subsequent years.

Faced with the critique of prenatal testing presented in this chapter, health care professionals may feel challenged by the requirement to provide full and balanced information about disability prenatally. Yet in an age of increasing access to information technology, this need not be impossible. I am currently working on a project in which individuals and families affected by the conditions currently screened for will be photographed and interviewed. Their edited testimonies and images will be made available, alongside information about the testing process, on a website <www.antenataltesting.info>. This will be publicized to people entering maternity services, so that they can understand in advance the issues involved in testing and terminating pregnancies affected by impairments. Balanced, full, and accessible information, including information about termination and its psychological impacts, will empower individuals to make the decision that is best for them and their families. The accessibility of these information resources means that high school students and trainee doctors and nurses also have the potential to explore them. The genomic age demands investment in information technology and interpersonal support services, if scientific knowledge is to create benefits and avoid harms.

In this chapter, I have argued that the decision about prenatal testing and selective termination has to remain a personal one, and that bioethics cannot generate an objective or universal "right decision."

There is no single rational answer to the range of dilemmas presented by our new technological capabilities. Yet, in both moral and political terms, this is not the end of the discussion. While I have defended the moral acceptability of prenatal testing, I cannot defend actually existing prenatal testing. On the contrary. There are important criticisms that can be made of the social context of screening programs at various levels. On moral and political grounds, there is a duty to reform the current regime for genetics and obstetrics, and to improve the wider attitudes toward and treatment of disabled people. Only when these injustices have been rectified will women and men be able to exercise true reproductive autonomy, and to make the decisions that they sincerely believe are best for them and their families.

NOTE

Thanks to the participants in the Washington symposium for the helpful comments and stimulating discussion, and in particular to the editors of this volume for their patient and insightful advice on improving this chapter.

REFERENCES

Barnes, C. 1991. *Disabled People in Britain and Discrimination*. London: Hurst.
Beresford, B. 1994. *Positively Parents: Caring for a Severely Disabled Child*. London: HMSO.
Britton, J., and Knox, A. J. 1991. "Screening for Cystic Fibrosis." *The Lancet* 388: 1524.
Clarke, A. 1991a. "Is Non-directive Genetic Counselling Possible?" *The Lancet* 388: 998–1001.
Clarke, A. 1991b. Non-directive genetic counselling (letter). *The Lancet* 388: 1524.
Davis, D. 2001. *Genetic Dilemmas: Reproductive Technology, Parental Choices and Children's Futures*. New York: Routledge.
Farrant, W. 1985. "Who's for Amniocentesis?" In H. Homans (ed.), *The Sexual Politics of Reproduction*. London: Gower, pp. 96–122.
Green, J. 1994. "Serum Screening for Down's Syndrome: The Experience of Obstetricians in England and Wales." *British Medical Journal* 309: 769–72.
Green, J. 1995. "Obstetricians' Views on Prenatal Diagnosis and Termination of Pregnancy: 1980 compared with 1993." *British Journal of Obstetrics and Gynaecology* 102: 228–32.
Green, J., and Statham, H. 1996. "Psychosocial Aspects of Prenatal Screening and Diagnosis." In T. Marteau and M. Richards (eds.), *The Troubled Helix: Social and Psychological Implications of the New Human Genetics*. Cambridge: Cambridge University Press, pp. 140–63.
Kerr, A., Cunningham-Burley, S., and Anos, A. 1998. "The New Genetics and Health: Mobilising Lay Expertise." *Public Understanding of Science* 7: 41–60.

Lippman, A. 1994. "Prenatal Genetic Testing and Screening: Constructing Needs and Reinforcing Inequities." In A. Clarke (ed.), *Genetic Counselling: Practice and Principles*. London: Routledge, pp. 142–86.

Lippman, A., and Wilford, B. S. 1992. "'Twice-told Tales': Stories about Genetic Disorders." *American Journal of Human Genetics* 51: 936–7.

Lukes, S. 1974. *Power: A Radical View*. London: Macmillan.

Maclean, A. 1993. *The Elimination of Morality: Reflections on Utilitarianism and Bioethics*. London: Routledge.

Marteau, T., and Drake, H. 1995. "Attributions for Disability: The Influence of Genetic Screening." *Social Science and Medicine* 40: 1127–32.

Marteau, T., Drake, H., and Bobrow, M. 1994. "Counselling Following Diagnosis of a Fetal Abnormality: The Differing Approaches of Obstetricians, Clinical Geneticists, and Genetic Nurses." *Journal of Medical Genetics* 31: 864–7.

Marteau, T. M., Johnston, M., Plenicar, M., Shaw, R. W., and Slack, J. 1988. "Development of a Self-administered Questionnaire to Measure Women's Knowledge of Prenatal Screening, and Diagnostic Tests." *Journal of Psychosomatic Research* 32: 403–8.

Marteau, T. M., Plenicar, M., and Kidd, J. 1993. "Obstetricians Presenting Amniocentesis to Pregnant Women: Practice Observed." *Journal of Reproductive and Infant Psychology* 11: 5–82.

Parens, E., and Asch, A. 1999. "The Disability Rights Critique of Prenatal Genetic Testing." Special supplement to the *Hastings Center Report*, September–October.

Parker, M. 2001. "The Ethics of Evidence-based Patient Choice." *Health Expectations* 4: 87–91.

Porter, M., and Macintyre, S. 1984. "What Is, Must Be Best: A Research Note on Conservative or Deferential Responses to Antenatal Care Provision." *Social Science & Medicine* 19(11): 1197–1200.

Rapp, R. 2000. *Testing Women, Testing the Fetus: The Social Impact of Amniocentesis in America*. New York: Routledge.

Shakespeare, T. 1999. "'Losing the Plot'? Medical and Activist Discourses of Contemporary Genetics and Disability." *Sociology of Health and Illness* 21(5): 669–88.

Shakespeare, T. 2000. "Arguing about Disability and Genetics." *Interaction* 13(3): 11–14.

Steinberg, D. L. 1997. *Bodies in Glass: Genetics, Eugenics, Embryo Ethics*. Manchester: Manchester University Press.

Vehmas, S. 1999. "Discriminative Assumptions of Utilitarian Bioethics Regarding Individuals with Intellectual Disabilities." *Disability & Society* 14(1): 37–52.

Wald, N. J., et al. 1992. "Antenatal Maternal Screening for Down's Syndrome: Results of a Demonstration Project." *British Medical Journal* 305: 391–4.

236

Chapter 9

Disability and Health Systems Assessment

JEROME BICKENBACH

WORLD HEALTH REPORT, 2000: FROM HEALTH PROMOTION TO HEALTH SYSTEMS PERFORMANCE

With much fanfare, the World Health Organization in June 2000 set out a framework for assessing and ranking the performance of health systems around the globe (WHO, 2000). The media responded to the *World Health Report, 2000* by latching onto its remarkable rankings, such as the worldwide first place position of France and the relatively low ranking of the United States (thirty-seventh). Ministries of health around the world either proudly displayed their unexpectedly high rankings, used their relative positions as an argument for reform, dismissed the exercise as an invidious "health Olympics," or else immediately expressed concern about the quality of the data, or the methodology, that the WHO relied on. For their part, academics began to pick apart the methodology and the advisability of the ranking exercise, while rehearsing arguments for and against the various components of the framework. On its release, WHO Director General Gro Harlan Bruntland insisted that the WHO was committed to its assessment framework and planned yearly recalculations based on more valid and reliable country-level data. A few months later, facing a minor rebellion at the executive board meeting, some of Bruntland's enthusiasm was muted as she allowed that many of the concepts and measures used in the exercise "require refinement and development."

The *Report* represents a shift in WHO's health promotion agenda. Two decades earlier, in the joint WHO/UNESCO Declaration of Alma-Ata (1978), universal access to primary health care was presented as the key to achieving "health for all" within the century. Significantly as well, the Declaration highlighted the common concern about social inequalities of health – namely, inequality in health status between and within countries associated with income, gender, race, and other features. A decade later, the Ottawa Charter (1986) reaffirmed the importance of social and economic inequalities, as well as environmental degradation, as the principal determinants of ill health around the world. This stance was echoed and extended in subsequent international pronouncements and calls for action (Adelaide, 1988; Sundsvall, 1991; Jakarta, 1997) in which the clear message was that health promotion is a matter of social and economic inequity, demanding coordinated and comprehensive strategies across all social institutions, not just within systems for the provision of health care.

While not abandoning the Declaration of Alma-Ata, the *Report* nonetheless argues that health systems and, in particular, their level of performance are now the WHO's primary focus for improving world health. It criticizes the Declaration for focusing on health care *needs*, rather than on people's *demand* for health care, thereby ignoring the efficacy problems that arise when consumer demand and presumed health care needs do not match and the supply of health services cannot be made to align with both. The *Report* also argues that the goal of providing all forms of health care for everyone ("classical universalism") must be abandoned in favor of the "new universalism" of "high quality delivery of essential care, defined mostly by the criterion of cost-effectiveness, for everyone." Some have argued that the WHO was not allowed by the world's political powers to take Alma Ata seriously in the first place, and that as soon as the ink was dry, "prefabricated" global initiatives were adopted that served the special interests of the rich countries at the expense of the poor (Banerji, 1999). But, at least in its move toward efficiency reasoning, the WHO is clearly aligning itself with agencies such as the Organization for Economic Co-operation and Development and the World Bank, which view health systems as powerful engines of economic development, and which themselves have proposed cost-effectiveness frameworks for assessing health systems performance (Hsiao, 1995; OECD, 1998, 1999).

It has not escaped notice that implicit in this shift is the assumption that health systems, and their efficiency, are the principal factor responsible for good health outcomes. Vincente Navarro, for example, baldly states that there is no evidence at all for this presumption, and insists rather that all the evidence points to a link between political intervention, in the form of wealth and income redistribution, and mortality (e.g., Wilkinson, 1996; Berkman and Kawachi, 2000; Navarro, 2000).

Elsewhere, Navarro chides the WHO for succumbing to political pressures and adopting the "conventional wisdom in US financial and political circles" that health problems can be resolved only by technological interventions, without reference to social, policy, or economic environments (Navarro, 2001).

On the question of a causal link between health outcomes and the performance of health systems, the *Report* has a response, although a somewhat cagey one. Navarro is probably correct that there is precious little evidence of a link between *medical* care and mortality and morbidity, but the *Report* shrewdly defines "health system" very broadly (not to say analytically) as including "all the activities whose primary purpose is to promote, restore or maintain health." This means that, in addition to medical care, all forms of health promotion, disease prevention, and social rehabilitation actions, as well as health-enhancing interventions that improve road, environmental, and work and occupational safety – the full range of public health activities – make up a nation's health system. There are borderline examples as well, such as a policy of increasing educational opportunities for girls, which has been shown to have direct population health consequences, although, arguably, these are not activities whose primary purposes are health-oriented. A critic like Navarro is on shakier ground when he denies that there is a plausible link between population health and the performance of health systems, so broadly conceived.

But Alma-Ala also spoke of social inequalities in health, and here the shift represented by the *Report* is more profound. In the *Report*, health inequalities certainly form part of the assessment criteria, but they measure in terms of the size of differences in health status across ungrouped individuals, rather than in terms of comparisons between social groups identified by income, gender, or race. That means that the WHO is not committed to collecting information about how health outcomes are distributed socially. This has moved one commentator to argue that the *Report* "effectively removes equity and human rights from the public health monitoring agenda," since, for example, the WHO will not be concerned to collect data that would help determine whether progress was being made in closing gaps in nutritional status between children in poor and nonpoor families, or whether racial or ethnic disparities in infant mortality are being reduced (Almeida et al., 2000; Braveman et al., 2000; Braveman et al., 2001: 679).

To be sure, the *Report* does not reject the claim that social inequalities are associated with health, but it does suggest that the relationship is both indirect and bidirectional: improvements to population health are economically beneficial, and countries with improved economies can raise the floor of absolute poverty – even while making income inequality worse – thereby allowing even the poorest to afford what it takes to avoid ill health. In a recent response to this objection, Christopher Murray – the driving force behind the *Report* and the WHO health system performance agenda – has argued in effect that the WHO is better serving its mandate by providing data on the full extent of health inequality in a population, while leaving to others research as to the – perhaps highly indirect and complex – factors that explain this inequality (Murray, 2001).

This would be a fair response, except for two further points. First, even the most fervent advocates of the social determinants of health inequality agree that the relationship between social, economic, and political conditions and health is complicated, and that it is mediated through ill-defined theoretical constructs such as social cohesion and political ideology (Kawachi and Kennedy, 1997a, 1997b; Kawachi et al., 1997; Coburn, 2000). But for all that, there is empirical evidence that health inequalities track income and other social inequalities, and it is difficult to understand why the WHO has made it policy to ignore this body of evidence. Second, developing countries in particular rely on the WHO to provide usable health information: these countries do not have the resources to do it themselves. By choosing to measure inequality across the population, rather than selectively, the data the WHO will produce in the future will be of limited use to them in monitoring social inequalities (Houwelling et al., 2000).

More fundamentally, the *Report* is vulnerable to objections directed to the utilitarian or consequentialistic theory of distribution implicit in its reliance on cost-effectiveness analysis as a determinant of health system performance. There are many such objections, but an important class of these deals with how a health policy geared to the demands of increasing "performance" deals with the lives and health of persons with disabilities and chronic health conditions. For example, if we are to assess health systems by weighing health attainment against resource expenditure, then the WHO seems to be advising countries to adopt modes of resource allocation that sacrifice the lives or the well-being of persons whose present or future health states create poorer and more costly health outcomes. Though "economically rational," it strikes many as unjust to sacrifice the interests of persons with disabilities, the elderly, and fetuses and infants with severe disabilities in order to maximize average health attainment and reduce costs. To make matters worse, when, as in the *Report*, health attainment is measured by a summary measure of population health – in particular, disability-adjusted life expectancy or DALE – the result will be policies that are discriminatory against persons with disabilities and others with health or functional limitations (e.g., Harris, 1987; Williams, 1987; Lockwood, 1988; Brock, 1989, 1992, 1995, 1997; Hadorn, 1992; Nord, 1993; Edgar et al., 1998).

Unlike the earlier WHO-sponsored Burden of Disease Study, in which disability-adjusted life years or DALYs were first used (Murray and Lopez, 1996), the *Report*'s framework for assessing health systems performance has been designed to address these objections, and indeed explicitly integrates justice considerations into the assessment process. In order to see how this is accomplished, we need to look more closely at the assessment framework as it was originally described in the June 2000 *Report*.

THE WHO'S ASSESSMENT FRAMEWORK

The *Report* opens by enumerating the intrinsic goals of health systems, in order to delimit the outcomes for which it is plausible to hold health systems accountable. Although the bulk of the *Report* concerns organizational functions (service delivery, investment, financing, and stewardship) that make achievement of these goals more likely, and offers suggestions for improving their efficiency, it is when examining the basic building blocks of the framework that considerations of justice typically arise and need to be addressed.

The *Report* identifies three intrinsic goals of a health system: health, responsiveness, and fair financing. That health systems exist to improve health is no surprise (although WHO has yet to operationally clarify what it means by "health"). In addition, health systems must respond to legitimate expectations concerning both how health services are delivered and how they are financed. The oddly named goal of "responsiveness" incorporates values of respect of persons and client-centered orientation in health delivery. The first value is further analyzed into the linked values of dignity of the person, confidentiality, and autonomy. Client orientation, for its part, is composed of four specific subgoals: prompt attention, amenities of care (such as cleanliness, space, and privacy), access to social supports, and choice of provider.

The goal of fair financing addresses two sources of unfairness created by the nature of health needs. First, since health expenses are often

unforeseeable, people can face catastrophic expenses they have not prepared for. These expenses, moreover, tend to be regressive, in the sense
that those least able to pay are hit the hardest. Given these unavoidable
features of health care provision, the *Report* argues that financial fairness can best be achieved by prepaid, risk-spreading insurance joined
with cross-subsidization to ensure equal access to the poor. This approach to health financing can rightly be called, following Navarro, the
"conventional wisdom" of health economists (as well as the World Bank
and the International Monetary Fund), although a close reading of the
Report fails to support Navarro's claim that it implicitly favors private
insurance arrangements.

Levels of the attainment of health and responsiveness across a population can be measured as an average, a not implausible metric of the
quality of the health system. But, as the *Report* clearly sees, equity is a
different matter. The average health attainment across a population may
be high, even though unequally distributed (a characteristic feature of
the situation in the United States, as it happens). Because of this, the
Report incorporates an equality criterion (although, as noted, one that
does not identify inequality by social ground, but across the population). Similarly, a health system may score well on the responsiveness
subgoals because of the manner in which services are delivered to a
fairly high proportion of clients, while at the same time a minority is
flatly denied these amenities and rights. When this occurs, the equity of
responsiveness suffers.

Fairness in financing, on the other hand, can only be seen as an issue
of equity or distributional fairness. The financing issue vis-à-vis levels
of attainment of the two other goals – namely, how much of a country's
overall resources are allocated to the health system – is, the *Report* argues,
not a question about the performance of the health system as such; this
highly political macro-allocative issue is outside the scope of health
system assessment.

In sum, the WHO framework identifies five distinct goals of a health
system (two of which include a total of seven subgoals): the average
and equality of health attainment, the average and equality of responsiveness, and fair financing. Together, these goals are said to capture
core considerations of both goodness and fairness, where "[g]oodness
means a health system responding well to what people expect of it [and]
fairness means it responds equally well to everyone, without discrimination" (WHO, 2000: xi).

The *Report* describes in general terms how each goal is operational-ized and measured (leaving the details to a collection of technical pa-pers). Since the five goals cannot be measured in terms of a single scale, in order to create the composite measure the goals have to be weighted. In order to avoid controversy (and to satisfy the requirements of "non-ideological, evidence-based" evaluation), the WHO conducted two in-ternational key informant surveys to establish the relative weights, first of each of the components of responsiveness, and second of the relative weights of each goal. Needless to say, this method has been heavily crit-icized. In any event, the resulting weight distribution was as follows:

Health	Overall or average	25%
	Distribution or equality	25%
Responsiveness	Overall or average	12.5%
	Distribution or equality	12.5%
Fair financial contribution	Distribution or equality	25%

The results are not counterintuitive: health attainment is the most im-portant (indeed, defining) goal of the health system. The goodness and the fairness of health attainment, moreover, are equally weighted, indi-cating recognition of the equal importance of distributional concerns. Responsiveness (also equally weighted between average and equitable achievement) and fair financing are equally important, although, as in-trinsic goals, secondary to health. The *Report* speculates that respon-dents' rankings indicated their belief that responsiveness and fair fi-nancing indirectly contribute to health achievement (by increasing and facilitating the use of the health system), while at the same time, re-spondents recognized that "a well-functioning health system should do much more than simply promote the best possible level of over-all health" (WHO, 2000: 39). This undoubtedly reads too much into a dubious and highly unrepresentative method.

So, the first step in the assessment of health systems is to determine, for each goal, the level of attainment that each country has reached. The *Report* provides tables of attainment rankings for each goal for all 191 member countries. A table of overall or weighted goal attainment is also given (with estimates of uncertainty for each value).

Although it would hardly be prudent given the meager country-level evidence upon which these rankings are based, it is tempting to seek patterns. And patterns emerge: rich countries can afford to spend more on health and enjoy higher levels of health attainment; in addition, rich countries can afford the amenities and rights of responsiveness and as a rule have public, prepaid financing schemes in place. As a result, ranking by overall attainment is closely related to country wealth.

A second pattern is more interesting. Since equity issues carry significant weight, countries that are not at all rich but that have managed to attain a high level of equality of distribution of health resources rank relatively high (Andorra, Cyprus, and Cuba, for example, all fall within the top forty). Because of exceptionally high life expectancy, Japan leads the list for health attainment, although falling to sixth for responsiveness and eighth for fair financing. The United States is first in responsiveness, but thirty-second in equality of health attainment and fifty-fourth in financial fairness, yielding a composite ranking of fifteenth.

Composite attainment of the five health system goals, though interesting in itself, is but the first step in health system performance assessment. Next, considerations of economic efficiency must be factored in by adding the cost side of the ledger, so that we can compare attainment level with the cost of attainment. This analysis, and the significant role it plays, makes it clear that the *Report* offers a comparative economic assessment of health systems, rather than a comparative ranking of health system goal attainment.

Indeed, even if the *Report* did not turn to efficiency explicitly but merely discussed ways in which health systems could improve attainment levels, it would still, implicitly, be offering an economic assessment of health systems. This is because the fair financing goal makes progressive prepayment an implicit objective (perhaps instrumental, perhaps intrinsic) – first, because such a financial scheme shelters all households from catastrophic expenses and subsidizes essential health services for the poor, and second, because it is an economically efficient way of financing health care. Economic efficiency, in short, is assumed to be an essential goal of a health system – although, admittedly, a goal whose impact on overall attainment is blunted by its 25 percent weighting.

Summing up, both directly and implicitly, the WHO has committed itself to economic efficiency as the basis for performance assessment of health systems. High levels of health attainment alone, however admirable, do not guarantee a high performance ranking if the health system is inefficient and wasteful of resources. In a word, complete population health need satisfaction (assuming we could operationalize the notion of "health need" uncontroversially) is not optimal performance. Performance is a multifactorial notion, rooted equally in economic efficiency and health attainment.

But how does the *Report* answer the tricky question of how we know when performance is lower, or higher, than it "should be"? The performance of a health system is a comparison of actual composite attainment with the best the health system could have accomplished, as measured by two variables representing resource input. The first is the country's actual financial expenditures on health (measured in the *Report* as a proportion of GNP). The second – the country's average level of educational attainment – is a measure of human capital, which serves as a proxy measure for the country's contribution to factors outside of the health system that contribute to health status, degree of responsiveness, and the financing of the health system. (Relying on educational attainment, it should be noted, is a transitional step: the WHO is committed to seeking out better proxy measures.)

Together, these variables account for a country's input into health systems, both direct and indirect; they also establish, for each country, a relevant "frontier" or upper limit of performance – the most that could be expected of that health system given that level of resourcing. A country's actual performance is thus a proportion of this upper limit. In fact, the *Report* estimates two performance relationships. The first relates resource input only to average health-status attainment, measured in DALEs; the second relates that same input to the overall composite attainment.

Although only the second of these indicators is consistent with the WHO's insistence on a composite indicator derived from the five goals of health systems, the first indicator provides interesting information as well. It not only indicates that there is a direct correlation between level of expenditure and average health attainment, but also shows a threshold effect: if its health budget is below $10 per person per year, no country can hope to achieve more than 75 percent of the life expectancy that should be possible. Comparing the two indicators suggests that to a considerable extent the high achievement of some wealthy countries lies not so much in their average health attainment as in their ability to afford the costs of achieving high attainment on the other two measures of responsiveness and fair financing. Whereas the United States ranks seventy-second in performance on health levels, it raises dramatically to thirty-seventh when responsiveness and fair financing levels are added in.

This brief synopsis makes it clear that, theory aside and taken on its own terms, the usefulness of the WHO's framework is entirely dependent on the quality of the information relevant to each of the five separate component measures – without which, of course, the framework is an idle exercise. In the event, this has turned out to be the *Report*'s Achilles' heel. In a carefully prepared critique published in *The Lancet*, Dr. Cilia Almeida and colleagues make the point that the data required to calculate four of the five component measures for overall goal attainment were absent for 70–89 percent of the 191 countries that are ultimately ranked in the league tables, a fact not acknowledged in the *Report* (Almedia et al., 2001). In these cases, the WHO used imputed values without adequately describing the various nonstandard assumptions, methods, and key limitations of the approach used – provoking one influential critic to dismiss the imputed values as "fiction" (Williams, 2001a). The causal reader who skips to the back of the *Report*, where league tables confidently rank 191 countries of the world on performance, might not realize that these composite indices have very little empirical basis.

As noted, in response to explicit complaints about data quality voiced at the WHO executive board meeting in early 2001, Director General Bruntland acknowledged that "refinements" were in order and established a technical consultation process to obtain ongoing input from member states as well as an expert advisory group to evaluate the methodologies and recommend changes. At the moment, and for at least the next two years, the WHO is engaging in one of the largest international health and responsiveness surveys on record (involving nearly eighty countries) in an attempt to fill the substantial data gaps for subsequent reports.

The data problem is undoubtedly a substantial one. Yet even with better data, the question remains whether the WHO's assessment framework escapes the kinds of criticisms that its predecessors have attracted.

GENERAL JUSTICE QUALMS ABOUT HEALTH SYSTEM PERFORMANCE ASSESSMENT

In order to assess health system performance, we need a measure of attainment and a standard of performance. In theory, we could use the measure of attainment itself to set the standard – for example, by defining appropriate units of outcome and measuring performance in terms of an optimal, an ideal, or (as in the *Report*) a "frontier" level of outcome. But it is far more sensible to measure performance as a function of outcome in light of the costs of producing that outcome.

Though mention of the word "cost" brings immediately to mind some form of financial or monetary expenditure, we could easily also add (or substitute) costs understood as the violation of human rights; the limitation of freedom, equality, or well-being; or indeed, a limit on any other value, individual or social. For example, Amataya Sen has long argued that in order to assess levels of development, "efficiency" must be measured in terms of the cost in freedom (Sen, 1999). Whatever our choice, and however multifactorial, in order for assessment to be meaningful, this "cost" must be measurable and linked to outcome.

On the attainment or benefit side of the cost/benefit ledger, summary measures of population health are the tool of choice among health economists. Summary measures are particularly attractive to the WHO as well, given its constitutional mandate is to collect comparable health data on a global scale. Promoting the "international public good" of valid and reliable health information is arguably WHO's best strategy for furthering international health cooperation. (Jamison, Frenk, and Knaul, 1998), and that enormous task is made feasible by a single summary health measure.

But there is more to summary measures than convenience. For decades, the health of a population was captured by mortality data alone. But cause-of-death data, or the common proxy of infant mortality rates, or even symptom-oriented measures of illness or morbidity do not capture all that we mean by "health" at either the population or the individual level. In addition, health is a function of the level of capacity or performance of basic human functions, activities, and roles. In short, health is a matter of both fatal and nonfatal outcomes. As it happens, there are numerous functional status measurements in the literature (see Bowling, 1991; McDowell and Newell, 1996). But these clinical tools are cumbersome for the purpose of identifying population health status, so the WHO has followed the standard practice of using a short list of core functional items that together give, if not a portrait, then at least a sketch of functional status.

The summary measure DALY thus combines information about mortality (in the form of life expectancy data) and nonfatal health outcomes ("disability") into a single number, understood as a portion of a year of life (Murray, 1996). Assuming that a state of perfect health has a weight of 0 and death that of 1, living with a disease-related disability has a weight somewhere between these end points. In the original Global Burden of Disease study, a representative core set of states of nonfatal health outcomes were described, and to each of these "disabilities" relative weights or values were assigned. Angina was given the weight of 0.223, major unipolar depression 0.619, quadriplegia 0.895, and so on. Thus a year lived in one of these health states is "discounted" by the appropriate disability weight: a year lived with angina is equivalent to 78 percent of a fully healthy year, living with depression is 38 percent, with quadriplegia 10 percent, and so on. To the degree that we have reliable data on the prevalence of these conditions, it is then possible to calculate for a population the overall "burden" of each condition. Given that we have a common metric in disability-adjusted years lost, it is possible also to compare the relative burdens of different health states across different populations.

Assuming we also have data on the cost of prevention measures, treatment, and cure of particular diseases and nonfatal health outcomes, it is a natural next step to give an economic value to the prevention of a unit of DALYs for each condition (Murray, Salomon, and Mathers, 2000). The move to comparison of cost and benefit, even for the noneconomist, is so natural as to be inevitable. Joining together these data, we can determine, across the health system, the relative economic value of alternative therapies for the same disease, or the opportunity cost of moving resources from prevention to cure, or the relative benefit (in reduced DALYs) of funding treatment of one disease rather than another, and so on. Assuming full and accurate information, the DALY measure joined with cost-effectiveness analysis appears on all accounts to be an ideal, evidence-based framework for making resource allocation decisions across the health sector.

There is, however, a missing step. Comparing costs and benefits is not itself a decision-making standard; it merely lays out the options, ranking them in terms of a ratio between cost and outcome. What is missing is the normative claim that resources ought to be used in the most, as we say, "cost-effective manner possible." The standard of economic efficiency, stripped to its core intuitive meaning, entails that we ought to aim at producing an output at the least cost (or aim at producing a maximal outcome for a fixed budget). Although economists are reluctant to admit it, this is plainly an ethical axiom, akin to the underlying maximization claim of utilitarianism. And this is the heart of cost-effectiveness analysis.

Although there certainly are strong advocates of the use of cost-effectiveness analysis in health care generally, and in making resource-allocation decisions in particular (see, e.g. McKie et al., 1998; Ubel, 2000), there is also a substantial literature pointing to ethical concerns about the overall justice or equity of the theory and practice of cost-effectiveness analysis in the health domain. Here are four representative justice concerns:

UNFAIR CONSTRUCTION OF SUMMARY HEALTH MEASURES: Several critiques of quality-adjusted life years (QALYs) and DALYs have argued that the weights or evaluations given to specific nonfatal health outcomes are unfairly produced. The standard approach is to generate these weights through a consensus of health professionals rather than by asking people who actually live with the conditions being weighted. The concern is not merely that this produces inaccurate or prejudicial weighting (although that is certainly arguable), but also that it is fundamentally unfair to deny a voice to those whose lives will be most directly affected by the results of the weighting exercise (e.g., Loomes and McKenzie, 1989; Brock, 1995; Menzel et al., 1999).

UNJUST USE OF COST-EFFECTIVENESS FOR ALLOCATION DECISIONS: Since allocation of health resources involves fundamental matters of life, death, and well-being, and because these matters involve value conflicts, these decisions must be made as part of a fair, participatory, and accountable political process. Turning the issue over to experts who rely on utilitarian calculation, disguised as neutral and objective science, is unjust (e.g., Daniels 1993, 1998; Daniels and Sabin, 1997).

COST-EFFECTIVENESS ANALYSIS IS DISTRIBUTIVELY NEUTRAL: More generally, it is argued that cost-effectiveness analysis ignores considerations of distributive justice. For example, a higher average health attainment might be achieved by cutting off the flow of expensive health resources to a few very ill or disabled individuals and spreading those resources over a huge pool of individuals, each of whom will enjoy a very small improvement of health – although this total improvement is larger than the health loss of the few. This is an intuitively unjust result (e.g., Broome, 1988; Williams, 1988; Kamm, 1993; Anand and Hanson, 1997, 1998; Brock, 1997).

ALLOCATION DECISIONS MAY DISCRIMINATE AGAINST SPECIFIC POPULATIONS: Individuals with disabilities and the elderly, it has been argued, are treated unfairly by summary health measures in a cost-effectiveness analysis for making allocation decisions. Because of pre-existing health conditions, fewer years to live, or both, these populations will achieve lower health outcomes from interventions than people who are younger or healthier; therefore, they will be discriminated against in making allocation decisions, in part because their very lives are devalued (e.g. Harris, 1988, 1994; Lewis and Charny, 1989; Brock, 1995, 2000; Arnesen and Nord, 1999; Koch, 2000; Rock, 2000).

These critiques are typically grounded in moral and political theory, or in some cases in historical analysis. Some build on empirical research – drawn from surveys, key informant interviews, and focus groups – seeking evidence of public views about the values inherent in rationing decisions. For example, in his recent book, Norwegian economist Erik Nord reviews this empirical work and concludes that the basis for QALY determination – and by implication, for DALY determination as well – ignores salient, and well-documented, social preferences that run directly counter to the presumptions of cost-effectiveness and disability weighting (Nord, 1999; cf. Menzel et al., 1999). Although the point cannot be debated here, it is a nice question how these two approaches interact. Suppose there were overwhelming evidence of social preferences that were blatantly discriminatory. Would that suffice to remove the moral objection? Without a bridging theory that merges empirical evidence and moral and political theory, it is difficult to answer this question, although some recent work on "empirical ethics" has tried to develop a strategy for doing so (Richardson, 2002).

Luckily, we can set this question aside, since the present concern is not affected one way or another. Of concern here is whether, if we grant that these objections have prima facie merit, they have been addressed and answered within the WHO framework. Although the detailed work still needs to be done, there is reason to think that the framework does not satisfactorily address these justice issues.

JUSTICE CONCERNS AND THE WHO FRAMEWORK

Subtle refinements notwithstanding, the WHO framework for health systems performance assessment assumes that the construction of DALEs is unproblematic. To be sure, a considerable amount of effort has gone into the technically sophisticated task of estimating – in the face of a dearth of solid evidence about the prevalence of disability around the world – the DALE average scores for the 191 countries in the WHO survey (Mathers et al., 2000), and data from ongoing surveys will considerably increase the empirical credibility of these values. Yet the fact remains that as a summary of the expected number of years to be lived in equivalent to full health, the DALE measure adopts without relevant alteration the methodology and the disability weights of DALYs. And this remains true for the most recent modification of the summary measure, namely HALEs or healthy life expectancy (Evans et al., 2001). The underlying methodology for weighting has always been the source of the problem.

Searching through the *Report* and its background technical papers, all that one finds to address the concern that people with disabilities have not fully contributed to determining how the quality of their life is limited by their condition is the following brief comment: "These weights do not represent the lived experience of any disability or health state, or imply any societal value of the person in a disability or health state. Rather they quantify societal preferences for health states in relation to the societal 'ideal' of good health" (Mathers et al., 2000: 13).

This begs the question – in fact, two questions. First, what needs to be shown – either empirically or by argument – is that the methodology used to determine the relative disability weights (the "person trade-off" exercises involving health professionals, described and critiqued in Nord, 1999) truly represents a societal value rather than a professional proxy (and a dubious one at that) for such a value. Second, in practice, there is no meaningful distinction between "quantifying societal preferences for health states" and expressing a "societal value of the person in a disability or health state." In rationing contexts, if resources are restricted or denied by disability type, the effect is to restrict or deny resources to people with that disability. In short, the *Report* fails to address or answer this first concern.

As for the second justice concern, the *Report* makes a determined effort to respond to the objection that health policy in general, and allocation issues in particular, ought to be debated and settled within the political process rather than behind the scenes by experts. It is, admittedly, no criticism of the WHO to observe that, as an international agency, it cannot make political recommendations relevant to the process by which health policy is determined. Nonetheless, the *Report* does state that the responsibility for the performance of a country's health care system lies with its government, which is charged with the task of efficient and sensible management of resources. However, a government's obligation to provide "stewardship" need not include any form of direct participation by the citizenry. Perhaps it was felt that the equity goals could stand as surrogates for a more fully participatory process, on the assumption that the outcome of such a process would seriously consider justice considerations of how health resources should be distributed.

Of course, this does not answer the basic challenge that Daniels and others make, that distributive justice demands a fair and deliberative process, not only because there is no a priori mechanism for deciding difficult allocation questions, but also because there is no stable consensus about how these issues should be addressed. The *Report* merely assumes what we have no clear evidence about – namely, that there is a social consensus (applicable around the globe) on rationing issues.

More to the point, all of this rests on the assumption that the framework already adequately incorporates distributive justice values. This assumption is precisely what the third justice concern challenges by way of insisting that, however sophisticated, cost-effectiveness analysis will always be distributively neutral. To this, the *Report* has a clear response: cost-effectiveness as an analysis is relevant only for achieving the best overall or average health; but this is but one of five intrinsic goals of health systems by which attainment is defined and measured. Moreover, except in the richest countries, cost-effectiveness analysis is of limited practical value even here, since it requires detailed information about intervention costs and results that is not available. In order to offset these obstacles, other, more technically complex versions of the cost-effectiveness analysis were used to prepare the *Report* (Murray et al., 1999).

It is instructive to measure the *Report*'s reaction to cost-effectiveness analysis against two other approaches, both of which favor a role for cost-efficiency considerations in the allocation of health care resources. One approach argues that distributive neutrality is the primary virtue of using QALYs or DALYs in a cost-effectiveness analysis. By separating health maximization from distributional concerns, the argument goes, we can more clearheadedly make allocation decisions, and we can then adjust them to satisfy whatever considerations of distributive fairness society at large decides upon (see McKie et al., 1998). This makes more sense, not only because of the imminent rationality of using cost-effectiveness in health resource allocation, but also because health, for all its importance, remains but one component of well-being, opening up the prospect of further securing justice by means of compensation or by using some other redistributive technique.

The second approach begins by flatly denying that it is possible to compensate for ill health and concludes that the role of cost-effectiveness must therefore be restrained or limited by an independent array of values, including distributional equity (Richardson and Nord, 1997; Menzel et al., 1999; cf. Culver and Wagstall, 1993). These values (or "equity weights") might identify the desirability of giving priority to the severity of illness, to lifesaving, to ensuring that everyone has a fair chance at a normal life span, or to some other important consideration. Needless to say, the question of how the precise allocation answers given by pure cost-effectiveness analysis are to be "adjusted" by incorporating these other factors poses a challenge to this approach.

The *Report* does not adopt, or even acknowledge, the first approach, as it focuses exclusively on health system performance. Nor does the *Report* adopt the second approach, since cost-effectiveness analysis is not modified by the proposed equity goals. Instead, health equality, responsiveness equality, and fair financing are independent of cost-effectiveness analysis. Or at least they are at the first stage. In stage two (the performance determination), these goals are wholly dependent on economic assessment. For although no direct form of economic analysis is used to determine the levels of attainment of these equity goals, performance determination is itself nothing more than a direct application of economic productive efficiency.

So, unlike the compensation and equity weight approaches, the *Report*'s approach applies an unmodified form of efficiency analysis. Performance is economic efficiency by another name. This raises the suspicion that though the *Report* insists that it is taking equity and distributive justice issues seriously, it in fact endorses a purely economic analysis of health systems. Even though distributive concerns are incorporated into the framework, the overall performance assessment is distributively neutral. At the end of the day, the equity goals are implicitly transformed into efficiency goals.

Moving to the last justice concern, it is arguable that the very choice of intrinsic health system goals is, if not discriminatory against the interests of people with chronic health conditions, then at least prejudicial to their interests. The *Report* argues that whereas health, responsiveness, and fair financing are intrinsic goals of a health care system, considerations such as accessibility are merely instrumental aims. For people with disabilities, however, accessibility has always been a major concern; for them, it is not a trivial issue whether health services are available when they are needed, or whether they are provided in physical and social surroundings to which individuals with mobility, sensory, and communication functional limitations actually have access. Why does the *Report* view responsiveness and fair financing, but not accessibility, as intrinsic goals?

The argument given is this. A goal is intrinsic when we agree that to raise the level of achievement of that goal, without lowering the attainment of other intrinsic goals, represents an overall improvement. According to this test, health is indisputably an intrinsic goal. But so too are both financial equity and the package of responsiveness subgoals. These are intrinsic goals, since people would be generally unhappy with a system that failed to meet these goals, even when the health outcomes were satisfactory (WHO, 2000: 24). Accessibility of services is different. Accessibility of services may be an explanation of good or bad health attainment, but it is not in itself an intrinsic goal, since it is possible to imagine a situation in which accessibility is increased without health being increased.

The argument is circular, since it assumes that people will not be unhappy with decreased accessibility to the health system unless they perceive their health to be directly affected by inaccessibility. This may be true of people who are generally healthy or who do not perceive themselves to be vulnerable to ongoing or episodic downward shifts in health status – such as are experienced by individuals with severe disabilities, chronic health conditions, and the elderly. For people with disabilities, securing a guarantee of accessibility to health care undoubtedly looms larger than ensuring that they have a choice of health care provider, good quality hospital food, confidentiality, or access to social services – the features of the purported intrinsic goal of responsiveness.

Even if, with some tinkering, accessibility could be incorporated into the responsiveness goal, another concern strikes deeper at the overall fairness of the framework, replaying arguments made by persons with disabilities against summary measures and cost-effectiveness as a standard of health system performance.

First, given the way DALEs are calculated, the fairness goal for health attainment would not rank a health system lower in attainment (or in performance) merely on the grounds that people with disabilities were given fewer or poorer health care services than people without disabilities, so long as the decrement in health attainment that people with disabilities experienced as a result of the poorer service did not produce in them a greater discounted life expectancy than they already possessed, given their disability.

The reason for this is somewhat technical. DALEs (and the new replacement, HALEs) are constructed by calculating adjusted survival at each age – that is, the sum of all disability effects for each age group (which is, for complicated reasons, the product of the disability weight and the complement of the country-level prevalence rate for that disability). These survival "shares" are then divided by the initial population, resulting in the average number of equivalent health life years for a newborn. This means that the downward adjustment in survival is not itself a health inequality – or, more to the point, that it is not something that the health system is responsible for producing. So the subpopulation of people with disabilities cannot complain on the basis of their health system's performance when the health services they get as a group do not yield DALE values of the same level as could be produced, with the same services, for people without disabilities.

Another way of putting this point is that the health equity goal built into the WHO framework catches differences in health service associated with age, race, and sex, but not (analytically) those associated with disability. This means that people with disabilities are, solely by virtue of their disability, treated differently in a way that is disadvantageous to them. Such treatment would prima facie qualify, in jurisdictions with antidiscrimination laws, as discriminatory treatment.

Once the cost-effectiveness component is factored in, the situation becomes more dire for people with disabilities. The central message that the WHO is sending to member states is that it is both possible and desirable to improve health system performance. Since performance is a matter of both goal attainment and resource expenditure, there are various paths open to improving performance. The responsible agency can either hold costs constant and improve attainment, or hold attainment constant and lower costs, or improve attainment and lower costs. More subtle options are always possible, such as altering the system to reduce both attainment and costs, but to reduce costs proportionally more.

Generally, it is easier to lower costs than to improve attainment levels, certainly in the short run. Improving overall attainment invariably incurs short- and medium-term costs in terms of shifting priorities, initiating and carrying out research into new methodologies, changing patterns of service provision, altering the workforce, and other changes that are costly and may not immediately produce better levels of health or responsiveness.

As a tool for summarizing health improvements, DALE helpfully extends our notion of health outcomes, expanding the goal from mere extension of life to include quality of life. Yet such measures assume that disabilities are always a burden, both for the individual (in terms of lower health-related quality of life) and to society (in terms of a variety of costs and expenses). A life with disabilities, in the words of the *Report*, is a "stunted" life, a life composed of years that are "shorter" than full, healthy years. Understandably, this aspect of summary measures is offensive to people who live with disabilities.

If we combine what is arguably a devaluation of life with economic efficiency in a rationing context, we come face to face with the objection that has been repeatedly expressed in the literature: on efficiency grounds, providing health resources to people with disabilities is an economically suspect proposition, since, at least in comparison to people without disabilities, the same health expenditure yields a lower health outcome. Disabilities, in other words, are inherently costly and burdensome to the health system. For this reason, attempts to reduce costs will disproportionally prejudice the interests of people with disabilities and others with compromised health, including, as a matter of course, the elderly (but for a justification for such practices, see Walters, 1996).

From this premise, any number of consequences would follow if health policy were guided by this approach: people with disabilities would be more vulnerable to service cutbacks than others; when services were rationed, they would be less likely to receive them, irrespective of the level of benefit they might receive; in end-of-life situations, resources would not be wasted on keeping their "burdensome" lives going when cost savings could be secured either by letting them die or by more active forms of euthanasia (see Koch, 2000; Rock, 2000). All of these consequences involve sacrificing one group of people for the greater health benefits of others – once again, a prima facie case of discriminatory treatment.

Is there anything in the WHO framework that would mitigate these practical consequences? Arguably, the framework flatly disallows these results, since health attainment implies not one, but two goals: "the best attainable average level – goodness – and the smallest feasible differences among individuals and groups – fairness" (WHO, 2000: 26). The second of these goals is characterized as equality of distribution of health expectancy (that is, the expected number of years lived in full health) (Gakidou et al., 2000).

Conceding the objections already noted about the methodology that the WHO uses for measuring inequality, could we nonetheless be confident that the health equity goal answers the objection that the framework is potentially discriminatory? Though the discriminatory impact of the framework may be blunted, it certainly will not be eliminated. The health equity goal has the same weight as the health average goal, so improvements in either translate into potential improvements in overall performance (assuming no budget change). Each country must therefore decide whether it is more feasible, with the same budget, to improve average health attainment or to reduce the gap between those with the lowest and those with the highest health expectancies. It is not obvious which is more efficient, nor does the *Report* give guidance here. We are left with the fact that, at least in theory, overall improvements can be made by rigorously restricting access to health resources to those with the worst health. The rationale is straightforward: if these individuals were to die, both population health average and equality of distribution would improve.

Making this point, of course, is highly provocative, since it suggests that health planners would seriously consider restricting health resources to people for whom the prospect and amount of health improvement is less than it is for healthier individuals. But this is just the point: if our ultimate evaluation of a health system is economic, then, as the *Report* clearly states, we must look not at health resource needs (as in Alma-Ata) or at health outcomes alone, but at the cost of achieving them:

In economic terms, performance is a measure of efficiency: an efficient health system achieves much, relative to the resources at its disposal. In contrast, an inefficient system is wasteful of resources, even if it achieves high levels of health, responsiveness and fairness. That is, it could be expected to do still better, because countries spending less do comparably well or countries spending a little more achieve much better outcomes. (WHO, 2000: 42)

But we should add that performance improvement will also result from spending less and attaining poorer outcomes, if the savings outpace the loss in attainment.

Without data, we cannot tell whether this option will be the most attractive to health planners. We don't know whether people with disabilities, the elderly, and other groups whose health expectancy is low will become the most cost-efficient targets of this strategy for health systems performance improvement. But at the same time, it is not an option that the *Report* rejects, regrets, or even comments on. By being agnostic about the potential efficiency of discriminatory practices, the *Report* grants the possibility that a responsible government could create and implement such a policy. If justice considerations – as operationalized by the three intrinsic equity goals – are outcomes that are weighted against other outcomes, then circumstances may arise when the values they represent must simply give way in the face of performance improvement strategies.

To sum up, the *Report* is a highly sophisticated version of a modified cost-effectiveness protocol for assessing health systems that distils into DALEs all data on health attainment. The *Report* gives a nod to those who object to the application of cost-effectiveness analysis to health resource rationing, but without altering any fundamental aspect of that analysis or its operationalization. Despite the enthusiasm with which advocates of cost-effectiveness insist that all justice considerations can be factored in as side constraints to cost-effectiveness (Ubel, 2000), when justice conflicts with cost-effectiveness the fans of cost-effectiveness will never grant that justice, in Ronald Dworkin's original phrase, should trump. In short, if the original collection of objections were damning before, they continue to be so.

ASSESSING HEALTH SYSTEMS: ANY ALTERNATIVE?

But do we have any options? If health resources are scarce, and if it is pointless to assess the performance of a health system exclusively in terms of needs met or health goal reached, without any reference to cost, then perhaps policies that sacrifice some group of people are just inevitable. Sacrificing people with low health outcome expectations at least has the virtue of being relevant to the domain of distribution at issue (compared, for example, to sacrificing an ethnic minority, or those too poor to buy health insurance). In the face of scarcity, will we inevitably reach a point where goodness and fairness are irreconcilable?

Before we succumb to pessimism, we should take another look at the machinery that has led us in that direction.

First of all, although the notion of a summary measure combining mortality with functional status is attractive, we need to be clear about what it purports to measure. Despite the recent move to HALEs, and the removal of the controversial term "disability," the underlying rationale remains that of measuring the level of "burden" associated with a particular nonfatal functional state. Although the debate over the appropriate "model" of disability has a long history (see the general discussion in Bickenbach, 1993), there is a consensus that disability is not an inherent trait of a person but an interaction between features of the person (disease conditions, injuries, impairments) and physical and social environmental factors. What "disables" a person is, at least in part, a feature of the overall context in which the person wants to, or is required to, perform certain activities. Moreover, limitations in the range of roles that a person can perform, and in the major life activities they can participate in, are direct causal consequences not only of impairments, but also of the environmental demands, barriers, and facilitators that create the lived experience of having a disability. In this sense, disability is a universal human condition that reveals various perspectives, some biomedical, some social and political (Imrie, 1997; Bickenbach et al., 1999).

This account is the standard one in the literature on disability, but it has profound consequences for the notion of summary measures of health. If the "burden" of having a disability is not entirely a matter of a person's health-related functional status, then what limits the quality of the life lived with a disability is not entirely a biological or biophysical limitation. Quality of life is limited by stigma and discrimination; lack of accommodation and other facilitating resources; denial of opportunities, respect, and basic rights – social factors that are external to the individual. If this is the case, then the weighting exercise required to make sense of DALEs should take into account the extrinsic sources of the "burden" of a functional state. But it cannot do so and remain a summary measure of "health," since, plainly, the external sources of the burden of a disability are not aspects of health.

When a measure like DALE is used to determine the performance of a health system, questions of validity merge with concerns about fairness. If we use a performance assessment framework that relies on DALEs to rationalize allocation judgments, we run the risk of prejudicing ourselves against people with disabilities by implicitly ascribing to their health condition "burdens" caused by social arrangements. These arrangements may be cheaper to alter – or, once altered, may have additional economic benefits that far outstrip their costs – than health interventions. The burden of disability, in short, may be relieved by means of interventions that are not health interventions at all and are therefore, from the point of view of the health system, costless. To deny health resources to a population of persons with disabilities on the ground that an improvement in DALEs generated by one use of resources is less effective than that generated for another population, when the burden can be relieved without cost, is unjust.

In short, summary measures of health face a dilemma: either they utterly misrepresent the source and nature of the "burden" of a condition (thereby treating people with that condition unfairly), or they cease to be measures of health and become something far more global (and become useless for measuring health attainment).

This leads to a second reason to be skeptical of the WHO framework. Why should we assume that the only relevant "cost" in a cost-effectiveness analysis is financial? Health economists make this assumption for purposes of theoretical simplicity: monetary assessments are commensurable and expressible in a single metric. As we noted, the minimal technical requirements for a cost-effectiveness analysis are measurability and linkage to outcome, not necessarily a single cost metric. Of course, in order to broaden the scope of the cost of decrements in health to include, for example, limitations on human freedom or well-being, we would have to operationalize these somewhat abstract notions, but the rewards would be a vastly more realistic assessment of the value of health.

Finally, is there really no alternative to a scheme that informs ministries of health of the overall, relative performance of their health systems? Ministries of health need to make decisions about how much to spend on health promotion, prevention, diagnosis, treatment, rehabilitation, and social support; they need to allocate resources between primary and secondary care and to prioritize intervention modalities; they need to determine how much and what kind of health research they can afford; and they need to establish levels of fair and efficient remuneration for health care workers. It is not at all clear how any of these decisions are informed by the WHO framework or the comprehensive league tables found in the *Report* (Williams, 2001b).

There are other ways to proceed. For example, Norman Daniels and colleagues have proposed and subjected to limited testing a scheme of proposed "benchmarks of fairness" for assessing health care reform (Daniels, Light, and Caplan, 1996; Daniels et al., 2000). Daniels's benchmarks represent a nuanced policy tool for analyzing and evaluating the fairness of health care reforms. The benchmarks capture facets of fairness that are parallel to, but extend far beyond, the goals specified in the *Report*: intersectorial public health; financial barriers to equitable access; nonfinancial barriers to access; comprehensiveness of benefits and tiering; equitable financing; efficacy, efficiency, and quality of care; administrative efficiency; and democratic accountability and empowerment (Daniels et al., 2000). Each benchmark is operationalized to apply to specific outcomes or processes.

The benchmark approach differs from the WHO framework in many respects. Daniels provides a moral/political account of the value of health, and he then uses it to show the relevance of each fairness indicator. Briefly, he argues that ill health is a disvalue precisely to the extent that it compromises or reduces the opportunities open to individuals and that the principle of equal opportunity should govern the regulation of a health care system. The WHO *Report* lacks this perspective and appears to float in midair: we are left wondering why the goals of the health systems are worth pursuing. Of course, the WHO must tread softly on political matters, but the *Report* suffers accordingly.

Of more practical significance, the benchmark approach looks at health intersectorially, integrating the health care system into the myriad other organizations and social agencies involved in the known determinants of health. The first benchmark, in particular, identifies a wide range of determinants – nutrition, housing, clean air and water, sanitation, health education, public safety, and violence reduction – that need to be reviewed in order to evaluate the efficiency of any proposed health reform. In this way, the benchmark approach boldly confronts an issue that the WHO framework only gestures at – namely, the role of the health care system in the production of health.

Lastly, Daniels's benchmark scheme does not churn a single summary numerical value of the fairness of a health reform. The benchmarks represent indicators of fairness that are jointly relevant to an overall assessment of the fairness of a health reform. These indicators (unlike the *Report*'s assessment goals) are not always commensurable, nor is there a predetermined weighting for each benchmark. These are matters for public discussion, which may yield different results in different countries. What is required for fairness in health reform, as specified by the last benchmark, is procedural fairness for arriving at judgments about the fairness of the reform, within each jurisdiction. Procedures for assessing reform, and especially for making resource allocation decisions, must be transparent and publicly accountable.

The WHO framework is undoubtedly a technically polished version of a political-economic approach to health systems assessment that is more attuned to the ideological temper of the times. Whether it provides ministries of health with information that they can use to improve their countries' health delivery systems – not to mention their countries' level of health – is not at all clear. We have canvassed a few of the more salient justice complaints regarding the use of cost-effectiveness analysis in health care in general, and features of the components of the WHO *Report* in particular. People with disabilities are not the only group that has a legitimate complaint here, but they are the most prominent, since, ultimately, they include everyone who lives long enough to experience some form of functional limitation. There are many other concerns and objections that have been raised. The WHO enterprise is a bold and risky one, and certainly should not be criticized on those grounds. The benchmark approach shows that there are other ways to assess health systems, other ways to analyze fairness and efficiency. As long as the issues are not lost in the drama of ranking exercises, progress can be made.

REFERENCES

Almeida, C., et al. 2001. "Methodological Concerns and Recommendations on Policy Consequences of the World Health Report 2000." *The Lancet* 357: 1692–7.

Anand, S. and Hanson, K. 1997. "Disability-Adjusted Life Years: A Critical Review." *Health Economics* 16: 685–702.

Anand, S., and Hanson, K. 1998. "DALYs: Efficiency Versus Equity." *World Development* 26: 307–10.

Arnesen, T., and Nord, E. 1999. "The Value of DALY Life: Problems with Ethics and Validity of Disability Adjusted Life Years." *British Medical Journal* 319: 1423–4.

Banerji, D. 1999. "A Fundamental Shift in the Approach to International Health by WHO, UNICEF, and the World Bank: Instances of the Practice of 'Intellectural Fascism' and Totalitarianism in Some Asian Countries." *International Journal of Health Services* 29: 227–59.

Berkman, L., and Kawaci, I. (eds.). 2000. *Social Epidemiology*. Oxford: Oxford University Press.

Bickenbach, J. E. 1993. *Physical Disability and Social Policy*. Toronto: University of Toronto Press.

Bickenbach, J. E., Chatterji, S., Badley, E. M., and Ustun, T. B. 1999. "Models of Disablement, Universalism and the ICIDH." *Social Science and Medicine* 48: 1173–87.

Bowling, A. 1991. *Measuring Health: A Review of Quality of Life Measurement Scales*. Guildford and King's Lynn: Biddles.

Braveman, P., Krieger, N., and Lynch, J. 2000. "Health Inequalities and Social Inequalities in Health." *Bulletin of the WHO* 78: 232–4.

Braveman, P., Starfield, B., and Geiger, H. J. 2001. "World Health Report 2000: How it Removes Equity from the Agenda for Public Health Monitoring and Policy." *British Medical Journal* 323: 678–80.

Brock, D. M. 1989. "Justice, Health Care, and the Elderly." *Philosophy and Public Affairs* 18: 297–312.

Brock, D. M. 1992. "Quality of Life Measures in Health Care and Medical Ethics." In A. Sen and M. Nussbaum (eds.), *The Quality of Life*. Oxford: Oxford University Press, pp. 95–132.

Brock, D. M. 1995. "Justice and the ADA: Does Prioritizing and Rationing Health Care Discriminate against the Disabled?" *Social Theory and Policy* 12: 159–84.

Brock, D. M. 1997. "Considerations of Equity in Relation to Prioritization and Allocation of Health Care Resources." In Z. Bankowski, J. H. Bryant, and J. Gallagher (eds.), *Ethics, Equity and Health for All*. Geneva: CIOMS, pp. 60–72.

Brock, D. M. 2000. "Health Care Resource Prioritization and Discrimination against Persons with Disabilities." In L. Francis and A. Silvers (eds.), *Americans with Disabilities: Exploring Implications of the Law for Individuals and Institutions*. New York: Routledge, pp. 223–235.

Broome, J. 1988. "Goodness, Fairness and QALYs." In J. Bell and S. Mendus (eds.), *Philosophy and Medical Welfare*. Cambridge: Cambridge University Press, pp. 57–73.

Coburn, D. 2000. "Income Inequality, Social Cohesion and the Health Status of Populations: The Role of Neo-Libralism." *Social Science and Medicine* 51: 135–46.

Culyer, A., and Wagstall, A. 1993. "Equity and Equality in Health and Health Care." *Journal of Health Economics* 12: 431–57.

Daniels, N. 1993. "Rationing Fairly: Programmatic Considerations." *Bioethics* 7: 224–33.

Daniels, N. 1998. "Distributive Justice and the Use of Summary Measures of Population Health Status." In M. Field and M. Gold (eds.), *Summarizing Population Health: Directions for the Development and Application of Population Metrics*. Washington: National Academy Press, pp. 58–71.

Daniels, N., Light, D., and Caplan, R. 1996. *Benchmarks of Fairness for Health Care Reform*. New York: Oxford University Press.

Daniels, N., and Sabin, J. 1997. "Limits to Health Care: Fair Procedures, Democratic Deliberation, and the Legitimacy Problems for Insurers." *Philosophy and Public Affairs* 26: 303–50.

Daniels, N., et al. 2000. "Benchmarks of Fairness for Health Care Reform: A Policy Tool for Developing Countries." *Bulletin of the World Health Organization* 78: 740–50.

Edgar, A., Salek, S., Shickle, D., and Cohen, D. 1998. *The Ethical QALY*. Haslemere, UK: Euromed Communications.

Evans, D. B., Tandon, A., Murray, C. J. L., and Lauer, J. A. 2001. "Comparative Efficiency of National Health Systems: Cross National Econometric Analysis." *British Medical Journal* 323: 307–10.

Gakidou, E., Murray, C., and Frenk, J. 2000. "Defining and Measuring Health Inequality: An Approach Based on the Distribution of Health Expectancy." *Bulletin of the World Health Organization* 78: 42–54.

Hadorn, D. 1992. "The Problem of Discrimination in Health Care Priority Setting." *Journal of the American Medical Association* 368: 1454–9.

Harris, J. 1987. "QALYfying the Value of Life." *Journal of Medical Ethics* 13: 117–23.

Harris, J. 1988. "More and Better Justice." In J. Bell and S. Mendus (eds.), *Philosophy and Medical Welfare*. Cambridge: Cambridge University Press, pp. 75–96.

Harris, J. 1994. "Does Justice Require That We Be Ageist?" *Bioethics* 8: 74–83.

Houwelling, T. A. J., Kunst, A. E., and Mackenbach, J. P. 2001. "World Health Report 2000: Inequality Index and Socioeconomic Inequalities in Mortality." *The Lancet* 357: 1671–2.

Hsiao, C. 1995. "A Framework for Assessing Health Financing Strategies and the Role of Health Insurance." In D. Dunlop and J. Martins (eds.), *An International Assessment of Health Care Financing*. New York: World Bank, pp. 15–29.

Imrie, R. 1997. "Rethinking the Relationships between Disability, Rehabilitation, and Society." *Disability and Rehabilitation* 19: 263–71.

Jamison, D. T., Frenk, J., and Knaul, F. 1998. "International Collective Action in Health: Objectives, Functions, and Rationale." *Lancet* 351(9101): 514–17.

Kamm, F. M. 1993. *Morality/Mortality: Volume One. Dealth and Whom to Save from It*. Oxford: Oxford University Press.

Kawachi, I., and Kennedy, J. P. 1997a. "Health and Social Cohesion: Why Care about Income Inequality?" *British Medical Journal* 314(7086): 1037–40.

Kawachi, I., and Kennedy, J. P. 1997b. "The Relationship of Income Inequality to Mortality: Does the Choice of Indicator Matter?" *Social Science and Medicine* 45(7): 1121–7.

Kawachi, I., Kennedy, J. P., Lochner, K., and Prothrow-Stith, D. 1997. "Social Capital, Income Inequality, and Mortality." *American Journal of Public Health* 87(9): 1491–8.

Koch, T. 2000. "Life Quality vs. the 'Quality of Life': Assumptions Underlying Prospective Quality of Life Instruments in Health Care Planning." *Social Science and Medicine* 51: 419–27.

Lewis, P., and Charny, M. 1989. "Which of Two Individuals Do You Treat When Only Their Ages Are Different and You Can't Treat Both?" *Journal of Medical Ethics* 15: 28–32.

Lockwood, M. 1988. "Quality of Life and Resource Allocation." In J. M. Bell and S. Mendus (eds.), *Philosophy and Medical Welfare*. Cambridge: Cambridge University Press, pp. 33–55.

Loomes, G., and McKenzie, L. 1989. "The Use of QALYs in Health Care Decision Making." *Social Science and Medicine* 28: 299–308.

Mathers, C., Sadana, R., Salomon, J., Murray, C., and Lopez, A. 2000. *Estimates of DALE for 191 Countries: Methods and Results*. (Global Programme on Evidence for Health Policy Working Paper Paper No. 16) Geneva: World Health Organization.

McDowell, I., and Newell, C. 1996. *Measuring Health: A Guide to Rating Scales and Questionnaires*, 2nd ed. New York: Oxford University Press.

McKie, J., Richardson, J., Singer, P., and Kuhse, H. 1998. *The Allocation of Health Care Resources*. Aldershot: Ashgate.

Menzel, P., Gold, M., Nord, E., Pinto-Prades, J-L., Richardson, J., and Ubel, P. 1999. "Toward a Broader View of Values in Cost-Effectiveness Analysis of Health." *Hastings Center Report* 29: 7–15.

Murray, C. 1996. "Rethinking DALYs." In C. Murray and A. Lopez (eds.), *The Global Burden of Disease: A Comprehensive Assessment of Mortality and*

Disability from Diseases, Injuries, and Risk Factors in 1990 and Projected to 2020. Cambridge, MA: Harvard University Press, pp. 1–98.

Murray, C. J. L. 2001. "Commentary: Comprensive Approaches Are Needed for Full Understanding." *British Medical Journal* 323: 680–1.

Murray, C., Evans, D., Acharya, A., and Baltussen, R. 1999. *Development of WHO Guidelines on Generalised Cost-Effectiveness Analysis.* (GPR Discussion Paper No. 4) Geneva: World Health Organization.

Murray, C., and Lopez, A. (eds.). 1996. *The Global Burden of Disease: A Comprehensive Assessment of Mortality and Disability from Diseases, Injuries, and Risk Factors in 1990 and Projected to 2020.* Cambridge, MA: Harvard University Press.

Murray, C. J. L., Salomon, J., and Mathers, C. 1999. *A Critical Review of Summary Measures of Population Health.* (GPE Discussion Paper No. 2) Geneva: World Health Organization.

Navarro, V. 2000. "Assessment of the World Health Report 2000." *The Lancet* 356: 1598–1601.

Navarro, V. 2001. "The New Conventional Wisdom: An Evaluation of the WHO Report Health Systems: Improving Performance." *International Journal of Health Services* 3: 23–33.

Navarro, V. (ed.). 2000. *The Political Economy of Social Inequalities.* Amityville, NY: Baywood.

Navarro, V., and Shi, L. 2000. "The Political Context of Social Inequalities and Health." *Social Science and Medicine* 52: 1–11.

Nord, E. 1993. "Unjustified Use of the Quality of Well-Being Scale in Oregon." *Health Policy* 24: 45–53.

Nord, E. 1999. *Cost Value Analysis in Health Care.* Cambridge: Cambridge University Press.

Organization for Economic Co-operation and Development. 1998. *Health Outcome Measurement in OECD Countries: Toward Outcome-Oriented Policy Making.* Paris: OECD DEELSA/ELSA/WP1 (98)6/ANN.

Organization for Economic Co-operation and Development. Health Policy Unit. 1999. *An Assessment of Health System Performance across OECD Countries.* Paris: OECD DEELSA/ELSA/WPI (99)3.

Richardson, J. 2002. "Economic Evaluation and Ethics." Paper presented to the WHO Consultation on Generalised Cost-Effectiveness Analysis, Geneva, January 2002.

Richardson, J., and Nord, E. 1997. "The Importance of Perspective in the Measurement of Quality-Adjusted Life Years." *Medical Decision Making* 17: 33–41.

Rock, M. 2000. "Discounted Lives? Weighing Disability When Measuring Health and Ruling on 'Compassionate' Murder." *Social Science and Medicine* 51: 407–17.

Sen, A. 1999. *Development as Freedom.* New York: Knopf.

Ubel, P. 2000. *Pricing Life.* Cambridge, MA: MIT Press.

Walters, J. (ed.). 1996. *Choosing Who's to Live.* Urbana: University of Illinois Press.

Wilkinson, R. 1996. *Unhealthy Societies*. London: Routledge.

Williams, A. 1987. "Who Is to Live? A Question for the Economist or the Doctor?" *World Hospitals* 13: 34–45.

Williams, A. 1988. "Ethics and Efficiency in the Provision of Health Care." In J. Bell and S. Mendus (eds.), *Philosophy and Medical Welfare*. Cambridge: Cambridge University Press, pp 60–74.

Williams, A. 2001a. "Science or Marketing at WHO? A Commentary on 'World Health 2000'." *Health Economics* 10: 93–100.

Williams, A. 2001b. "Science or Marketing at WHO? Rejoinder from Alan Williams." *Health Economics* 10: 283–5.

World Health Organization. 1978. *Declaration of Alma-Ata*. International Conference on Primary Health Care, Alma-Ata, USSR, 6–12 September.

World Health Organization. 1986. *Ottawa Charter for Health Promotion*. (WHO/HPR/HEP/95.1) First International Conference on Health Promotion, Ottawa, 21 November.

World Health Organization. 1988. *The Adelaide Recommendations*. (WHO/HPR/HEP/95.2) Conference Statement of the Second International Conference on Health Promotion, Adelaide, South Australia, 5–9 April.

World Health Organization. 1991. *Sundsvall Statement on Supportive Environments for Heath*. (WHO/HPR/HEP/95.3) Third International Conference on Health Promotion, Sundsvall, Sweden, June.

World Health Organization. 1997. *The Jakarta Declaration on Leading Health Promotion into the 21st Century*. (WHO/HPR/HEP/4ICHP/BR/97.4) Fourth International Conference on Health Promotion, Jakarta, 21–25 July.

World Health Organization. 2000. *The World Health Report, 2000*. Geneva: World Health Organization.

Index